Dressing Smart for Women

Books by JoAnna Nicholson

Dressing Smart for Men:
101 Mistakes You Can't Afford to Make
& How to Avoid Them

Dressing Smart for Women:
101 Mistakes You Can't Afford to Make
& How to Avoid Them

Secrets Men Have Told Me:
What Turns Men On and What
Turns Them Off

Dressing Smart in the New Millennium:
200 Quick Tips for Great Style

110 Mistakes Working Women Make
& How to Avoid Them:
Dressing Smart in the '90s

How to Be Sexy Without Looking Sleazy

Color Wonderful

Dressing Smart
For Women
101 Mistakes You Can't Afford to Make . . . and How to Avoid Them

JoAnna Nicholson

IMPACT PUBLICATIONS
Manassas, VA

ISBN: 1-57023-200-8

Library of Congress: 2002117048

Publisher: For information on Impact Publications, including current and forthcoming publications, authors, press kits, online bookstore, and submission requirements, visit our website: www.impactpublications.com

Publicity/Rights: For information on publicity, author interviews, and subsidiary rights, contact the Media Relations Department: Tel. 703-361-7300, Fax 703-335-9486, or email: info@impactpublications.com.

Sales/Distribution: All bookstore sales are handled through Impact's trade distributor: National Book Network, 15200 NBN Way, Blue Ridge Summit, PA 17214, Tel. 1-800-462-6420. All other sales and distribution inquiries should be directed to the publisher: Sales Department, IMPACT PUBLICATIONS, 9104 Manassas Drive, Suite N, Manassas Park, VA 20111-5211, Tel. 703-361-7300, Fax 703-335-9486, or email: info@impactpublications.com.

Layout and Design by Donna B. McGreevy.

Contents

Dedication

To my Mother
I can still feel your love

Acknowledgments

I am so appreciative and honored that my life has been touched by so many *smart* women.

My Mom encouraged me to develop my own sense of style by praising and supporting my creative nature.

My sisters Jane and Daphne prove daily that a woman can look great every day no matter what her budget, size, or age.

I love watching my nieces, Shannon, Randen, and Jessy, develop their own sense of style.

My best friend, Phyllis (she's so amazing), has proven over and over again that *smart*, classic, conservative dressers can still be "spicy." And, speaking of spicy/sexy, my good friend Estela is that woman who appears in every man's dream. My newest best friend, Corinne, is the epitome of old world European elegance with just a touch of whimsy.

My wonderful friends Talitha, Tracy, Trina, Mary Frances, Sachi, Sandra, Leslie, Winnie, Dorothy, Marilyn, Shu Shu, Marcia, Beth, Beverly, Elizabeth, Ina, Isabelle, Florence, Nicole, Allison, Hue-Chan, Marcelena, and Audrey are my ongoing source of creativity, inspiration, wisdom, courage, clarity, and compassion. Extra special thanks to Phyllis, Mary Frances, and Leslie for taking the time to help edit my books—I am forever grateful!

My exceptional Color 1 Associates, who are international image and style consultants, are showing women and men around the world how they can look *smart* every day. I am grateful for their trust in me and our concept. Special thanks to my Directors of Training, Kate, Lea, Sachi, Marianne, Debbie, Maggie, Diane, and Kathleen, and to my Associates Leslie, Ellen Rae, Denise, Janna, Susan, Barbara, Wonder, Heidi, Maggie L., Camille, Emily, Marilyn, Debbie P., Sylvia, Terri, Sidney, Pam, Beth, Chardon, Jan, Valerie, Margaret, Ann, Judi, Natalie, Elizabeth, Kayo, Charles, Myra, Claudine, Rachel, Ardith, Carolyn, Sally, Nancy, Judi, Usha, Deanne, Evelyn, Allegra, Elsa, Masami, Janet, Yoshiko, Rosemary, Keiko, Trish, Rebecca, Mimi, Fumi, Linda, Judy, Thelma, Sandra, Bonnie, June, Peggy, Joanne, Pat, Jane, Leona, Donna, Sue, Makiko, Marietta, Bonnie, Darlene, Joyce, Ruth, Dorothy, Debra, Jill, Misako, Jeanne, Takako, Rosemary, Lucy, Harumi, Karen, Yuko, Gisel, Maria Christina, Michiko, Sadako, Mabel Jean, Connie, Marlene, Melvye, Jeannine, and Lyra.

I am especially thankful to **The Photographer's Gallery** in Washington, DC, for the terrific photos that bring the Color 1 concept to life in this book, and I'm eternally grateful to the artists who took them, Len De Pas, the unforgettable founder of The Photographer's Gallery, and photographer Paul Zambrana for their exceptional work and comprehension of the "color story" the photos needed to tell. Check out their terrific website at ThePhotographersGallery.net

A very special thanks to **Macy's**—especially the Tysons Corner, Virginia, store—for allowing me to use some of their shoes and boots to help illustrate this book and to The Industrial Union in Bellingham, Washington, for sharing their dress code with me.

This book wouldn't exist without my publishers, and my dear friends, Caryl and Ron Krannich—I am forever appreciative for their belief in me and my life's work. And to Mardie Younglof for her patient and detailed editing.

Dressing Smart for Women

ARE YOU A SMART DRESSER?

Do you look as great as you could? Do you wish you could look like a million dollars without spending a fortune? Do you think anyone is whispering behind your back about the way you look? What image do you want to present when you walk into a room?

If you are like most women, you probably make several wardrobe mistakes that may visually detract from your appearance. Perhaps you have difficulty picking out styles and colors that would make you look fabulous. Or maybe you let someone else make those critical decisions for you!

The way you dress sends an instant message about who you are. Right or wrong, you are judged first by the way you look instead of by what you know and who you are. You have to look the part or you may not get to play the role—whether it be a leadership position in your dream job or being #1 with your dream of a man.

One negative impression at the wrong moment can hinder your career or the personal future you are wishing for. One instant positive image could change your life. A quick look at any woman can convey the following:

- Classy or common

- Appropriate or inappropriate

- Decision maker or invisible

- Creative or cookie cutter mentality

- Poor, rich, or somewhere in between

- Careful or careless

- Smart, not so smart, or doesn't have a clue

- Elegant or pedestrian

Dressing Smart for Women is your passport to good taste—not for just appropriate looks but for fabulous elegant attire regardless of your job, budget, age, or size. It's designed to help you develop an eye for dressing your very best for all occasions. Outlining 101 mistakes you can't afford to make, the following pages offer sage advice on how you can quickly become your own expert so you can dress smart for both work and play. Each mistake is examined and tips provided so you can avoid mistakes in the future.

If you are uncertain what wardrobing mistakes you make, start by taking the following True/False quiz:

WHAT'S YOUR DRESSING SMART I.Q.?

1. The way you look has nothing to do with helping you get a job or a promotion.   T   F

2. Wearing opaque stockings with sandals, sling-backs, and a sundress is fine.   T   F

3. Wearing black shoes with a navy dress is fine and can actually work better than a navy shoe, which in some cases looks too "matchy."   T   F

4. It's okay to wear sandals when all of the rest of you is covered up (i.e., long sleeves, high neck).   T   F

5. It's okay to carry a handbag/shoulderbag that doesn't relate to your outfit—everybody does.   T   F

6. Wearing a top in a color that is barely visible in the print of the bottom (and vice versa) is fine.   T   F

7. Wearing bright, bold Pucci-like prints when your *coloring* is delicate looking will help "brighten" you up.   T   F

8. Mixing bright colors with toned-down muted colors in the same outfit just makes the look more interesting.   T   F

9. Wearing black makes you look slimmer.   T   F

10. A ribbed turtleneck is perfect for minimizing a full bustline.   T   F

11. In the new Millennium, anything goes.   T   F

12. Fishnet and other patterned stockings are a great way to update more traditional clothing.   T   F

13. It's fine to wear large hoop earrings with classic business attire.   T   F

14. Shoes with wedge soles look great with knee length skirts.   T   F

15. It's okay to go bare-legged with suits in the summer.   T   F

Answers

1. False. AND there are many *"it depends upon"* to deal with. All suits/ dresses in medium tones will look better with a nude (skin tone) stocking. With suits in darker colors, for women who have *delicate* coloring and light to medium hair color, nude will still be the best choice (yes, hair color is one of the *"it depends upon"*). Nude stockings may also be the best choice for darker-haired women—judge on an outfit by outfit basis; and *it depends on* the time of year—in the spring and summer, even with a darker suit, a nude tone is often more flattering. For much more information on stockings, please read ***Dressing Smart in the New Millennium***.

2. False. Unless you are a trendy, funky, or eccentric dresser, opaque stockings are only to be worn when it's cool or cold outside. Think about it. Sandals and sundresses are "open/bare" to keep you cool; opaque stockings are dense and look warm.

3. False. Under ALL circumstances, a navy shoe with a navy dress or suit will *always* be the far better choice—much more elegant and pulled-together looking. Just because it's "acceptable" for men do it, doesn't mean that it's a great look for us.

4. False. Sandals are for warm weather (or semiformal and formal affairs) and when you wear them with long sleeves and a high neck, they look out of place and out of balance. The same goes for mules because the heel is bare. The uncovered skin at your foot needs to be balanced by skin showing elsewhere—short sleeves/pushed-up sleeves or skin showing at the neck. Bare, or nude-toned, legs don't count because they are right next to the sandals and can't help balance the look.

5. False. Your handbag doesn't have to match your shoes (but it's great when it does), however, it does need to relate in some way to you and what you're wearing.

6. False. Even if you see the color in the print when you are standing right next to it, it needs to be visible from a distance or you won't look well pulled-together. Walk a few steps away from a full-length mirror, then turn around. If the color of your top isn't *obviously* one of the colors in your bottom (or print top with solid bottom), don't wear them together. How do you pick the best coordinating color from a print—one that will always look great? You can't go wrong with the background color! Second choice is any other color prominent in the print that is flattering to you.

7. False. Everyone can look super in prints but the brightest and boldest only look wonderful on women with stronger coloring like Winona Ryder, Lucy Liu, Catherine Zeta-Jones, Diahann Carroll, Monica, and Ruth Bader Ginsberg. They totally overpower delicate color types like Gwyneth Paltrow, Cameron Diaz, Tyra Banks, Claire Danes, Cybill Shepherd, Janet Jackson, and Annette Bening.

8. False. The bright colors can make the toned-down colors look dirty, and the toned-down colors can make the bright colors appear garish. Each of you is enhanced by one specific clarity—either bright and bold, delicate looking brights, slightly toned-down, or toned-down.

9. False. It is an absolute myth that darker colors, like black, make you look slimmer! The only time they do is when it's dark outside and you are outside, too, or when you are standing in front of a dark background. The idea is that if you can't make out the size of your silhouette, you will look slimmer. Think about it! Most of our background colors are LIGHT, not dark. If you put a dark color in front of a light background, the silhouette looks LARGER, instead of smaller! Try it if you don't believe me! All colors that look great on you can be slimming, including black, but it is the way a garment is *styled/ shaped* and what you combine it with that makes the difference between *WOW*, so-so, and "OH NO!"

10. In general, all ribbed tops *maximize* the size of your bosom, not minimize it!

11. True for only the trendy, funky, or eccentric dressers. The rest of us will avoid mixed *statements* like: wearing sandals with a warm coat; a warm wooly sweater with a chiffon skirt; boots with a sundress; a glitzy button on a classic tweed jacket; boots with a chiffon evening dress; wool knee-high stockings with spike-heeled, calf-high boots; and chunky/clunky heavyweight shoes with an evening dress (all looks featured in fashion magazines).

   Yes, fashion should be fun and, without being "over-the-top," we can have amazing style from some unusual mixes like borrowing the jacket from one of our best suits to wear with jeans or other casual pants and skirts.

12. Not exactly. If you wear them with a traditional suit, you will look like "you don't have a clue." There are two *wonderful* ways to wear fishnet and patterned stockings that will bring admiring glances instead of raised eyebrows. First, choose the smallest patterns and net—they are more flattering. Wear them with a solid color dress that is the same color as your stockings; match your shoe as well.

Although it's not impossible to get a great look using a contrasting color, it's definitely beautiful to have your trouser/skirt, fishnet stockings, and shoes match or be tone-on-tone of the same color. Try them with trousers so that just a touch shows. Can just that small touch make a difference? Indisputably! **Sometimes the biggest "Wows" come in tiny, subtle touches.**

13. Please don't—they make different statements. You're probably wondering WHAT'S considered *large*. It's best to stay under 1¼" with your classic business looks.

14. False. Because of the mass of the sole, all wedges are heavyweight looking and, therefore, do not look great with skirts that "hover around" between your knee and your ankle or with very slim-cut trousers.

15. False. Wearing a suit gives a polished, finished, "dressed" look. Especially with a classic suit, it's important to wear stockings because bare legs look *unfinished* and, with a suit at work, unprofessional. For the same reason, please remember to wear makeup.

101 Mistakes You Can't Afford to Make!

 Instant Impression

1 Not making your best first impression.
2 Comparing yourself to impossible illusions.
3 Believing bad advice.
4 Not looking promotable.
5 Thinking that it takes a lot of money to be able to have an elegant look.
6 Not knowing how to look great every day.
7 Being afraid to wear the same look often.
8 Being afraid to stand out.
9 Dressing too casually.
10 Sacrificing comfort for looks and looks for comfort.
11 Not looking as if you have a sense of style.
12 Not dressing correctly for your industry or your job.

 Color Power

13 Not knowing how to use color to give yourself an advantage.
14 Wearing colors that make you look drab or garish, or that muddy, sallow, or gray your skin tone.
15 Thinking you look safe or elegant in a color just because it's a neutral.
16 Not taking your coloring into account when you shop for clothing and makeup.
17 Wearing color combinations that make you look ill, garish, or headless.
18 Wearing pure white when it looks inexpensive on you.

CHANGING THE WAY THE WORLD LOOKS AT YOU

19 Utilizing only 25% to 50% of your wardrobe in any given season.

20 Not understanding that you don't have to be thin, young, or look like a model to have a fabulous appearance.

21 Buying things that aren't equal to or better than the best look you have right now.

22 Not taking the time or making an effort to get the training that could change your life.

23 Believing old myths.

24 Not knowing how to use illusion to create great style regardless of your size or shape.

25 Looking less expensively dressed because you buy two suits and fail to have them tailored to fit you, instead of buying one and having it tailored to fit you perfectly.

26 Wearing the wrong size patterns.

27 Not realizing the importance of wearing a jacket.

28 Wearing a skirt with the wrong style of shoes.

29 Wearing your pants too short.

30 Wearing your tops too tight.

31 Wearing your tops too long.

32 Wearing tops for business that look as if they belong at a party.

33 Wearing dress styles that look like tents or little girl's jumpers.

34 Dressing like all of the other applicants for an interview.

35 Not knowing how to combine separates to create great looks.

36 Not knowing what's the smartest top and bottom you could own.

37 Not understanding how to mix and match the separates in your closet to make super outfits.

38 Wearing too-sheer fabrics to work.

39 Wearing too-heavy, clunky shoes and boots.

40 Wearing the wrong color shoes.

41 Not knowing what shoes are the best, most flattering, and basic shoes you should own.

42 Wearing your stockings too dark or too light.

43 Wearing opaque stockings with classic skirt lengths.

44 Carrying the same handbag with everything.

45 Not taking the gold- or silver-toned detailing on your handbag into account when choosing your other accessories.

46 Carrying the wrong color or style of handbag for your attire.

47 Wearing a belt that doesn't compliment your body structure or your outfit.

48 Thinking that you can't wear a belt if you don't have a small waist.

49 Not considering your belt buckle when selecting your other accessories.

50 Wearing jewelry that doesn't make the same statement as your attire.

51 Wearing competing pieces of jewelry.

52 Wearing "party earrings" with a classic business suit.

53 Wearing a necklace that is the wrong shape for the neckline of your top/jacket.

54 Wearing too many rings with classic business attire.

55 Wearing a sporty looking watch with a "strictly business" outfit.

56 Not knowing how to tie a scarf to flatter you and your attire.

57 Wearing the wrong shape of glasses for your face.

58 Wearing glasses with lenses that are tinted in colors that cast an unbecoming color under your eyes.

59 Wearing frames that make your eyes look close together or your nose appear to be large or strangely shaped.

60 Wearing bras in the wrong size so your bosom appears to be an odd shape.

61 Showing VPL—visible panty lines.

62 Letting your slip show in the slit of your skirt.

63 Letting your bra straps show.

64 Wearing a dark bra under a light top or the other way around.

65 Not looking stylish in your business casual attire.

66 Not understanding the boundaries between day and evening clothing.

67 Stressing out about being overdressed or underdressed.

68 Not understanding the subtleties of style.

69 Wearing competing necklines.

70 Not knowing that knits look fabulous on women of all shapes and sizes.

71 Not owning a coat that works well with almost everything you own.

72 Wearing coats that make a less than great arrival and departure statement.

73 Wearing warm scarves and gloves to work that look like they belong at a football game.

74 Not wearing makeup or wearing too much or too little makeup.

75 Wearing the "in" looks that aren't flattering to you.

76 Wearing too dark, too pink, or too ashy looking foundation.

77 Wearing lipsticks that are too brownish or too bright for your skin tone.

78 Wearing orangy or brownish blush.

79 Putting blush on your forehead, nose, and chin.

80 Wearing a lipstick and blush that don't compliment each other.

81 Wearing lip and blush colors that don't go with your attire.

82 Doing your eye makeup in such a way that it makes your eyes look small or closer together.

83 Placing your blush in the wrong place.

84 Using concealer incorrectly.

85 Using too reddish or too dark an eyebrow pencil.

86 Over-plucking your eyebrows and/or not extending your eyebrows when they are "missing" on the outside edge.

87 Not brushing your eyebrows up.

88 Not removing dark hair from your upper lip and chin.

89 Wearing too much fragrance.

90 Wearing your hair in an unflattering style.

91 Letting dark or white roots show and/or having your hair color too brassy or too ashy-blonde.

SMALL DETAILS WITH A BIG IMPACT

92 Wearing your nails too long and/or too squared-off.

93 Wearing the wrong color polish for your coloring or your outfit.

94 Not knowing what to pack for a trip.

95 Wearing shoes in need of repair.

96 Not understanding that small details can make a big difference.

97 Perceiving yourself differently than others perceive you.

98 Not standing out from the crowd.

99 Having a wardrobe that is out of control.

> Right or wrong, you are first JUDGED by the way you look instead of by what you know and what kind of a person you are—almost everybody does it, including you. You have to look the part or you may not get to play the role—whether it be that of a leadership position in your dream job or being #1 with your dream of a man.— JoAnna

INSTANT IMPRESSION

WHAT MESSAGE ARE YOU SENDING?

One negative impression at the wrong *moment* could hinder your career. One instant positive image could change your life. You never know just when you might run into "fate" in the form of person who has the power to make your life different. Always be dressed for the part you want to play for the next five years. Use clothing as a *tool*—think of learning to dress well as a necessary skill that is needed to get the job you want, the future you desire.

The way you dress sends an instant message about who you are—you just want to make sure that you are sending the message you want people to get. One quick look at any woman can convey the following:

- Classy or common

- Competent or doesn't have a clue

- Smart, not so smart, or dumb

- Creative or cookie cutter

- Caring or not

- Poor, rich, or somewhere in between

- Decision maker or not

- Careful or careless

- Appropriate or inappropriate

- Entry level, worker bee, middle management, or executive

- Elegant or pedestrian

You can look *smart*, creative, caring, rich, appropriate, successful, and attractive no matter your size, age, or budget—that's a fact! Six things set one woman apart from another:

- Knowledge

- Self-assurance, self-confidence, self-esteem

- A unique sense of style

- Attitude

- Heart and soul

- The aura of *easy elegance*

These attributes, gifts, and characteristics have a symbiotic relationship, each taking turns helping, rescuing, and strengthening the other. No matter which attribute is strongest at this very moment, learning one new skill is going to give you the gift you've always wanted—that of *feeling* attractive, intriguing, confident, successful, and stylish. How? *Continue......*

> Class and elegance have nothing to do with money—they are a look and an attitude. You can have both if you are willing to invest the time to learn a new skill. — JoAnna

NEVER COMPARE YOURSELF TO AN ILLUSION

JUST THE BASICS

◆ Judging yourself against the impossible illusion of a model or movie star can hurt the way you feel about yourself now.

◆ Less than 99.9% of these celebrities look, in real life, the way they appear in a photo or on the screen.

BEYOND THE BASICS

Almost without exception, the pictures you see of a woman in a magazine have been re-touched—probably a dozen times. Our self-esteem and, therefore, our self-confidence, are *directly* tied to how we feel about the way we look. Our confidence is difficult enough to maintain without comparing ourselves to an impossibly perfect manmade image.

Do you realize what is most often done to a picture before we see it? Even on a 15-year-old dressed like a 30-year-old the "re-toucher" will make her nose look smaller or narrower; move her eyes farther apart and make them bigger, more open; add and lengthen eyelashes; reshape eyebrows; erase circles, lines, spots, and blemishes; make her lips fuller; clean up her hairline and add highlights. Someone else's eyes can even be "popped in" digitally. If they *have* to do all of this to a model, imagine what they would do to you or me.

What about in the movies? If we wore all that makeup, were seen only under special lighting, and had weeks of filming edited down to two hours, only our "best side" would be seen by millions. Given what we're up against, how can we stand out—what will give us an edge?

In this book you will find that I "talk" to you about looking great—the purpose of this highly detailed text is for you to have a reference guide to show you how. This is a little book with a lot of power. Much more than just advice that tells you to wear a *power* suit, this information, put into practice, will give you an **edge**—higher odds that you will reach your career and personal aspirations.

HAVING AN EDGE ⚡

JUST THE BASICS

⚡ When it comes to color and color combinations, as in most things, you can't believe everything you see, read, or hear.

BEYOND THE BASICS

If what you are wearing is appropriate and it fits well, there is only one reason why you might not look good—the colors you are wearing. Either your colors don't work together, or they are making you appear insignificant, washed-out, or like you aren't feeling very well.

⊘ **Bad *advice is rampant*!** When it comes to color and color combinations, don't believe everything you read or see in books and magazines or hear from sales personnel, your significant other, or your best friend. Significant others and best friends you may understand, but when it comes to "experts," surely I must not know what I'm talking about because why would they showcase something that wasn't correct. Why should you believe what I say? When you have trained your eye to see what works for *you*—or not—you will embrace my advice.

I wish that I could tell you otherwise, but magazine fashion editors, stylists, salespeople, and other "experts" continue to give really bad advice about color, and often about style. Why? For one main reason. Just because a person writes about fashion or sells clothing, it doesn't mean that he or she has had any color training, or even wardrobe training.

Absorb and practice all of your *dressing smart tips* and train your own eye so that YOU can decide whether to copy a look you see or follow advice. When you've trained your eye, you can take charge of what you wear *from a color standpoint,* and you'll learn to recognize when something looks great on you, and, if it doesn't, you will know why. Until you do, you are **susceptible** to misleading words and pictures.

Here and there in this book you will see the words *"BAD ADVICE."* The examples are from magazines written to advise women on their wardrobe. My contradiction will follow the bad advice—please don't get them mixed up. The following is the first example.

⃠   **Bad Advice:**   For work, sheer black stockings go with everything except a light-colored suit.

①   **My Advice:** Absolutely not true! You will be learning *more than you ever wanted to know* about your best colors for stockings, so for right now, I'll just say that most suits in medium tones look better with a nude (skin tone) stocking and that it's not automatic that darker colored stockings, even in a sheer, will work best with dark suits—there are many "it depends upon" to deal with.

Who am I to give advice on color and color combinations and why take my advice instead of "theirs"? I'm one of the founders of the image and color consulting industry, and since 1977 my company, Color 1 Associates, International Image and Style Consultants, has been training color and wardrobe consultants all over the world. We specialize in helping our clients make a great **instant impression**—*every day*.

> "When a man gets up to speak, people listen, then look. When a woman gets up, people look; then, if they like what they see, they listen."
> —Pauline Frederick

It takes only a few seconds to form an opinion about someone. The trouble is, if the opinion, *the impression*, is a bad one, it can take weeks, months, or years to reverse. Our clients can't afford to get it wrong. They include the president of a country, ambassadors, cabinet secretaries, senators, congressmen, Fortune 500 companies, rock stars, an Academy Award nominee, two Miss Americas, and women like you.

When you want to get it right every time, the most important skill you can learn is how to combine colors in a way that gives YOU a great look. This skill is not just one of learning what works with what, but learning what makes *you* appear attractive, successful, healthy, and effective. When you master this art, you will have an *edge* over everyone who doesn't know how.

Some women don't care about clothes and that's fine, but since you are reading this book, I'll assume that you do care about the way you look. If you think that you have your business and business casual "uni-forms" down pat and you don't need to learn this additional skill, you may continue through life looking good—just from the neck down. From the neck up, you may be looking washed-out, like you don't feel so well, or you may simply be looking ineffective—not an image that will help you move ahead.

Learning this new skill **now** will serve you well for the rest of your life. Read about it, understand it, integrate it, enjoy the compliments and the feelings and success that being self-assured will bring. Looking exceptional **every day** will become second nature to you—you'll get up in the morning, get dressed with *ease and elegance*, forget about the way you look and get on with your day, your life. Any woman can put on a suit and get on with it. I want you to look *better*. There is a very strong color section in this book because *color* is the missing link that makes the difference between your looking bad, just okay, or fabulous!

LOOK PROMOTABLE NOW

JUST THE BASICS

 If you don't look the part, you may not get the role.

 If you are feeling overwhelmed, confused to the point that you won't absorb the information in this book, or if you just don't have much time right this minute because you need to run out and buy an interview suit, review the **"Just the Basics"** that appears at the beginning of each section and **"Ace the Interview"** on page 89. When you do head for the store, there is an abbreviated **" Just the Basics *Quick* Reference"** at the end of the book.

BEYOND THE BASICS

My Associates and I have had hundreds of calls throughout the years from firms and organizations who request our assistance in upgrading or updating the image of employees they are "grooming" (obviously in more ways than one) to move "up." One was for the president of a successful small company, a woman who was going to have to start making presentations (selling) to a giant company. Another was a U.S. senator, and yet another was a vice president of a multinational company who was being sent overseas to head up one of their offices in Europe. All of these individuals knew their "stuff"—they just didn't *look* like they knew what they were doing. How much faster would they have risen through the ranks if they had *looked the part* earlier in their careers?

> Look great and you look as if you know most everything. Look as if you don't have a clue and you'll look like you don't know anything—even if you have a Ph.D. — JoAnna

Looking the part for any given industry is made up of a series of small, but significant, details. If you are feeling a bit apprehensive, don't give up. Just like a mountain of work becomes manageable when you tackle one thing at a time, understanding the **details** allows you to start *dressing smart* from your first purchase—from your first day on the job, for the rest of your life.

BREAKING THE RULES
TO WIN THE GAME

JUST THE BASICS

- You can break every old rule except two.

- Always look elegant—this word may have more meanings than you know.

- Follow any dress code guidelines, spoken or unspoken, until you get to make the rules—even if they seem foolish to you.

- Look far better than merely appropriate every day.

- In order to successfully break a rule, you have to know the rule.

BEYOND THE BASICS

Some businesses don't have a dress code, and others have gotten so casual that "business casual" means that you can wear anything you want—right? For someone else, yes. For you, not exactly. No matter how casually you are *allowed* to dress, there are a couple of "rules" that **you** will want to make for yourself.

Rule #1
Always Look Great.

Whether you are wearing classic business, business casual, trendy, feminine, vintage, up-fashion, arty, romantic, funky, ethnic, formal, eccentric, or workout clothes, you will look *equally* as great.

When you read the words "always look great," did you just think, "Now I have to be slim and rich, too"?

Great looking, accomplished women come in all shapes, sizes, and ages. They may be on a tight budget, rich, or somewhere between. They may be shy, outgoing, or both, depending on the circumstances. Although they may spend very little, or a lot, on their clothes they do have one thing in common: they all have *developed* a great look—they have great style— and they all look *elegant*. Yes, even in their workout clothes.

Just what does the word *elegant* mean? Lots of things, all good, including:

◆ Behaving nicely toward others—being gracious.

◆ Walking gracefully instead of stomping or clomping.

◆ Sounding elegant—both the tone of your voice and what you say.

◆ Having a "pulled-together" look—being fashionable, polished, and stylish.

◆ Having charm.

◆ Never making someone feel inelegant or *less*.

◆ Dressing and behaving appropriately for your work and for the occasion—A CLASS ACT.

You work on being gracious and charming (*attitude*) and we'll work together on the rest. One thing you will find is that, as your self-assurance gets stronger, you will automatically feel and act more charming and gracious.

Rule #2
Dress Smart, Look Smart, Be Smart!

This means, among other things, playing by any dress code "guidelines" your workplace or industry has (written or understood) until you get to the top, at which time **YOU** get to set the standard.

Right now, create a look for yourself that is even more stunning, yet *businesslike,* than the code suggests. Look totally **elegant** every day and avoid creating any "visual barrier" that may keep you from reaching your career goals.

Wearing clothing viewed as "appropriate" for your workplace gives the impression that you are highly competent and a team player—it can make you appear to have more knowledge and know-how than others. But be aware, it doesn't take the place of other necessary skills.

Dress equal to, or better than, the top female in your company. Easy elegance, not overdone. Think quality, not quantity. Never be afraid to wear the same smart look often. — JoAnna

Dressing smart also means looking the part EVERY DAY, no exceptions. It's what you'll want to do if you want to get a job, keep your job, get a promotion, and *maybe* even meet the man of your dreams.

ACCIDENTALLY LOOKING GREAT

> If you don't look great every day, it means that on the day you did look great it was an accident! — JoAnna

JUST THE BASICS

- Because you don't consistently look great, it shows that you don't know how you did it. It was a fluke.

- Don't disappoint—it causes doubt.

BEYOND THE BASICS

Is the way you look really that important? In a restaurant, if the server is sloppy, surely the food is bad or the kitchen is dirty. Even if you go back and everything seems perfect, the first impression will linger. If you walked into a store (any store) and it appeared messy and ill kempt, you would probably think that the merchandise was low quality. The least this negative image would do is cast a *doubt* in your mind. *Don't give any person room for doubt.* It's so easy to create the right image and it takes too long to erase even one bad impression.

Although it happens every day, it's hard to give you a real life "business example" of what can happen to you when you don't *dress smart* because women don't generally go around saying, "Gosh, I got passed over for a promotion because I don't look like I could handle the job."

On the other hand, I do have many stories about women rejecting men, and men rejecting women, because of the way they dress. A great looking, *smart* (and picky) male friend of mine and I were at a gathering of "strangers" one evening and, wanting him to meet someone *nice*, I volunteered to go talk with a woman standing nearby that I didn't know (but I thought looked really lovely) and then I would introduce them. We were about six paces apart. He *assessed* her and said, "No, I don't want to meet her." I asked him what was wrong. He replied simply, "She's wearing too many rings." I took a look at her hands and she was only wearing one ring on each hand and neither were large or flamboyant. Shallow on his part? Most of you just said, "Yes." See how easy it is to judge someone else? He judged her at a glance (he prefers *really* subtle elegance), and you have probably just judged him for judging her.

All it takes to consistently look great is:

♦ Becoming aware.

♦ Gaining knowledge.

♦ Training your eye.

♦ Applying this knowledge and your trained eye to your specific lifestyle.

♦ The willingness to put your new knowledge into practice every day.

♦ Maintaining your sense of humor and not forgetting to "play."

♦ A desire for *easy elegance*.

EFFECTIVE PACKAGING

JUST THE BASICS

▪ Never fear showing your best side.

▪ You can stand out without standing out.

▪ Wear boardroom looks instead of backroom looks.

▪ Investing in a wardrobe that works for you, not against you, is an investment in your future.

▪ Stop buying—don't buy anything at all unless it is *equal to or better than the best look you have right now!*

BEYOND THE BASICS

Who made the rule that you need to look *less than fabulous* in order to accomplish your work in an exceptional way? Heaven forbid that you might turn heads when you walk into a meeting—what's this world coming to? Will the meeting accomplish less? I suppose that there are those who feel that it would be better (more businesslike) if you looked forgettable instead of stunning. I would call them imperceptive or, perhaps, jealous.

If more women looked great all of the time, the only "distraction" would be a woman who didn't! Men would be only too happy to get used to women who look fabulous all the time. How do I know? I asked them. If you are fearful that you will look *overdone* and that people will be gazing at you with raised eyebrows instead of admiration, keep your look totally understated, yet *elegant*. As these *smart tips* help you become more accomplished and certain about yourself, you can *go for the gold*.

Invest in a Wardrobe That Works for You

When you shop, do you just fatten your closet? Most women really only use about 25% of their wardrobe in any given season. They buy things (lots of them) that they have *never* worn, may never wear, or have worn only once or twice. How many garments do you have that fall into this category? Do some still have the tags on them? Have they been hanging in your closet for several months? Several years?

Let me guess at some of the reasons why you aren't wearing something:

- You have nothing to wear it with.

- It was on sale and you just couldn't pass up the bargain even though....

- It doesn't fit—yet.

- You've decided that it's a bad color or that you don't really like it after all.

- It's scratchy.

- It's uncomfortable.

- The right occasion hasn't come along.

- You are saving it.

How would you like to leave the house every morning feeling dynamite about the way you look, never giving it a second thought no matter what you might do that day and no matter whom you might meet? Learn how to build a *smart wardrobe* that works for you—one that you can count on, one that makes you feel *great* every day, one that you love.

Wear boardroom looks instead of backroom looks. Throughout years of presenting wardrobe seminars to diverse audiences around the world, I've asked thousands of women to list their **"million-dollar looks."** What's a million-dollar look? Outfits that when you wear them you look and feel like a million dollars.

Without exception, no matter what group—wives of wealthy businessmen and powerful politicians, executive and professional women, women who work at home—*only* two or three women could list any thing at all.

From now on, don't buy anything unless it is *equal to or better than* the best look you have right now. For most women today, money and time are a huge investment and, after all that, if what you buy "sets you back" instead of moves you forward, it doesn't make sense. Be able to look in the mirror and say, "Yes, I look and feel like a million dollars." If you can't say it, leave it—you will find something perfect the next time you go shopping.

You don't have to spend any more money on clothing and accessories than you do now (probably even less) to have million-dollar looks. As a matter of fact, you probably already have a few **FREE $,$$$,$$$** looks hanging in your closet—free, because when I teach you to go shopping in your own closet and you find them, you won't have to pay for them.

A million-dollar look has nothing to do with how much money you spend on your clothing, but it does have everything to do with "investment"—a *lifetime investment*—because your future will be much brighter based on the way you look right now.

BE CAREFUL NOT TO GET TOO CASUAL — THINK BIG PICTURE 🎥

JUST THE BASICS

♦ Dressing too casually is a mistake.

♦ Dress better than you have to.

BEYOND THE BASICS

If you are dressed too casually for *your* workplace, you are making a **visual statement** that you don't know what's appropriate and/or that you don't care.

Some examples of styles and garments that are too casual looking for some businesses, but appropriate for others, are: jeans and khakis; loafers, sandals, and athletic footwear; T-shirts; and "ski" or other casual sweaters.

While none of these are appropriate classic business attire in a bank or law firm, each are befitting in some place of business: an interior designer wearing jeans and a nice T-shirt with a beautiful jacket; an assistant editor of a sports magazine wearing khakis and loafers; a saleswoman of outdoor clothing or sporting equipment in a ski sweater; a veterinarian in jeans and athletic shoes; and a hostess in a silk tank and matching sarong skirt and sandals seating people around a pool.

You are always making "visual statements." No matter where you are going or what you are doing, you are telling people something about yourself. Thinking "big picture" means that to get to where you want to be in three years, for example, you may have to pay extra close attention to those visual statements you are making today.

One of my Associates, who lives in the same lovely neighborhood as several of her clients, was preparing for a party—she had her hair in curlers and was down on her hands and knees waxing the floor when she ran out of wax. Now, I have to tell you that this is a woman who **never** has a hair out of place—casual, to her, means an incredible outfit that many women would wear "out." She doesn't even own jeans and she cooks dinner in a skirt and heels!

Saying a prayer that she wouldn't run into anyone she knew, she covered her curlers with a scarf and ran to the store. Just as she was paying for her wax, this woman came up to her and said, "Aren't you, so and so, the image consultant?" She waved her off as she turned to run to her car saying, "No, that's my sister."

Don't Sacrifice Comfort for Looks or Looks for Comfort

Just the Basics

- ◆ Comfort and sloppy are not synonyms.

- ◆ Wearing something that hurts, binds, or itches is not *smart.*

- ◆ You can have both style and comfort if you practice *smart tips* and a little restraint.

Beyond the Basics

Sloppy equals incompetence in the minds of many people. A sloppy appearance, created by poorly put-together, ill-fitting, unwashed, unironed, mismatched, or stretched-out clothing, sends the message that you don't care how you look and/or that "you don't have a clue." It makes a *LOUD* statement that you are not confident or competent in *at least one* aspect of your life—perhaps casting doubt on your competence in other areas.

On the other hand, comfort, grubby, baggy, and sloppy are not synonyms. Comfort can be found in any style and shape so it's never necessary to make this sacrifice. When you try something on, sit in it, walk around in it, and ask yourself how it feels on your body. Confining? Scratchy? Uncomfortably tight when you sit? Will you happily reach for it all of the time? Is one size larger the answer?

Most every day in your place of work someone, maybe you, has sacrificed comfort for style. You got a terrific bargain on a beautiful tweed suit, but it reminds you of your "itchy" pants when you were a little girl. Your new shoes look great, but even though they hurt when you tried them on, you bought them anyway because the salesperson assured you (or you convinced yourself) that your feet would stretch them. Clothing and accessories that annoy or cause discomfort start getting left at home, making you feel guilty (and less smart) because you wasted your money on them.

Follow the *smart* tip—don't buy it unless it is *equal to and more comfortable than the best look you have right now*. And carefully remove all scratchy tags before you wear something for the first time. If you don't, you may be tempted to "rip it out" in the middle of the day. The annoyance factor can *contaminate* the way you feel about the item, keeping you from wanting to wear it again.

DEFINING STYLE:

ALWAYS READ THE SMALL PRINT　

JUST THE BASICS

> Develop a sense of style that fits your personality, the person you *want* to be, and is more than perfect for the job you have right now.

BEYOND THE BASICS

ALL of the *smart tips* in this book will help you develop a stylish look uniquely your own. Each tip you put into practice will bring you closer to training your eye to see what works for you and what doesn't.

You'll look in the mirror and be able to say, "My stockings are too light (or too dark). I need a different jacket style with this particular trouser shape because this one is making me look short-legged and dowdy. My earrings conflict with the buttons on my jacket. My shoes are too heavy looking." Trust me, you will be able to tell—just put yourself in *class* until the end of the book and then put your new knowledge to work for you.

Style—it even sounds like a *smart* word but what does it mean? It's a word that has a myriad of meanings, all directly related to what you want to achieve.

One connotation is something you strive for, *being stylish*, as in looking fashionable, chic, contemporary, sophisticated, and pulled together.

Another has to do with the *shape* or *line* of a garment—there are many *styles* of jackets and trousers. Jacket styles range from feminine to tailored, short to long, and curvy to boxy. Trouser shapes vary from cigarette-slim to wide-legged, flared to tapered, from capri to cropped, and from pleated to flat-front. Wearing a suit, dress, jacket, pants, skirt, or top that has an interesting shape can give you style.

Finally, the word *style* can refer to a specific *style of attire*—western, funky, faddish, trendy, up-fashion, casual, business casual, classic (or formal) business, sporty, arty, vintage, eccentric, and sophisticated.

One day I had a call from a peripheral friend who wanted me to work with his new wife to give her a more sophisticated image. I had met several women that he had dated through the years but not his wife. The others ranged from *Cosmopolitan* "do's" to Cosmopolitan "don'ts," appearing a tad "too tight, too short, and too low" all at the same time. He was a multimillionaire businessman and needed his wife to look like she fit her new role, which included working in his company. The look that had seduced him was now inappropriate and perhaps a little embarrassing. At the time I was on a deadline for my last book, *Secrets Men Have Told Me: What Turns Men On & What Turns Them Off*, so I referred him to one of my Associates. The *lesson* I want you to get may not be the one you're thinking.

> It takes a rare man to understand that it's easy to change the cover of a book whose words cannot be altered, and it takes a discerning boss to notice your talent when your image makes you appear un-qualified. — JoAnna

If it complimented your career and personal aspirations, you could dress in any style you wanted or even in a *different* style every day if you like—having no "set" style is a style of its own.

As a young woman, I was told that I should find my own style and stick with it. What I *found* was that I like several different styles, depending on how I feel, where I am going, the person I am going with, and what I want to accomplish once I get there.

It only makes sense for me to dress differently for a meeting with the chairman of a conservative corporation who wants to talk about the services my company can provide than I do if I am going to lunch with a newspaper fashion editor. Of course, I dress even differently yet when meeting my friends for a Sunday brunch in Georgetown than when I'm presenting a seminar in Paris at the invitation of the American Embassy, going to a state dinner at the White House in honor of a king and queen, or heading into the jungle to go down the headwaters of the Amazon.

Can you still wear more "up-fashion" looks for business and pleasure when you are a woman of a *certain age*? Of course, but for those of you who are concerned, I'll be more specific. First we should define what that age is—but we can't. Because, it's not an age exactly, it is any time at which you would look ridiculous in what you are wearing. Before you get dressed in the morning, ask yourself the following: Where are you going? Who are you going with? What are you trying to accomplish there? What impression do you want others to have of you?

In other words, what image (what *style*) will best serve your needs at any given time? When you are going to a meeting with your boss, she/he needs to be proud to be seen with you, and, for both of your sakes, you need to "look" like you know what you are doing—no doubt. What image do you need if you are meeting/calling on clients who wear jeans and T-shirts or uniforms for a living? What if you are from a big city and they live in a small town in the middle of what you might think of as "nowhere"?

Consider the trust factor. Clients need to trust that you are giving them good advice (selling them what they need, for example), and your image can exude trust or doubt. They also need to feel that you are just enough like them that you understand them—so they can relate to you—you have common ground. All this boils down to the fact that you can't dress like them. You have to look like an expert in your field because an expert, not a neighbor or best friend, is what they need and want. — JoAnna

Vintage Style or Out-of-Date

Wearing clothes, makeup, and hair trends or fads from the past could make you look out of date, out of style, out of touch or, maybe, *special*. In part, the difference could simply be where you work and what you do there, with another important part being the item of clothing in consideration. A vintage suit, dress, or coat from the '40s, '50s, or even the '60s could be wonderful. A vintage miniskirt, hot pants, or baby doll top from the '60s could look as if it was right off the runway this year, but would certainly raise eyebrows in any year if worn in a classic business environment.

The three eyebrow raisers above are not classic but "trends" and "fads" from the past—and, depending on the year, the future. If you have true classics from any decade, assuming that they are in good repair and still fit you, you are in luck.

Trends and fads are usually short-lived fashions (worn from just one season to maybe a couple of years). Some are *wearable* for business and some are too extreme for the mainstream. Wearing "yesterday's news" can date you unless, of course, you wear it long enough that it becomes *vintage* and you look chic again.

Sometimes a woman's image grows with her and she gracefully glides from college, being a stay-at-home mom or from clerical worker to the executive office, while other women need to be gently nudged to "get it together." Some resistance may be natural because, after all, when you are used to seeing yourself the "old (comfortable) way," the *new you* may seem like a stranger you're not sure you can trust.

One client accustomed to her "ordinary" self was enticed (actually, I gently twisted her arm) into purchasing a simple red dress with a small slit on the side that opened just to above her knee. Until she got used to her new stylish image, she would make an amusing comment about herself in the dress looking like "socks on a rooster!" The first time she wore it, a delightful man said, "So, where exactly do those legs end?" She's only 5' 3" tall. **You, too, will learn the art of *illusion*.**

DRESSING SMART FOR YOUR INDUSTRY

JUST THE BASICS

♦ Look *better* than you are expected to look—*equal to or better than* the top woman in your company.

BEYOND THE BASICS

How are the executive women in your industry expected to dress—strictly business, more up-fashion, sophisticated casual? Once you identify the *required* look of your work realm, you can plan a wardrobe based on this "expected" attire. Why should you? To disappoint with your image can keep you from moving up. To stray too far from the expected could "get you noticed"—noticed in a positive way or negative way depends on which direction you stray.

For each field, there will be regional differences and differences even within regions, sometimes due to climate, "cultures," and big city/small town influences. There will also be differences even within the same city. In Washington, DC, for example, one would think that our government agencies would follow a specific dress code. But, no, each has different policies on what employees can wear to work.

Once when I was doing a wardrobe workshop for the Congressional Wives Club I had the "nerve" to tell them how extra important it was that they look great every day. No excuses. Why? Because everywhere they went, they represented **me** and every other American woman.

I explained that, in this country, women look at them and say, "Oh, that's the wife of Congressman so and so—look at what she's wearing." When traveling in foreign countries, the women say (pretend that this is written in French or Italian), "Look, that's Senator so and so's wife—that must be how American women are dressing now."

Whatever you do, I know you want to *look smart* but this is one area where you will want to ***think smart,*** as well. Play by the rules until you are able to take the lead. That does not mean that I advocate looking dowdy, drab, frowzy, frumpy, dumpy, or overly conservative just because top women in your field or place of business look this way. I do want you to stand out—in the best possible light, just be *smart* about it.

If you are in a conservative field such as investment banking, you will most likely be dressing in classic attire—please don't read boring, mundane, dowdy, or uninteresting into the word *classic*. Classic clothing is never really out of style. How fashionable classically styled clothing appears is almost always dependent on the "cut" or "design" of the items and the way you choose to combine them. Think classic with a *twist*—interesting shapes or patterns.

For example: Wear a pantsuit that has a very curvy jacket—yes, curvy jackets are classic and at the same time feminine and flattering to **all** figures. Combine a classic blazer with a "just above the knee" *pegged* skirt (it's narrower at the hemline than at the hipline) and you have a much more fashionable conservative look than if you paired the same jacket with a "regular" straight skirt—the difference is a subtle "wow" versus "borrrrrrrrrring."

Regardless of the length of a skirt, have all of your *straight* skirts "pegged." The taper that narrows the skirt starts just below the widest part of your hips and slims gradually to the hem. Very pegged skirts need a kick pleat or a slit so that you can walk gracefully in them rather than "mince" across the room. "Slits" for business attire should not be higher on your leg than the same place a short skirt would end—lower if short skirts are not worn in your place of business. If your industry is casual, understand really, really well that "casual" and sloppy, stretched-out, faded-out, and worn-out are not synonyms. Dress with a *studied* casualness—think sophisticated casual, *easy elegance*. If you work in a field where you may, or are expected to, dress more up-fashion or trendy, you will be constantly checking out the latest "must haves" in the fashion magazines and "zany" boutiques. If you are going to *"do"* one of these looks you'll more than likely need to do it head to toe for the right image. That often requires one or two additional purchases—a specific shoe style or bag, for example—so unless you can afford to, it's best not to buy a lot of the "in" because it's nearly certain to be *out* shortly.

Respect tradition: Sometimes it seems difficult to be true to your own personality, sense of style, and follow a company's attire *guidelines* at the same time.

What do companies do when an employee's image is hurting their business? It's a touchy matter, of course, because they cannot use the way you look as a reason to let you go, but it's very clear that if you don't look the part, they will find a (legal) way to get rid of you.

The idea behind business casual was that employees would be happier and therefore more productive. It was also hoped that they wouldn't "jump ship" and go to the much more casual high tech industry. What happened was that, not having to wear their familiar uniform of a suit, women got stressed out because they felt they needed a different wardrobe—one that they didn't know how to put together. Part of the problem is that there is a huge leeway between suits and denim, and many women chose attire too close to the casual end of the spectrum.

Examples of Dress Codes

The GAO (Government Accounting Office), an agency that one would think of as conservative, has a formal policy of 24/7 business casual all year (it started as Fridays, progressed to all summer, then went to all year). *But* their policy also states that employees have to dress for business if they have an outside meeting or if people are coming in from the outside to meet with them.

In the hospitality industry there are often some strict guidelines, such as uniform-like or furnished uniforms of dark suits for some high end hotels for front desk personnel or anyone who might be interacting with clients. Even in the office at the Ritz Carlton hotels, for example, the dress code is a suit. On the other hand, at the Marriott Hotels the guidelines are 24/7 business casual, including the front desk—formal business attire is an appropriate option.

An employee of one of the largest hotel chains in the world wasn't wearing a tie when he called on a client. The client called the chairman of this company and said, "How dare he come to see me without a tie." Yes, how you present yourself is very important—to your job and to your company.

I spoke with a senior partner in a typical Washington law firm where the dress code is business casual 24/7 but the lawyers are counseled to "dress for their day," meaning that if they had a client meeting they should assume that the client would be in a suit and tie and, therefore, so should they. When they first instigated this code, everyone took full advantage of it. Now, the attire seems to be divided by age. The "older" women are wearing suits and the younger women are more casually dressed. Would you like to guess into which group the partners fall?

Although it's important to always *feel* appropriate, "business dress" doesn't always mean a suit or dress. At the Industrial Credit Union in Bellingham, Washington, business dress is required Monday through Thursday and Friday is business casual.

Their business dress policy shows, as *optional*, suits, dresses, pantsuits, and jackets with skirts or pants. In the "required" column are pantyhose/socks, tops, bottoms, and shoes, which translates that just a blouse or sweater with a skirt or pants is appropriate when worn with stockings/socks and shoes. The "never" column is as follows: culottes, stirrup pants, leggings, overalls, athletic socks, denim, polo/golf shirts (knit shirts), flannel shirts, sweatshirts, T-shirts, tank tops (without jacket or sweater), halter tops, spaghetti straps, jeans (any color), sweat pants or warm-ups (any style), shorts (walking or Bermuda), leather topsider-style shoes, boots (cowboy or hiking), canvas shoes, tennis shoes (any type), running shoes, and sandals/ thongs.

For Friday business casual you can still "dress up" or you are required to wear an approved ICU shirt or sweater (they have the credit union's logo on them); jeans are allowed, as are tennis shoes, topsiders, cowboy boots, and hiking boots—Bellingham is on the northwest coast about 15 minutes from the Canadian border. Socks are still required, and the items on the "never" list are culottes, stirrup pants, leggings, athletic socks, sweat pants/warm-ups, shorts, overalls, running shoes, and sandals/thongs.

Sometimes it comes down to a matter of respect—respect of tradition, respect of others, respect of self. President George W. Bush is a casual kind of guy on his ranch in Texas but he will not enter the Oval Office without putting on a tie—neither will anyone else who works at the White House. When you understand the "rules," you will know when you can ignore them—I'm sure that in a national emergency the president and his staff would not stop to put on a tie before entering the Oval Office.

WHAT'S YOUR COLOR I.Q.?
TRUE OR FALSE

1. Every smart woman can wear yellow and look great.   T   F

2. There are individuals who look good in both clear/bright colors and toned-down, muted colors.   T   F

3. Black and white was very popular last year and remains so; every smart woman can wear black and white together effectively.   T   F

4. A short person should never wear bright, bold patterns.   T   F

5. Small, blended looking patterns in enhancing colors look wonderful on most shorter women.   T   F

6. It's taller women who can wear most anything and look great.   T   F

7. Brighter colors look better when you have a suntan.   T   F

8. A fresh, crisp, pure white blouse would be a super basic in every smart woman's wardrobe.   T   F

9. There are individuals who can wear every shade of a color like lime green, Kelly green, moss green, sea green, avocado, etc., and look great.   T   F

10. As smart women move into their 60s and 70s, wearing clothing in soft pastel colors will be a smart thing to do.   T   F

11. Your personality plays a part in what colors look best on you.   T   F

12. Fuller figured smart women look best in quiet looking, subdued colors.   T   F

ANSWERS

1. True. You are enhanced by at least one shade of yellow. In order for it to look great on you, the "clarity" (the brightness level) must also be your best! I'm certain many of you think I'm crazy but if you would wear just the perfect yellow for you, the compliments would change your mind.

2. False. You are definitely more enhanced by either clear, bright colors, slightly toned-down colors, or toned-down muted colors.

3. False. The six Gentle and Muted Color Types should avoid wearing the high-contrast color combination of black and white. Black with light beige will look much more expensive on these women.

4. False. For many Color Types this is true, but for a Contrast Color Type the look is one of her best regardless of her height. Her body's proportions may determine where she places these bold patterns.

5. False. Regardless of height, only Gentle Color Types look wonderful in small blended looking patterns. Your height has nothing to do with your best pattern sizes—your body's coloring is the determining factor.

6. False. Shorter women can look as fabulous in the same styles as taller women. It's getting the proportions right for your height and body that makes the difference.

7. False. If you are one of the six Color Types that are flattered by clear, bright colors, they will make you look radiant whether your skin is pale or dark. If you are one of the six Color Types that are overpowered by bright colors, having a tan won't help.

8. False. Only six of the twelve Color Types look stunning in pure white. On the other six, it will appear inexpensive instead of fresh.

9. False. No one is equally enhanced by all shades of a color. When it comes to green, for example, one or two shades will be far more flattering than the others.

10. False. As we age, It becomes even more important for us to wear colors and color combinations that help keep us radiant looking. Do not retire into retiring colors unless you are a Gentle Color Type and they just happen to look phenomenal on you.

11. False. Our personality has nothing to do with what looks great on us— it has to do with what we like and the styles we wear.

12. False. Wear flattering colors, in your best clarity, in great styles for you, and you will look fabulous. Wear the wrong clarity for your skin tone and you will appear to be a fuller figured woman who looks washed-out or overpowered—not a smaller woman.

Color Power

It's Your Most Important Accessory and It is Free

Just the Basics

 Wearing colors and color combinations that flatter you will give you an *edge*.

Beyond the Basics

Why am I calling color an accessory? Because it is an *adornment*. If you know how to work with color for *your coloring*, you will look more phenomenal, by far, than you can without this knowledge. Edith Head, the famous Hollywood costume designer, referred to color as a *powerful tool* that should be used as a precision instrument to bring out a woman's beauty.

Color has an amazing impact. According to research done by the Wharton School of Business and the University of Minnesota, color accelerates learning retention and recall by 55% to 78%; it improves and increases comprehension up to 73%, increases willingness to read up to 80%, and sells products and ideas more effectively by 50% to 85%. The Beach Boys, former clients of mine, wanted to know what *their* best colors would be for both their *signature statement* Hawaiian shirts and the backdrops for their stage sets.

I do not believe in any of the seasonal or cool/warm color theories. The following *smart tips* are what I *do* believe:

 Approximately 50% of you look stunning in bright, clear, vibrant colors.

The other half of you look amazing in colors that have less brightness—those that are more subdued or muted looking.

How can you tell which "clarity" is best for you?

Do You Look Essential ⭐ or Insignificant? ⭐

Just the Basics

⭐ If you wear colors that are too toned down for your coloring, you will look insignificant.

   ✯   If you wear colors that are too bright for your coloring, you could look ill. (Don't you just hate it when someone asks if you aren't feeling well when you're feeling just fine?)

BEYOND THE BASICS

What is *clarity*? Clarity has to do with the amount of "brightness," or lack of brightness, of a color—how "clear" or "toned down" the color appears. *ALL* colors (red, blue, green, and so on) come in different clarities—from very bright to very toned down.

     Picture the brightest red you have ever seen. Maybe it's fire engine red. Now picture a toned down, quieter version of the same red.

     Very bright, clear colors, such as fire engine red, lack brown or gray pigments. Toned down colors are clear colors that have been softened with gray or brown pigment. The more gray or brown pigment that is added, the more toned down the color becomes. There are:

   ✯   Bright, bold, vivid, brilliant, intense, vibrant, clear colors.

   ✯   Dazzling, radiant, lively, clear colors that are bright but more "delicate" or "subtle" looking (not as bold or intense) than those above.

   ✯   Gutsy (but not bright), rich, muted, burnished, spicy, slightly toned down colors.

   ✯   Restrained, reserved, calm, quiet colors that are more subdued, less gutsy than those just above.

     Don't be fooled by advice that muted, subdued tones are always elegant—they are only elegant for half of you, and the other half of you will just look insignificant if you wear them.

     If a color is *too* bright or *too* bold for your coloring, it can appear garish, and, by comparison, you will look washed-out and overly pale, even sickly. That's a clue that you are one of those women who will be more enhanced by subtle looking brights or by more subdued, muted, toned down colors.

     If, on the other hand, a color is **too** subdued or toned down for your coloring, it can gray, muddy, or even sallow your skin, causing you to look drab. That's your clue that you are in the approximately 50% of women who are more flattered by bright and bold, or bright but delicate, clear, vibrant colors.

     You can experiment in front of a mirror—it's very important to use good light. Hold different clarities up to your face. Work with any colors you like. If you don't have many colors around, do this in a store (don't pay any attention to raised eyebrows—you are training your eye and you will *live* through this experiment). Start with a comparison of bright colors—one **BOLD** and bright, the other **more delicate** yet still vibrant and bright. Holding up the boldest, brightest first, glance at yourself and see if your eye goes right to the color or whether it goes to your face and the color at the same time. What you are looking for is a good "fit" for your skin tone and hair color.

If you "hold your own" and your face looks fresh, radiant, and alive, the boldest, brightest colors will look outstanding on you. If your glance brings your eyes immediately to the color, this clarity is too bright and bold for your coloring.

Try a more delicate looking bright color next. If your face "lights up" and looks clear and healthy, you've found your best clarity. But, if the color still appears to "jump forward" or "jump off" your skin, and you look washed-out, pale, or sickly, you'll know that you need yet more subdued, toned down colors to make **YOU** look your best.

If you compare just *slightly* toned down, subdued colors to *very* toned down, subdued colors, you will find that you look more healthy in one or the other of these clarities. Watch for your face to "light up" versus appearing dulled or grayed. The right clarity "brightens" your face, making it appear healthy and alive, while the wrong clarity instantly dulls your skin (like a shadow has been cast upon it), taking away your healthy look.

SMART SHADES 👓

JUST THE BASICS

- 👓 You can look wonderful in at least one shade of every color in the spectrum.

- 👓 If you are going to wear a red suit, for example, make sure that the "shade" of red you choose looks exceptional on *you*, particularly, instead of somebody else.

BEYOND THE BASICS

> For an extraordinary appearance, wear your most flattering shade of every color in the spectrum. — JoAnna

Now that you have an understanding about the importance of clarity, we need to work on *shade*. There are many different shades of every color in the spectrum and you'll look beautiful in *your* red, for example, but not so hot in *mine*—remember that we are each wearing our reds in our best *clarity*.

Do women instinctively know what colors are flattering to them? Rarely. What most do when they look in the mirror is to check out everything "from the neck down"—the style and the fit. Because their eye hasn't been trained to see what the color is doing to their skin tone, they seldom comment accurately on the color. Even *I* was one of those women.

Once upon a time, a long time ago, I was a "creature" of fashion—I cared about style and the way something looked on my body.

I needed to buy a "perfect" dress, so I did. It was going to be the dress I changed into after my wedding (I think they used to call them *going away* outfits), and, much more importantly, it would be the dress I would be wearing to teas and receptions in "my life to be" as the wife of an Air Force pilot.

How did I know how to pick out a "perfect" dress? I was a professional fashion model and had taken university fashion and wardrobe classes, so I felt well prepared. What did it look like? It was:

- The epitome of *easy elegance*.
- Understated.
- Classic.
- Beige linen—I was headed south.
- A wrap style with a shawl collar.
- Fitted at the waist, but not tight.
- A mid-knee length.

Truly, over the next two years, it was the perfect dress for many occasions. There was only one problem—I wouldn't wear it. Why? It didn't look good on me but I didn't know why. All I knew was that I loved it, but every time I put it on and looked in the mirror, I had to take it off. With all my fashion knowledge, I couldn't figure out what was wrong. When I finally figured it out, it changed my life *forever*.

It was the wrong "shade" of beige for my skin tone. It made me look totally drab. Suddenly I knew that the perfect dress (or any other clothing item or accessory) is not perfect unless it is also **color perfect!**

Why was this realization so life changing? In exactly the same time frame, I met Judy Lewis-Crum and together we founded Color 1 Associates, our company of International Image and Style Consultants. We were the first firm in the world to train color and image consultants, making us two of the founders of a new industry—an industry that has changed the lives of countless women and men.

Clients have commented during color charting sessions, as they view for the first time all of the shades of colors that have just been selected just for them, that many of these exact colors represent all of their *old favorite outfits*—the ones they used to love to wear because they always brought so many compliments. Clients who are grandmothers (and even great-grand-mothers) are still receiving compliments—when you are in this age group and *young women* are telling you how fabulous you look, you know you are doing it right!

Every one of you can wear at least one **specific shade** of *every color* in the spectrum and look fantastic—on some of you, a few of your best shades may need to be combined or "accented" with another to create the right strength or delicateness for you. There are *numerous* different shades of:

- white ("white" is flattering to all, but *pure* white is a different story)

◆ beige	◆ camel	◆ brown
◆ gray	◆ green	◆blue-green
◆ robins egg blue/teal	◆ blue	◆purple
◆ plum/fuchsia	◆ raspberry	◆ red
◆ red-coral	◆ coral	◆ orange
◆ yellow and gold	◆ rust	◆ navy

- black (most, but not all, women can wear black effectively in some way)

I know that some of you have just decided that I'm crazy because I'm telling you that you can wear a particular color that **you're certain** you don't look good in—green, yellow, or brown, perhaps. Actually, if you haven't been wearing these colors I'm happy because if you don't know exactly which *shade* of each of these you look great in, it's easy to make a **MAJOR** mistake.

Of all of the greens—for instance, lime, celery, kelly, mint, olive, jade, parrot, spring, emerald, sea, forest, apple, moss, sage, grass—there is most often only one that will be wonderful on you. Yellow can be difficult, but when you get it right for you, it's amazing and it can be combined so well with all of your other best colors. Brown may be the most difficult to get right because if you don't get it perfect, it's a disaster as a clothing color. But when it's good, it's very, very good.

Everyone can wear both "cool" and "warm" colors but without working with you in person, it's difficult to guide you to your very best shades. How-ever, as you train your eye to see your best clarity, you will begin to notice how your face either glows (lights up) or looks sallow, grayed, or muddy—the *right* or *wrong* shades of colors do the same.

Even though I can't see you, I can give you some "colorful" smart tips:

- The most wearable shades of **green** have a touch of blue in them (like emerald green), versus the more yellow greens (such as lime green).

♦ **Blue-greens, turquoises, robins egg blue, and teal** are universally flattering colors—IF you wear them in your best clarity.

♦ A shade of **blue** that is closer to turquoise than it is to a blue-purple is more universally enhancing than the "royal" blues.

♦ Every one of you will be flattered by several shades of **purple**—the clarity, again, is very important.

♦ Each of you can wear some shade of **raspberry**. In the case of plum and fuchsia, most of you will have a becoming shade, but be very careful here—the wrong shade can really sallow your skin.

♦ You all have your best **red**—your body's natural red color is a deeper tone of the color you naturally blush, the same color as your fingertips and the inside of your lower lip.

♦ All of you can wear a shade of **coral**, and you can also wear a shade of red-coral—picture a shade that would fall right between your red and your coral.

♦ **Orange** is available to all of you, but the shade of orange that you may be *picturing* is wearable by only a few of you. The most flattering oranges have pink in them and are often very close in shade to your coral.

♦ Everyone can wear at least one shade of **yellow**—picture how many different shades of yellow there are, and that will help you understand that someplace between buttercup and lemon there will be a shade of yellow that is perfect for you. Beware of the more brownish golden yellows, like mustard, as they are rarely flattering to any coloring.

♦ What about **gold**? Not everyone can wear a shade of gold successfully. If you don't look equally as good in a gold as you do in your yellow, avoid it. If you *love* gold and want to wear it anyway, combine it with other enhancing colors.

LOOKING PERCEPTIVE—NOT PRIM

JUST THE BASICS

♦ Just because it's a "neutral" color doesn't mean it's *safe* or will be flattering to you.

BEYOND THE BASICS

Here are some guidelines that will help you select the best shades of neutrals for your coloring:

- You'll be learning all about your best **whites** soon.

- Your best **beige** matches your skin tone exactly or, if your skin is darker, it is a lighter version of your exact skin tone. If your hair is light, your best **camels** will match your hair, hair highlight, or be a darker version of it. Your **brown** will be a darker version of your hair color and/or your hair highlight color.

- If your hair is a medium brown, your best **camels** will be a darker version of your skin tone, your skin tone, or possibly a lighter version of your hair color and/or hair highlight color. Your best **browns** will be a darker version of your hair color and/or your hair highlight color.

- If your hair is brown, your best **camel** will be a darker version of your skin tone; match your skin tone; if your skin tone is darker, a lighter version of your skin tone or, possibly your hair highlight color. Your best **browns** will match your hair color and/or hair highlight color.

- If your hair is very, very dark brown or black, your best **camels** will either be a darker or lighter version of your skin tone, or they will match it exactly. Your best **browns** will be a darker version of your skin tone or, if your skin tone is darker, they will match it exactly. With very, very dark brown hair, **black** is often the better choice when it comes to clothing color.

- Your best **gray** will not have any brownish or muddy quality to it—more pure grays and blue-grays are more universally enhancing. Charcoal gray is an outstanding color for suits and a good option to black for those of you who find that black isn't flattering or is too heavy looking on you.

- Your best **rust** will not look burgundy, orangish, or brownish on you—it will look "rust."

- You may be able to wear several shades of **navy**, but they will all have something in common—they will all be lighter or darker versions of the same *"shade"* of navy which is very handy when you want to combine them. Avoid shades of navy that sallow or gray your skin.

- Other **dark neutrals**—forest green (varying shades of dark green) works best for those of you who are enhanced by slightly toned-down or toned-down colors. Drab burgundies that are brownish looking versus the color you see when light shines through a glass of red wine are rarely flattering to anyone. Burgundy and olive were the most over-rated colors of the last century.

◆ **Black**.

Ah, **black:** Most of you can wear black and look great—it's *how* you wear it that can make the difference between looking *elegant* and looking drab. On some of you black will need:

◆ A touch of color near the face.

◆ More skin showing—lower neck versus turtleneck.

◆ Less black—sheer tint of black stockings with black skirt/dress instead of opaque.

◆ A touch of *metallic*—jewelry. It could be gold, silver, or copper, but those of you who have golden skin tones, or golden, camel, caramel, or bronze colored hair or hair highlights will want to use gold. If your hair color is red or has red or copper high-lights, copper will look phenomenal.

◆ Black, or black and metallic, earrings or headband—you are "tying" the black into your skin tone and hair colors, creating balance and making it look like there is a *relationship* between your coloring and the black.

◆ A *delicate* use only, like black lace over a skin-toned fabric.

◆ To be worn only as a small amount in a print combined with your best colors and neutrals, or not at all.

How can you tell which is your most flattering way(s) to wear black? Your mirror will help you figure it out. Experiment with the various ways listed above. If you find that no matter what you do, black looks "out of place" or "foreign" on you, don't wear it.

Don't be disappointed! Knowing once and for all is liberating and I know that you definitely wouldn't want to show up in black at an interview or for a party, and compete with other women who look great in it. Pick another neutral that looks fabulous on you and designate it as **your** "black." Don't overlook cream—your "black" doesn't have to be a dark color.

Do you look *smashing* in PURE white or does it look *cheap* on you? I hate the word *cheap* but I'm using it because, in this instance, it is so descriptive that I know you'll pay extra close attention to what follows!

What am I talking about? As strange as it may seem, only 50% of you are flattered by **pure** white, while all of you can wear "clean-looking" *soft whites, off-whites*, and *creams*. Your mirror will help you figure out if you can wear pure white.

If pure white tends to "jump off your skin" and look visually too bright, or inexpensive (cheap), wear softer whites, off-whites, and creams. Sometimes whites, off-whites, and creams have a brownish "oatmeal" or grayish "putty/taupe" cast—*please* avoid these. And, unless your skin tone is golden, avoid yellowish looking whites, yellowish looking off-whites, and yellowish looking creams.

ESSENTIAL ACCENTS

JUST THE BASICS

- É If you look washed-out, try adding a color accent near your face.

- É Know what colors to avoid in general.

BEYOND THE BASICS

There are some colors that just work best when they are accented, near the face, with a touch of another color (sometimes the accent can be one of your best neutrals, as well). Not all of you will need this accent, but here's the list to be suspicious of:

- É beige, tan, and taupe

- É camel and khaki (the color)

- É brown

- É bronze

- É gray

- É rust

- É navy

- É very light colors

- É very dark colors

- É black

Some colors to avoid in general:

- ⊘ taupe

- putty

- oatmeal

- muddy or brownish grays

- khaki (the color) and olive green

- very yellowish greens

- orange the color of a pumpkin

- mustard

- very orangy rusts

- brownish burgundy

Every attempt has been made to match the colors/combinations of the clothing and accessories in the photos as closely as possible to that of the actual apparel. We have worked closely with the printer to ensure that the printed charts on the preceding pages match the actual Smart Charts as well. However, as printing runs may differ, there may be slight variations in shades and clarity. To order your own Smart Chart with actual color chips in a convenient purse size holder go to www.DressingSmart.com or call 202-293-9175. There's a free quiz on the website that will help you figure out your Color Type.

Some of the colors listed above may "work on you" but there will always be a better choice if you want to look *radiant*. If you are going to wear them, placing a flattering color next to your face is a good idea. At night, or when you are in the front of a large room making a presentation or in an important meeting, I hope you will choose a different color, but, if you don't, add a bit more makeup because these tones can drain color out of your face.

Whenever you are contemplating something new, find a dimly lit mirror (not hard in most stores) to check the color. If it fades out or blacks out (looks like a paler or darker color) you will probably look faded as well. No matter how beautiful the ensemble, it's not worth buying if it makes you look drab exactly when you want to look your best.

Creating Instant Impact

Just the Basics

> ✗ Understanding your unique personal color harmony is an essential key to looking great, so please take the time to figure out your *Color Type*.

Beyond the Basics

Let's assume that you are wearing your most flattering shades of each color in the spectrum in the best clarity for you. Can you combine these colors in any way you like and look great? Sorry, **NO.** You also have "most becoming" color combinations.

Color is the missing link—everything else can be perfect, but if the color, or color combination, is wrong for YOU it can cause you to look washed-out, sickly, or ineffective.

> Wearing the wrong color combination for your coloring can give you a "headless" look! — JoAnna

---

A few women have a wonderful sense of style in that they have a knack for creating great looks. Unfortunately, if a woman with this ability doesn't pay attention to *her* best colors, clarity, and color combinations, she may be looking stunning only from the neck down.

Why? Half of you have "strong" coloring and are very complimented by gutsier color combinations for your clothing and makeup. The other half of you have "delicate" coloring and are very enhanced by using delicate color combinations for your makeup and clothing. Once you know your "Color Type" I'll give you the *specifics* on **your** best combinations.

What Is a Color Type?

First the *fun* descriptions. Your coloring, which has nothing to do with your personality, can be described as being "exotic and dramatic," "sexy and alluring," "romantic and sensual," or "provocative and sultry."

Now for the "nuts and bolts," hardware and software, buttons and bows. A Color Type is simply a *description* of your coloring (skin tone and hair color) and/or a *description* of your best "look" for clothing and makeup. For example, I have an ivory skin tone and very dark brown hair—there is a great deal of "contrast" between my skin tone and hair color. Therefore I am a Contrast Color Type and my very best looks for clothing and makeup all revolve around my creating **needed** *contrast*. Not all Contrast Color Types have contrast between their skin tone and their hair color (the reason for the "and/or" above). Their skin tones may be medium or dark, but they also absolutely **need** the same *contrast* in their clothing and makeup looks—no other look is as fabulous.

Finding Your Color Type

The following lists of well-known women with their Color Type, best clarity and the designation of "strong" or "delicate" will help you make a decision that will be **LIFE CHANGING**. Why so serious, suddenly? Because, if you want to look your **absolute best** *FOREVER*, nothing is as important!

Although I have made only four lists, there are really 12 different Color Types because MANY people are a cross between two—half delicate coloring and half strong coloring, for example. If this is you, you will find that you walk a fine line between being overpowered and being underpowered. For some of you, a "light" just went on—now you know why it's been so hard for you to get it *right*. Now that you know, your full-length mirror will help keep you on track. More about "Cross Color Types" soon.

How dark or light your skin is has nothing to do with your Color Type—I am referring to all women and especially black women. The darkest skin tones and lightest skin tones are found in **all** 12 Color Types.

Also, there are no single categories for all blondes, all brunettes, or all redheads, nor are there for all Black, Asian, Hispanic, Native American, or Caucasian women. There is a huge variety of coloring among all women, whatever race. Black, Asian, Native American, Hispanic, and Caucasian women are found in all 12 Color Types. Black and brown hair are in all 12. Natural blondes in at least 6 different Color Types (could be more, it depends on what you think of as "blonde"). And redheads are found in about 4 (again, depending on what you think of as a "redhead").

Four Major Color Types

◆ **Contrast Color Types—Bright, Bold Clear Colors and Strong Coloring—"exotic and dramatic":**

Jacqueline Kennedy, Toni Morrison, Elizabeth Taylor, Liv Tyler, Winona Ryder, Toni Braxton, Connie Chung, Cher, Alicia Keys, Audrey Hepburn, Giselle Hernandez, Queen Elizabeth, Carole Simpson, Demi Moore, Jessica Yu, Rita Moreno, Minnie Driver, Judith Dench, Diahann Carroll, Courteney Cox, Lucy Liu, Catherine Zeta-Jones, Joan Collins, Barbara Bush, Lynn Whitfield, Julianna Margulies, Christina Ricci, Monica, Dixie Carter, Irina Dvorovenko, and Ruth Bader Ginsberg.

Natural hair colors are dark brown or black. Skin tones range from clear ivory, clear camel, and clear olive to clear dark brown.

◆ **Light-Bright Color Types—Bright, but Delicate, Clear Colors and Delicate Coloring—"sexy and alluring":**

Faith Hill, Princess Di, Tyra Banks, Reese Witherspoon, Jewel, Hillary Clinton, Janet Jackson, Marilyn Monroe, Claudia Schiffer, Sharon Stone, Ce Ce Winans, Faith Ford, Cameron Diaz, Kristi Yamaguchi, Diana Ross, Melanie Griffith, Ivana Trump, Mary Hart, Dolly Parton, Sandra Day O'Connor, Deborah Norville, Charlize Theron, Heather Locklear, Courtney Love, Portia de Rossi, Vivica Fox, Elizabeth Shue, Ashanti, and Diane Sawyer.

Natural hair colors range from golden blonde to black (but do not include red). Skin tones range from clear ivory, clear golden ivory, clear golden camel, to clear dark brown with probable golden tones.

◆ **Gentle Color Types—Toned-Down, Subdued Colors and Delicate Coloring—"romantic and sensual":**

Gwyneth Paltrow, Katie Couric, Annette Bening, Candice Bergen, Beverly Johnson, Calista Flockhart, Jane Leeves, Nicole Kidman, Elizabeth Hurley, Drew Barrymore, Kim Basinger, Meryl Streep, Beverly Johnson, Glenn Close, LeAnn Rimes, Jane Seymour, Jane Pauley, Phylicia Rashad, Michelle Pfeiffer, Betty Ford, Kate Moss, Cicely Tyson, Claire Danes, Jodi Foster, Roma Downey, Cybill Shepherd, and Linda Evans.

Natural hair colors range from blonde to black and include some redheads. Skin tones range from ivory and pink beige to dark brown with probable pink tones.

◆ **Muted Color Types—Slightly Toned-Down Colors and Strong Coloring—"provocative and sultry":**

Cindy Crawford, Oprah, Julia Roberts, Beyonce Knowles, Barbara Walters, Jennifer Lopez, Bai Ling, Naomi Campbell, Sophia Loren, Mariah Carey, Debra Messing, Salma Hayek, Whitney Houston, Shirley MacLaine, Nancy Reagan, Whoopi Goldberg, Maria Shriver, Barbra Streisand, Gloria Estafan, Tina Turner, Jennifer Esposito, Geena Davis, Christine Lahti, Patti La Belle, Lauryn Hill, Carmen Electra, Sheryl Crow, and Susan Sarandon.

Natural hair colors range from blonde to black and include some redheads. Skin tones range from ivory beige to golden beige and from olive to dark brown.

When your hair turns "gray," silver, or white, your Color Type stays the same. Sun-damaged skin, skin rashes/diseases, high doses of some chemicals and some vitamins might change the color of your skin tone and, if permanent, might change your Color Type. Also, looking beautiful in clear or toned-down colors has nothing to do with your age—the only way a bright color could make a woman look older or less chic is if she is wearing "bright" when her most flattering clarity (from birth to death) is more toned down. Yes, you can tell a baby's Color Type. — JoAnna

Cross Color Types

There are as many Cross Color Types as there are straight Color Types. Here are some *smart tips* to help you find yourself:

♦ **Contrast/Muted Color Types** might look just like a straight Contrast Color Type but instead of clear colors, they look best in slightly toned down colors. The natural hair color is very dark brown (with probable reddish highlights) or black.

♦ **Muted/Contrast Color Types** on the other hand, look best in clear colors instead of slightly toned down colors. They are not straight Contrast Color Types because their color combinations need to look more "muted"—you're "blending" brighter colors. The natural hair color is dark brown (with possible reddish highlights) or black. Pure white in any amount will look "inexpensive."

♦ **Contrast/Light-Bright Color Types** have half-strong, half-delicate coloring and may need to *slightly* "take the edge off" their clear bold colors, making them just a hint more delicate looking. The natural hair color is dark brown (with probable golden highlights) or black. A "typical" Light-Bright look in makeup and clothing will look weak and a "typical" Contrast look will appear overpowering.

♦ **Light-Bright/Contrast Color Types** have half-delicate, half-strong coloring and usually need slightly more powerful color combinations than a straight Light-Bright Color Type. The natural hair color is brown to dark brown (with golden highlights) or black. Again, "typical" Light-Bright looks will appear a touch weak, yet a straight Contrast look will overpower.

♦ **Light-Bright/Gentle Color Types** might look like a straight Light-Bright Color Type but they need slightly toned down colors instead of clear, bright delicate looking colors. Natural hair colors range from blonde to black.

♦ **Gentle/Light-Bright Color Types** need clear, delicate looking bright colors instead of a straight Gentle Color Type's toned down colors.

Natural hair colors range from blonde to black, and pure white will only look good in a small amount in a print.

◆ **Gentle/Muted Color Types** have half-delicate, half-strong coloring so some of the very blended small patterns that look ethereal on a straight Gentle Color Type may look weak, so strengthen color combinations when necessary. Natural hair colors range from blonde to black and include some redheads.

◆ **Muted/Gentle Color Types** have half-strong and half-delicate coloring so some of the darker or gutsier color combinations that look so rich on straight Muted Color Types may look "heavy" or overpowering. Lighten darker color combinations when necessary. Natural hair colors range from blonde to black and include some redheads. Pure white, even a small amount in a print, will look "inexpensive."

Looking Powerful or Weak

Just the Basics

◆ Avoid wearing navy and white, or black and white, together unless you know that it is not overpowering you.

Beyond the Basics

Are "you" the center of attention *or* is your outfit? Yet another *technical* thing to discuss—"high-contrast." Believe me, I wouldn't be writing about it if it weren't very important. How important? If 50% of you do "it," you aren't looking your best—to be truthful, you're looking pretty bad.

High-contrast is created by wearing:

◆ Black with white—like a black suit with a white blouse; a black and white striped sweater with black trousers; or a black dress with white pearls.

◆ Black with off-white or light cream/winter white—like a winter-white suit with a black necklace and black shoes; or a black and off-white print blouse with black trousers.

◆ Navy with white—like a navy suit with white piping on the jacket; a navy skirt with a white top; or a white suit with a navy shell and navy shoes.

◆ Navy with off-white or light cream/winter white—like a navy suit with a navy and off-white scarf.

◆ And sometimes very dark brown with white—like dark brown

leather pants with a white sweater. If your hair is very dark brown, you may be able to handle this contrast; if not, it's best to avoid it.

All three Contrast Color Types and all three Light-Bright Color Types look great in high-contrast. However, all three Gentle and all three Muted Color Types are overpowered by these high-contrast color combinations—that means that if you are wearing them and you walk into a room, your outfit will enter ahead of you. They can give you a "headless" person look.

Not sure about your Color Type? Your mirror will tell you if you should avoid high-contrast—try it and see where your eyes go. If they go to the color combination before they go to your face, you are one of the Gentle or Muted Color Types. Substitute your best light beige for the white and look at the **spectacular difference**. For you, beige with black or navy creates a slightly softer contrast and a much more stunning entrance! It is *your* high-contrast look—your powerful look.

Which Color Types are enhanced by "pure white"?

◆ Contrast Color Types can wear pure white head to toe.

◆ Light-Bright Color Types can do the same.

◆ Gentle Color Types can wear a small amount of pure white in a print or as a trim. You can wear soft whites (a white that still "looks" like white on you but isn't so bright-white that it jumps off your skin), off-whites, winter whites, and creams. Wear them with any color except black, navy, and *probably* dark brown.

◆ Muted Color Types should avoid pure white in any amount. Just like all Color Types, you can wear soft whites (they will still "look" like white on you without being so bright-white that they jump off your skin), off-whites, winter whites, and creams. Wear them with any color other than black, navy, and *probably* dark brown.

I would like for you to note a distinction between light creams and deeper creams—those that are deeper can generally be worn with black and navy by all Color Types. Your mirror will help you decide if the contrast level works with your coloring.

SMART COLOR COMBINATIONS

JUST THE BASICS

◆　If your coloring is *delicate* looking (Light-Bright and Gentle Color Types), you will want to make all of your color combinations delicate looking also. If your coloring is *strong* (all Muted and

Contrast Color Types), all of your best color combinations will have strength, gutsiness.

Beyond the Basics

"Picture" it. If you have a painting that needs to be framed, you would never pick out a powerful, bold looking frame for a delicate looking watercolor. Nor would you select a delicate looking frame for a bold graphic.

If your *coloring* is "delicate" (this term has nothing to do with your personality), **lighten up darker colors and dark, or strong, color combinations**—you could also avoid wearing them. For example:

◆ The strong color combination of a navy suit worn with a red blouse can be lightened up by putting gold buttons on the jacket and wearing gold, or navy and gold, earrings. But you can also easily solve the dilemma by wearing a pink, yellow, or other light color top, in place of the red.

◆ Could you add just a gold or silver necklace to lighten the dark combination of a forest green jacket and brown trousers? A tiny chain is not enough but a more substantial looking necklace and earrings will help, although you may still look "bottom-heavy" (not your bum, but your coloring, from the neck down). Adding a brown belt with a buckle in the same metal will give you better balance. Or, you can add a scarf that combines the green and brown with some lighter colors.

If your *coloring* is "stronger," "gutsier" looking, it's not necessary for you to lighten strong color combinations, but you will probably need to **lighten, strengthen, or brighten** other *specific* color combinations.

As you read the following examples, remember that we are discussing those of you who have STRONG coloring. By the way, you do know by now that your Color Type has nothing to do with your personality or body shape and size. Right?

If you are a Contrast Color Type, you will need to add a light or bright accent to an all dark color combination (the exception is black **if** you look great in it head to toe), and a bright or dark accent to an all light color combination (exceptions are white and cream). An example:

◆ A clear light pink top and cream trousers are strengthened by a black belt and black shoes. A dark purple top with a navy suit can be brightened by adding a scarf that combines the navy and purple with white/cream and/or any bright color. Or, you can always just change your top to one that is a bright color or a light color.

If you are a Muted Color Type you will not need to lighten dark color combinations **unless your hair is light**. If your hair is medium to dark in tone, you may need to strengthen light color combinations (add a medium or dark color) or wear them in large blocks of color like:

◆ A coral skirt with a yellow sweater or cream trousers with a light blue top—if these combinations look "weak," add belt and shoes in your hair color.

◆ Avoid wearing small patterns that combine light colors—they aren't "gutsy" enough for you.

I'm giving you some "unusual" examples on purpose to *stimulate* your imagination—you may substitute **your** favorite light, medium, or dark colors. **Here are your best *color combinations* by Color Type:**

CONTRAST COLOR TYPES

◆ Wear a dark color with a bright color—black and red; navy and fuchsia.

◆ Wear a bright color with a light color—turquoise and white; purple and bright pink.

◆ Wear two bright colors together—yellow and blue; fuchsia and red-coral (I mentioned that I'd be giving you some "unusual" color combinations—I wear my fuchsia suit with a red-coral top and "tie" it all together with a fuchsia and red-coral scarf).

◆ Wear a dark color with a light color—black and white; navy and a light, but bright, yellow.

◆ Avoid using two light colors together without adding a medium or dark color—cream and light gray with red; white and clear bright pink with black.

◆ Avoid using two dark colors together without adding a light or medium accent—black and dark (but bright) purple with white; navy and rust with clear light coral.

LIGHT-BRIGHT COLOR TYPES

◆ Wear a light color with a bright color—cream and bright robins egg blue; red and white.

◆ Wear two medium-toned "delicate" looking bright colors together—bright yellow and bright coral; bright pink and clear purple.

◆ Wear a dark color with a light color—black and white; charcoal gray and clear pink.

◆ If you wear two pastels together such as beige with light purple or light green with light yellow, you may need to add a contrasting accent (a bright or dark color) near the face or at the waist.

◆ Avoid wearing a bright color with a dark color without adding a light accent—red and black with gold buttons and/or gold jewelry.

◆ Avoid wearing two dark colors together. If you do, you will definitely need to lighten the color combination—dark blue and charcoal gray lightened with jewelry, matching metallic buttons and/or a large block of a light color (a white top, perhaps).

GENTLE COLOR TYPES

◆ Wear two light colors together—pink and yellow; light gray and light turquoise.

◆ Wear a light color with a medium color—light blue-purple and raspberry; cream and red.

◆ Wear two medium colors together—coral/purple; medium blue/camel.

◆ Wear a medium color with a dark color—medium green and dark green; medium plum and navy (light-haired Gentle Color Types will need a light accent near the face or at the waist).

◆ Avoid wearing the high-contrast combinations of black, navy, or dark brown with white/off-white/light cream—substitute your deeper creams, light beige, or any other light color. You may combine your white/off-white with any other dark color.

◆ Avoid wearing two dark colors together, especially if your hair is light to medium in tone. If you do, you will definitely need to lighten the color combination—dark red and charcoal gray lightened with jewelry, matching metallic buttons, and/or a large block of a light color (like a light gray top, perhaps).

MUTED COLOR TYPES

◆ Wear a light color with a medium color—beige and green; light blue-purple and raspberry.

◆ Wear two medium colors together—red and camel; medium blue and green.

◆ Wear a dark color with a medium color—black and purple; rust and teal.

◆ Wear two light colors together in larger blocks of color (coral trousers and yellow top) or accent lighter color combinations with a medium or dark color—light green and beige with rust; cream and light gray with camel.

◆ Wear two dark colors together (light-haired Muted Color Types will need a light or medium accent)—navy and rust; dark green and brown; dark purple and black.

◆ Avoid wearing the high-contrast color combination of black, navy, and probably dark brown with white/off-white/light cream—substitute deeper creams, your light beige, or any other light color.

If you love to wear "fashion" or "in" colors although they may not be enhancing to you, try to use your best *version* and clarity of these colors. If raspberry is *in*, for example, you can find many variations and clarities in the stores. You may be able to combine the latest "hues" with one of your best colors—keeping a great color next to your face (especially if your color combination has the *look* of your Color Type) can fool the eye.

CHANGING THE WAY
THE WORLD LOOKS AT YOU

CLASSIC AND CLASSY

> Being fashionable is always in style but to be considered fashionable one does not need to wear the current looks shown on the runway or in fashion magazines, spend a lot of money, be thin, or young.
> — JoAnna

JUST THE BASICS

- *Classics* are enduring, reliable, and *elegant*.

- If you want your clothing to look contemporary for several years, avoid buying fads, extremes in fashion, or anything flashy.

- Think twice before wearing a fad to work.

BEYOND THE BASICS

Clunky, chunky, heavy looking shoes are a terrible fad—they don't deserve to be called a "fashion" even though they have been around for a while. Clumsy, dumpy and inelegant, they make *perfect* legs look heavy, thin legs look like toothpicks, and they turn an otherwise good looking outfit into a look that makes people wonder, "What was she thinking?"

I asked an elegant Frenchman about clunky shoes when he was visiting the States and I happened to catch him grimacing when he saw a group of women wearing them. He said, "First, I blame the person who thought them up; second, I blame the manufacturer who made them; third, I blame the stores that bought them; and fourth, I blame the women who buy them and wear them—they look so ungraceful!"

> Some women are born wealthy, but no woman is born with elegance, class, grace, and charm. — JoAnna

Actually, even though my field is fashion and beauty, I've become nearly *anti-fashion* because I'm perturbed (to put it mildly and ladylike) at the designers for being ridiculous, and irked at magazines that continue to show mostly unwearable, inelegant, unflattering, or unattainable clothing and accessories (from a price standpoint) on undersized, under-aged models who have been airbrushed a dozen times to bring them closer to so-called perfection. *Yikes*—sorry for the long sentence!

The "fashion" sections of many magazines continue to be an arena for photographers to show how "talented and creative" they are by *shooting* leaping, crouching, sleeping, snake-wrapped, scary, drugged-out looking women. Shot in alleys, messy, dirty rooms, and sometimes with eight violent looking men shown pulling them apart, in many cases you can't even see what the "model" is wearing and when you can decipher the *fashion*, you usually wouldn't want it anyway.

Years ago, I used to "light up" when I got the latest issue of any fashion magazine because everything was so beautiful (not affordable, but wearable) and I could get ideas that helped me in my personal quest to be and stay stylish. Now, there is rarely a picture of anything I might want, and, for the most part, "lessons" designed to help you be stylish are filled with **really bad advice** or old myths.

Classic and Classy

Classic styles have perennial appeal, a long life expectancy, and they are used every day in some way by most of us. They look "stylish" for decades depending on the ways in which you combine them with each other or with newer "fashions."

> There is an art to being timeless, yet so current that you look like your knowledge and skills are up to the minute—modern. — JoAnna

Instead of telling you what is classic, it's easier to describe what **isn't:**

◆ Anything oversized, overstated, or extreme.

◆ Shoes and boots with platform soles over ¼".

◆ *Very* short skirts.

◆ Very wide pants.

◆ Sleeves that come down to your knuckles.

◆ Heavy-looking shoes and boots with very chunky heels.

◆ Glitz in the daytime.

◆ Large shoulder pads.

Can you identify the scarves below that would look super with your coloring? (Hint: there will be two.)

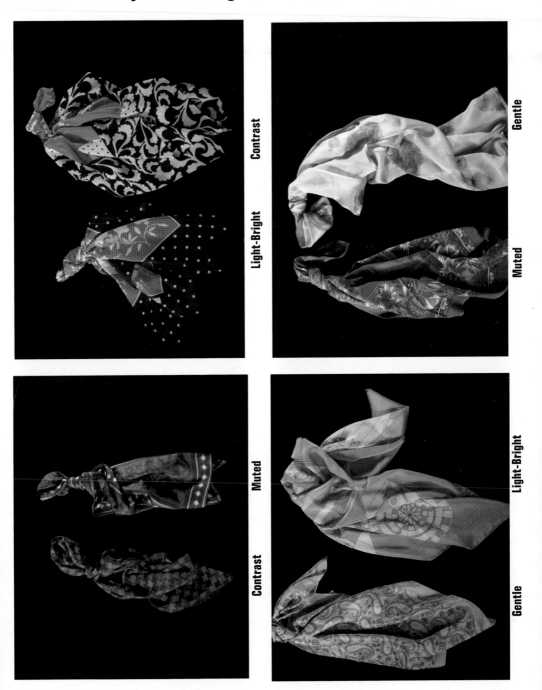

Clothing and accessories courtesy of JoAnna and Color 1 Associates.
Photos courtesy of The Photographer's Gallery.

Smart Chart for:

Muted Coloring

Smart Chart for:

Contrast Coloring

Smart Chart for:

Light-Bright Coloring

Smart Chart for:

Gentle Coloring

There are many shades of beige, camel, brown, and navy.

Your personal best beiges, camels, and browns will match your skin tone, be a lighter or darker version of your skin tone, and/or match your hair color and hair highlight colors. Wearing your most flattering shades of gray and navy are equally as important as selecting your best shades and clarity of every color. Black is a "possibility" for all color types, but will not be a great head-to-toe look for every individual.

Can you identify the three scarves below that would look super with your coloring?

Contrast   Gentle   Light-Bright   Muted

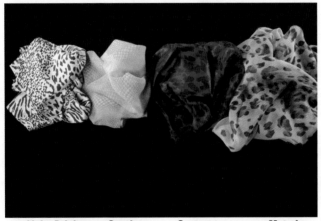

Light-Bright   Gentle   Contrast   Muted

Contrast   Light-Bright   Muted   Gentle

50% of you are most enhanced by a delicate mix of colors – the other 50% of you are most enhanced by a strong mix of colors.

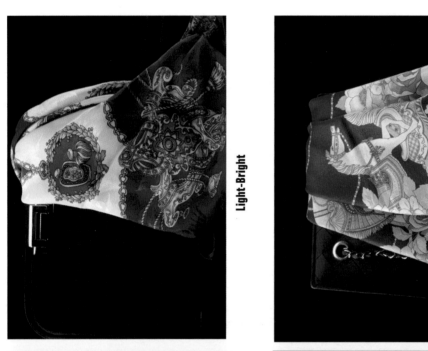

Light-Bright

Gentle

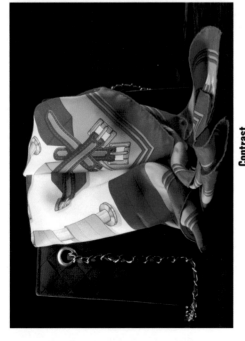

Contrast

Muted

- Brownish lipsticks and brownish or orangy blush.

- "Odd" colors of nail polish, such as purple, green, black, and blue.

- Long, square fingernails and embellished nails.

- Shoes and boots with very square or very pointed toes.

- Above-the-knee and thigh-high boots.

Sometimes something is considered classic in one region of our country but not in another. For example, in parts of the west and southwest, western attire is classic but not in New York City (except jeans, which are classic everywhere). Big hair may be classic in Texas but not in urban southern California cities or San Francisco.

Wearing "wearable art" is classic for women who have adopted it as their style, and it's a *fashion* for the rest of us. Funky is a wonderfully broad term that seems to be classic for some teens and, depending on the item, a fad or fashion for the rest of us.

Classic makeup looks include using lip and blush colors that are always flattering to your coloring instead of following trends like brownish lipsticks and blush. Classic ways to wear your hair do not include spikes, a lot of teasing, or hair "frozen" in place with hairspray (helmet hair).

Please note that classic and boring are not synonyms. — JoAnna

---

Fashion-Forward to the New *"Silhouettes"*

Many of us also wear styles that are currently "in"—one of the new suits that has a personality, for example. The fashions of today may have started as a fad or trend. And, some of these "fashions a la mode" may stay around for several years, if they are worthy of incorporating into our wardrobes. They are the odd pieces that can help keep us *contemporary* looking. Their life expectancy is "medium" (which is longer than a fad but shorter than a classic). Some fashions may actually stay around so long that they eventually are considered classic.

An example is very slim-cut or narrow-leg trousers. I'm not using tight and slim as synonyms. Since women have found out that this shape trouser made their legs look longer and their body look more slim-hipped and sleek, you can count on them to be around for many, many years—regardless of other pant shapes being pushed to the forefront of fashion.

Stirrup pants are classic only for skiing and horseback riding. For regular wear, years ago they were adopted as a fad until they were declared "OUT"—

we liked them because they were comfortable; they helped us create the slim-hip look mentioned above; and because we wore them with long sweaters and didn't have to worry if our tummies were flat at the moment.

Most of us replaced them with leggings—we didn't need the "stretch pant" look to get the effect we desired. Since leggings come and go in style, replacing them with very narrow-cut trousers, perhaps made out of a comfortable microfiber or another fabric that has "stretch," is the *smart* thing to do.

Fast forward fads and trends definitely make a statement—but is it a *smart* statement for you to make? The words "fad" and "trend" may, or may not, be considered synonyms—it can depend on which magazine you are reading, and it can depend on which fad or trend you are talking about.

Fads are usually considered pretty "wild" or "far-out" by current standards. However, they, too, may stand the test of time, become a *fashion,* and maybe even a *classic.* Today's fad of heavy-looking clunky heeled shoes will go the way of the headband of the late '60s (the one that went around your forehead, not the *classic* headband that goes over your head to keep your hair pulled back).

Although a trend and a fad are sometimes the same thing, a trend has another definition that fad doesn't have. For example, pantsuits are *classic* but wearing pantsuits to work started as a "trend" that continued to grow— it is not a fad but a viable option for women in every workplace, no matter how formal or conservative. I am talking about a pantsuit that is **equal** in quality and styling to your skirted suits—not just pants and a top. A tie worn with a pantsuit is a fad that comes and goes in fashion.

Trends are usually more *popular* than fads—more people will try them because, although they are a "stretch" for some women, they are usually less of a stretch than a fad.

LOOK SMART—BUY SMART

JUST THE BASICS

    💰 To get the most versatility out of your clothing pieces, buy classics in solid colors and in fabrics that can be combined and worn all, or almost all, year.

BEYOND THE BASICS

Before you invest in any garment or accessory, ask yourself if it will serve you well in your workplace and help you create the exact look you want. If the answer is yes, and the item is "trendy," ask yourself another question. Are you willing to spend your money on something that you may not be able to wear more than one or two seasons? Would you happily wear it once every week or two? Does it make you look and feel like a million dollars?

Buy *Smart Basics:* If you're on a budget and want every purchase to count, buy *smart basics.* Besides being "classic" in styling, what makes a garment a *smart basic*? All of the following:

- It's a solid color.

- All stitching matches the garment exactly.

- The color of the buttons match the garment exactly.

- There are no extra details on the garment like epaulets or contrasting trim or braid.

- Its fabric can be combined with many other fabrics.

- It can be worn with many different things.

- Nothing is oversized, such as collars, lapels, shoulders, and so on.

- It's perfectly plain and simple—do not think boring—think *easy elegance*.

Buy Quality Instead of Quantity: It's much more difficult to have a lot of bad choices because it can be confusing—that's one of the reasons you will hear women who have a closet full of clothes say, "I have nothing to wear!" What they are really saying is that they don't have anything that they *like* that they *want* to wear.

> If you really want to continually upgrade your look, you'll want to always apply the smart tip, "If it isn't equal to or better than the best look you have right now, leave it." — JoAnna

If you want to look great every day, when you shop consider the following:

- Invest in the right places—spend the most money on clothes you spend the most time in.

- Learn to pass up a bargain—It's NOT a bargain if it doesn't look like a million dollars on you.

- It is far better to wear the same outstanding look once or twice a week than to wear something else that looks so-so on you.

- Buy well the first time—well-made, well-cut, wonderful *basics* won't go out of style.

- Don't spend money on something that doesn't look great on you—even if it's *almost* free!

You can't afford to look great one day and not the next—it can give the impression that you don't know what you're doing. People who can be consistently counted on are the ones who are promoted, and your visual presentation is often even more valued than your work presentations. It doesn't sound fair, but that's the way it often works.

LOOKING AS IF YOU DON'T HAVE A CLUE

JUST THE BASICS

- To look great every day, all you need is to learn a new skill.

- You don't know what you don't know.

BEYOND THE BASICS

You are just beginning to know what you don't. No one can dress well without "training" or without a full-length mirror. Think about training for a minute and about how you would perform in your job if you didn't have the skills. *Dressing smart* is the same principle. Just because you are born *female* doesn't mean that you should be able to dress yourself, your children, and your significant other without training.

For example, every woman can type. Yes, you can. Those of you who took lessons type faster and more accurately than those of you who haven't had lessons—without lessons, you can still type but this is called the "hunt and peck" method. With your wardrobe, I call it "hit and miss."

If you've had lessons, do you remember your first typing test? I think that I typed 17 words a minute and made five mistakes. By my second test, I was up to 35 words a minute with three mistakes. *Eventually,* with practice, 80 words a minute, nearly perfect. After lessons, if typing is part of your life, you just get better and better at it. But, new *equipment* is constantly being developed and you may not know how to use it skillfully at first—a new program on your computer, new styles of shoes, pants in all widths and lengths, skirts in all shapes and lengths, textured stockings, and belts that would have dazzled Cinderella! Consider this book your *training* program for great style, and practice, practice, practice.

How does the full-length mirror help in your training? It helps you train your eye. To train your eye, you must look carefully at yourself **OFTEN** and do the "mirror test" whenever necessary. A woman can look at herself in a mirror and say, "I look fine," when she really doesn't (perhaps her stockings are too dark for her ensemble but she can't see this). This woman knows *less* than the woman who looks in the mirror and says, "Something is wrong but I don't know what."

Your level of knowledge is higher when you can tell what's wrong—"My stockings are too dark"—and greater even yet when you know how to fix the problem—"I need to change to lighter stockings; maybe a sheerer version of the same color will work."

A Mirror Image

Just the Basics

◆ Studying your image in a full-length mirror will help you know at a glance if you look great, just okay, or not so good.

Beyond the Basics

To start training your eye, you want to learn to do a mirror test. Place your full-length mirror where you can walk a few paces away from it—good lighting helps a lot. Study yourself coming and going. Turn around *fast.* If your eye goes immediately to the color or pattern you are wearing, it is probably too bright, too bold, and/or too large for you, causing you to look overdone or garish—certainly not a successful look.

If your glance reveals an overall "washed-out" or dull look, the color or pattern is more than likely too muted, too weak, and/or too small for you. Looking drab or mousy is not a radiant, successful look! If your eye goes straight to your belt, necklace, or earrings, for example, it may not be right for you and/or your outfit.

Learn to use your mirror to your advantage by letting it help educate you. Check everything, even if, in the beginning, you feel that you *don't have a clue* what to look for:

◆ Is your shoe too heavy looking? Is the color too light or too dark?

◆ Is your leg line being shortened by wearing a longer jacket with wider-leg trousers?

◆ Does your face look washed-out or overly made up?

◆ Is your outfit making you look pear-shaped—narrower at the shoulders and wider at your hipline? Are your colors balanced and coordinated looking?

◆ Do they really enhance you?

◆ Does your hairstyle make the statement **you** want?

◆ Do *you* love the way you look?

◆ Would you be happy about the way you are dressed if you suddenly happen to meet your favorite movie star or you were to run into your new "special" guy with his "old" girl friend?

LETTING GO OF LIMITATIONS,
⃠ BAD ADVICE & OLD MYTHS ⓘ

JUST THE BASICS

♦ You can create any look and wear any style you wish, as long as you get the scale, fit, and balance right for your size and shape.

♦ All bodies are right—only clothes are wrong.

♦ Stylish and attractive women come in all sizes and shapes. It's time to get over what *size* you are and get on with looking great.

♦ In most environments, black could actually be making you look larger, not smaller.

BEYOND THE BASICS

You really can create any look and wear any style you wish. All you need are a few lessons (*smart tips*), a full-length mirror, patience, perseverance, the willingness to train your eye, a good tailor, and a wonderful sense of humor.

If your size and/or shape have been a limitation to you in the past, it's only been because your head has been filled with less than accurate advice and a mind-set of old myths. A woman needs confidence and knowledge to challenge myths and years of bad advice. If you are full-figured, have full-figured body parts, or you are short, your life has probably been filled with so many *DON'TS* that you've had very few *DO'S* to work with—a vast injustice, because you can *DO* everything everyone else can.

⃠ **Bad Advice:** A sleeveless, thinly ribbed turtleneck, cropped at the waist is perfect for minimizing full breasts.

ⓘ **My Advice:** In general, all ribbed tops *maximize* the size of your bosom, not minimize it! Cropped tops can also maximize, and being sleeveless has nothing to do with making your bustline look smaller or larger. No cropped tops for most all *legitimate* business.

All bodies are right—only clothes are wrong! One of my friends has a **great** looking derriere—her husband speaks of it as "booty." She doesn't always need to cover it, she just makes sure that it always looks super. We both love "wild" jeans and some of our jeans have lycra or spandex in them and they are cut quite close in the upper leg. With some of them, she does cover her "booty" with a jacket because they tend to push her derriere "up and out," making it look like a lollipop (her words)! Always check the "view" you are giving others of your backside.

⊘ **Bad Advice:** Petite women look their best in sleek, structured designs.

① **My Advice:** Whoever wrote this advice was thoughtlessly telling all short women that they won't ever look good in more softly designed feminine clothing. Totally not true! First of all, sleek, structured designs do not add even a 1/8" of height to anyone. Secondly, having less height does not limit you in any way. Both very short women and very tall women can look great in long jackets and short jackets, long skirts and short skirts, and so on, as can very thin women and very full-figured women. It's all a matter of how you combine different styles and how each garment is scaled to your proportions.

Let's talk about the "issue" of weight and get it over with. Most women would prefer to be smaller. Most women postpone feeling attractive until they get small! Most women never get small or believe they are small enough. Many women never *feel* attractive!

This breaks my heart. You have no idea how *really* attractive and elegant you are, or can be, at the exact weight and size you are *right now*. I have proof! Fabulous non-skinny women include: Kirstie Alley, Queen Latifah, Emme, Kathy Najimy, Oprah, Lisa Nicole Carson, Camryn Manheim, Star Jones, Kathy Bates, Delta Burke, Cybill Shepherd, and my sisters, whom I adore.

My *much* older sister (she's really only 16 months older than me) decided a long time ago that, even if she wasn't the same size she used to be (before her first child), she was still pretty, she was still sexy, and she wasn't going to put off having fun, really living life. She is fabulous! You can ask her significant other or her boy friends—you can even ask her ex.

What size is she? Well, when she decided that she wasn't going to postpone feeling attractive, she was about four sizes larger than she used to be. She's at least two sizes smaller now.

My *little* sister (she's barely 5' tall and I'm 5' 8½") has the challenge of being a full-figured petite. Yet, when the company where she works needed someone to teach wardrobing classes to their employees, they asked her to be the instructor.

Why? Because she's the one who has developed a great stylish look—women follow her around and ask her advice. Is she sexy? Men leap out of their 4 x 4's (she lives in the northwest) when they see her just to talk for a few minutes—they even stop by work when they don't have any business to do! Well, maybe monkey business.

Now you are suspicious that I don't know what full-figured means. Without giving you her exact dress/suit size, when they asked her to teach the class, I'll just tell you that it was the fourth size up from the smallest size sold in the plus-size department. She's now the same size as the average American woman.

You may still be thinking that you'd rather be smaller than you are, but wouldn't you also like to feel pretty, confident, and sexy *right now*? If you've been hiding your body (or your "booty"), or wish you could, you've probably been denying yourself full love of self and life. Many women put their lives into a "holding pattern" until they are a smaller size—you can look terrific now, so why wait?

⊘ **Bad Advice:** Black, medium tones, and brights visually take off pounds if you wear them close to your body.

⊕ **My Advice:** First of all, it's a myth that black is slimming— it's only slimming if you are standing or sitting against a dark background or walking around outside at night. Most of our background colors are light. If you are wearing a dark color (close to your body, or not) and you are standing in front of a light-colored background your shape is totally *outlined*—the reverse of camouflage, it "stands out"! When you wear lighter colors in front of a light background, you blend in. All colors that look great on you can be slimming, including black, but it is the way a garment is *styled/shaped* and what you combine it with that makes the difference between it looking *WOW* or so-so on you.

As far as wearing clothing close to your body goes, I feel that it's wonderful for women of all sizes to show their curves. The problem comes in knowing the difference between *close to the body* and *tight*. Tight clothing can make you look larger—like you've just gained weight, when indeed, you may be so excited that you are now able to squeeze into a smaller size that you forgot this fact.

Actually, one of the reasons women *feel* smaller when they are wearing black is because they tend to wear *all* black—black top, bottom, belt, shoes and stockings. Any "all one-color look" can give a slimming appearance because the eye can easily travel around without interruption.

⊘ **Bad Advice:** If you are bottom-heavy, you should wear ankle-length skirts only.

⊕ **My Advice:** Yikes, nearly a whole country/world of women in really long skirts! Let me remind you that the "Bad Advice" I'm writing came out of popular women's magazines. You can wear any skirt length you want—it's all in the **shape** of the skirt and what you pair it with.

One day a client called to ask me to send her a gift certificate for her best friend. It had been about two months since our consultation and she told me that I was responsible for her having lost ten pounds. I thanked her but told her that I couldn't take credit for that difficult task. She insisted that it was my doing and explained that when she came to me to have her color chart done she didn't feel good about herself—basically because of her weight. With her chart in hand, she bought three new scarves and two new lipsticks that matched the colors on her chart. She wore them with *everything*. People kept giving her compliments that started with, "Gee, you look great!" and ended with, "Have you lost weight?" She explained to me that she hadn't lost even one pound but because of the way the praise made her *feel,* the weight just started coming off.

In reality, whether you are a size 4 or a size 20, you may do everything all other women can do—you may choose your own "exceptions"—there are always a few. For example, most women with legs that are heavier than they wish won't be wearing **very** short skirts, but they may choose to wear short skirts. Think about it for a second. If only women with *perfect* legs wore short skirts, very few short skirts would ever be worn (or sold).

> "The average man is more interested in a woman who is interested in him than he is in a woman with beautiful legs." — Marlene Dietrich

Change your focus from trying to look "smaller" and just concentrate on feeling great about the way you look every day.

THE ART OF CREATING ILLUSION

JUST THE BASICS

- If your shoulders *appear* wider than your hips you will look slimmer and more stylish.

- Small shoulder pads can work a miracle.

- A skirt that is narrower at the hem than it is at your hip can give you a very stylish look. The same goes for a pair of pants.

- No matter what your size, wear jackets that define your waist.

- Slim-cut pants are generally more flattering than those with a wider leg.

- Dowdy is not a disease, but if you have this malady, *easy elegance* is the cure.

BEYOND THE BASICS

Avoid looking dowdy at all cost! First, the good news. Dowdy is not a disease, although at times it seems to have reached epidemic proportions in parts of our country and has currently infected the footwear of many women.

Looking dowdy or frumpy is caused purely by lack of knowledge, and no woman should ever have "that" thought about herself or have anyone else think "that" about her. In this day and age, women who look less stylish are likely to be viewed as behind the times, out of the loop—not a positive business or social image. All it takes to look *smart* is **good advice** and practice.

The Eye Goes Where the Line Leads It: Part of creating *illusion* is in the understanding that certain designs or styles can make you appear "squashed," or they can create a "down-line" where you need an up-line (like the upside-down "V" that can make you appear pear-shaped). If the line and design (the shape) of a garment, or the pairing of garments, can create an unflattering look, then the line and design of a garment, or the pairing of garments, can create a flattering look.

For everyone, the best way to get a great stylish look is to create a V shape each time you get dressed. It will give you a flattering slimmer-hip, broader-shoulder look. You create this V shape by making sure that your hipline *looks* narrower than your shoulder line. All you have to do to check this out is to look in the mirror—remember, you are training your eye.

First, take a close look at yourself just in your underlovelies. Some of you will find that your natural shoulder line is wider than your hips and others of you will see that your shoulder line looks narrower (or about the same). If your shoulders look narrower, all you have to do is to make sure that each of your outfits makes your shoulder line look a little wider, most often by using shoulder pads in your tops and/or jackets. **Don't panic,** I don't mean large, football-player pads. The tiniest pads, placed *just right*, can turn dowdy into *elegant*.

A great "balancer" for both hips and for full upper arms, shoulder pads can instantly create a V shape. By the way, the opposite of a V shape is the dreaded pear-shape.

What do your upper arms have to do with your shoulder line? The widest place on your upper body may be across your upper arms—you may actually be wider here than at your shoulder line. If you are, you will want to make certain that your shoulder pads are placed far enough out so that the end of the pad is as far out as the fullest part of your arm.

Did you think that women had given up their shoulder pads? Not until men do—pads give them the same flattering V shape they give us. Most jackets, many blouses, and some sweaters come with padding—most have just gotten smaller, but you can easily change the size when necessary (heavy-weight fabrics may need a slightly larger pad).

If your natural shoulder line is at least a touch wider than your hips, you can do without pads in *some* garments. Those garments that make your shoulders look sloped or narrow in comparison to your hipline will need a little padding.

Shoulder pads aren't like money, more is not better. Besides paying attention to the size of shoulder pads, you need to watch the "layering" of pads—all you need is one. If you place a jacket with pads over a blouse with pads, you often have one too many (football, anyone?). If you then place a coat with pads over your jacket, you probably have two too many.

What to do? If you always work with your jacket on, you won't need shoulder pads in your tops. If you always, or sometimes, take it off, your tops may need padding (keep the pad very "thin") and your jacket padding may need to be scaled down. Since coats are worn over jackets and tops, take a good look at the total effect and remove or scale down the coat padding as necessary. Too large, or too many, pads can make your head look really small in comparison to the rest of your body, and it can also make your neck look scrawny. Full-figured petites need to be especially aware of this, as do those of you who wear your hair very short or pulled tightly back.

Placement is critical: Be aware that many blouses, some sweaters, and some jackets come with the pads situated too closely to the neck—simply move them out farther. Pin them in place first and take a look in the mirror before you sew them in. Feel awkward around sewing needles? Your cleaners or your best friend will help you.

Speaking of placement, I no longer "assume" that anyone knows which end of a shoulder pad aims which way. A client, who had gone from frazzled and frumpy (her words) to so elegant that she was mistaken for the mistress of a wealthy European businessman at a conference they were both attending, was excitedly relating the story when I realized that she had her shoulder pads in backwards. Without interrupting this fun, I simply reached inside the shoulder of her knit top and switched them around.

Did I need to explain what I had done? No, she was, after all, the president of her own company. She just smiled and I knew she would never put them in that way again. I will, however, explain to you that the thickest part of the pad goes toward the outside edge of your shoulder and the thinnest part goes toward your neck—just in case you don't know.

What was this *American woman* wearing at the noted conference that made her look not only European but *interesting* enough to be a "kept woman"? She had told me that she needed something for a cocktail party and dressy dinner the evening before the conference started, but her budget and lifestyle did not support the purchase of strictly cocktail attire. I suggested that she could wear something that we had already added to her wardrobe, an off-white wool gabardine suit.

At my suggestion, she wore it with her matching silk jewel neck blouse, matching very sheer stockings, matching low-cut "pumps" (a pump to her is a 1½" heel), and matching bag and pearls. Yes, she wore off-white head to toe and she looked phenomenal—so can **all** of you.

Back to the subject at hand, there are other ways to help you create the figure-enhancing V shape:

◆ Wear straight skirts that are pegged.

◆ Wear curvy jacket styles that give you a small waist/broader shoulder look.

◆ Avoid A-line skirts—they are an upside-down V shape—exceptions are short A-lines and A-lines coupled with the curvy jacket mentioned above.

◆ Wear trousers that are cut narrow in the leg.

◆ Wear tapered-leg trousers (they get narrower as they leave the upper leg and head toward the ankle).

◆ If you are going to wear a boxy-style jacket or a classic-cut blazer, pair it with a pegged skirt or narrow or tapered leg trousers.

Looking stylish instead of frumpy is simply a matter of how you "put things together" for **you,** how they fit, and how you choose to accessorize them. It's the total effect of the combination of small details.

TAILORED FOR ELEGANCE ✂

JUST THE BASICS

✂ Make elegance out of mundane—stylish out of pedestrian.

✂ Take the time and money to get it *more* than right—if not, don't buy it to begin with.

✂ Costly garments will look less expensive if they fit poorly, and less expensive garments can look high-priced (if the fabric is good) when they are tailored to fit you.

BEYOND THE BASICS

When it comes to style, any silhouette can look good on you. How is this possible? It's the fit, the silhouette that works for **your** proportion, that creates elegance. You are training your eye to work with your body as well as with your unique coloring.

There is an important visual difference between "tailored" clothing that looks like it was made for you and something that is almost right. Not many women can put on a suit and walk out of the store looking fabulous.

Develop a good relationship with a skilled tailor/dressmaker and spend the extra money to get the fit right. If you are into quality instead of quantity, you will probably be able to afford this extra expense. If not, **never *ever*** buy anything that doesn't fit right to begin with. You'll regret it with the first wearing and you'll hesitate wearing it again because you won't "feel" confident or attractive when you do.

"Things" That May Need Tailoring

- ✂ Jacket fits in shoulders or do not buy.

- ✂ Placement of shoulder pads—remove, scale down, or add.

- ✂ Overall shape of jacket—at least slightly defined at the waist unless you are going for a boxy style.

- ✂ Sleeve length—ends slightly below wrist bone at the bottom of the indentation just below the bone. Petites may want to consider having sleeves slightly tapered toward the wrist but not to the point that it restricts freedom of movement.

- ✂ Trouser length—covers the back of shoe (much more information in *Smart* **Looking Shoes and Boots**).

- ✂ Skirt length—many lengths will work well on you depending on the shape and your choice of jacket, stocking, and shoe.

- ✂ Unless they are slim-cut, taper trousers from the hip toward the ankle.

- ✂ Buttons moved—lapels, pleats, and pockets do not spread or gape.

Clothes that fit too tightly can make you look like you just gained several pounds even if you've just lost 10—they actually make you look bigger instead of smaller.

If a garment is "too" tight, especially across your bustline or your derriere, you won't look *elegant*. You must judge, or ask a chic, but not over-the-top, friend to help you judge if you simply look stylish and feminine (and maybe just a touch sexy), or too sexy for your workplace. Anything too tight is appropriate for only one occasion—a private party of two!

Jackets that fit too tightly across your derriere are such a prevalent mistake that they deserve their own *smart tip*. Make sure that the buttons aren't "pulling" in the front and check your "rear view" as well.

For a little extra ease, move your buttons over if you can, or ask your tailor if they can let out the jacket. If you can't get any extra room, wear the jacket open—only if it looks good that way. In the front, it should hang as "vertically" straight as possible. If it hangs open in an upside down V shape, don't wear it (remember the pear).

A jacket that is too big in the hips (sometimes referred to as having too much fabric in the "skirt" of the jacket) can create a frumpy look. I keep wishing that I could come up with different words than "dowdy" and "frumpy," but I haven't. You have to admit that they are pretty descriptive. Sometimes a jacket looks as if it fits perfectly from a front view, but from a side view you'll see too much fullness in the back. It's easy to remedy—*please* have it done as it will make all the difference in the world between your looking ordinary and looking extraordinary.

The *poor urchin* look of too long sleeves gives the impression that you are wearing hand-me-downs (I have always loved hand-me-downs), your hands are cold, or that you do not know what size you wear. Do you need a petite size only in blouses and jackets? Sleeves with ruffles that are "supposed" to hang down over your hand are fine if they go with your total look, and you assure me that you won't ask your company for disability if they get caught in a machine. Have too long sleeves shortened, push them up, or roll them up.

You can also push up, or roll up, sleeves that are too short. Sometimes you can get the sleeve length you need by buying blouses and jackets a size (or sometimes even two) larger than you would normally need and then have the body taken in. Before you do this, make certain the shoulders still fit properly because that's nearly impossible to change without remaking the entire garment.

INTERPRETING PATTERNS

JUST THE BASICS

- ◆ If a pattern size is too small for you, it can make you look totally insignificant—the opposite of a **powerful**, successful image.

- ◆ If a pattern size is too large for you, it can completely **OVER-POWER** you, making you look washed-out by comparison.

- ◆ Don't be afraid of prints, plaids, and patterns—just learn which ones will flatter you.

BEYOND THE BASICS

I'll bet you think that pattern size has to do with your height and size. Enhancing pattern size has to do with your body *coloring*. Yes, I know this is contrary to what you may believe, but it's true! Except for "placement," it has nothing to do with how tall you are, or aren't, or with your size or shape.

- ⊘ **Bad Advice:** Short figures are flattered by small, low-contrast prints.

① **My Advice:** The author of this fashion magazine article is telling all short women that they will look their best in small, blended looking prints. As remarkable (and unbelievable) as it may seem, your height doesn't have anything to do with flattering pattern size and/or the amount or lack of contrast in a print. Pattern size and your body structure could dictate *where* you place larger patterns but it's your natural body coloring—your skin tone and hair color—that determines your best look when it comes to the size.

For example, a woman who is 5' tall, with clear ivory skin and very dark brown or black hair (a Contrast Color Type), will be more enhanced by medium to large patterns that have high-contrast and boldness. She will appear washed-out in small blended looking patterns. And a woman who is 5'10" and has pink tones to her skin and ash blonde or ash brown hair (a Gentle Color Type) will be more flattered by small and medium-sized patterns that are blended in appearance. Larger patterns can look overwhelming on her, even though she's tall, unless they have a light background and the pattern is very delicate and airy looking.

Before we go into pattern size, here's another *very* important detail. All patterns should have at least two of your best colors prominent in them, AND the background color should also be flattering to you.

◆ Everyone can wear medium-sized patterns, but not everyone looks great in small patterns or large patterns. There are always a couple of "it depends upon."

◆ If your coloring is more delicate looking, Gentle and Light-Bright Color Types, you'll look terrific in small and medium-sized patterns, and (here's one of the "it depends upon") very lightweight, airy, delicate looking larger patterns that have a light background. If you are a Light-Bright Color Type, you will want to avoid small patterns that are *blended* looking (where all of the colors seem to run together).

◆ Those of you who are Muted Color Types look great in medium-sized patterns, small patterns that have some strength, and (another "it depends upon") very *blended* looking large patterns.

◆ If you are a Contrast Color Type, medium and large patterns look wonderful on you. Small patterns that have extremely high-contrast, like black with white and navy with white, can be effective if you accent them with a bright color, or with the dark color.

If you are a full-figured Contrast Color Type who is concerned about wearing large patterns, just be aware of *where* you place them on your body. If you are a petite Contrast Color Type and are worried that large patterns will overwhelm you, don't be. The proof will be in the compliments you get when you finally decide to wear a *color-perfect* large pattern.

LOOKING *SMART* IN SUITS AND JACKETS

JUST THE BASICS

- ◆ Wearing a suit is the answer to the most *easy elegance* of all.

- ◆ To get the look of a "suit," your jacket doesn't have to match your skirt or trousers.

- ◆ Wearing a jacket gives you personal presence and the look of *easy elegance*.

- ◆ All styles and lengths of jackets are possibilities for you regardless of your height and body structure—it all depends on the shape and length of your skirt or pants.

BEYOND THE BASICS

We are experiencing a return to elegance and more "formal" business attire —many charming women never left this look behind. Even without *having* to, more women are choosing to wear suits while others, who used to be able to dress business casual, are being "required" to wear a suit or a dress.

Jackets can create great style for an otherwise "ho-hum" ensemble. You rarely see a stylish Parisian or New York woman without one, even (especially) when she is wearing jeans or other casual pants.

Personally, I collect jackets in various colors and styles and I definitely have more than I need. Do I wear them? Almost every day, both casual and dressy—they are one of my *signature statements*. I definitely recommend that you *steal* your jackets off your "good" suits and wear them with your casual looks. Truthfully, I wouldn't have nearly so many if I didn't wait for them to be marked down to at least 50% to 75% off the **outlet** price!

There are lots of *smart tips* on jackets throughout this book—here are some more:

- ◆ You can wear any style jacket whatever your size or height—all you have to do is pair a specific style with the right shape/style bottom.

- ◆ Wear narrower trousers and pegged skirts with all jacket styles.

- ◆ Longer jackets and classic blazers usually look more "contemporary" with narrow trousers and pegged skirts (of all lengths).

- ◆ Short and very short skirts (pegged, flared, flip, or pleated) work well with a large variety of jacket styles. When a very short skirt is paired with a longer jacket, the look is a touch more conservative.

◆ Avoid wearing a "standard" classic blazer with wrap or sarong style skirts—a curvy shorter jacket would look great.

◆ Shorter jackets of all styles can be worn with most all styles of trousers and skirts including the pegged skirts and narrower cut trousers that work so well with longer jackets. Guess, then, which you should have more of in your wardrobe?

◆ Jackets that look almost like a "blouse" are very feminine looking and, when paired with the right skirt or trousers for their particular length and shape, can be flattering to all.

⊘ **Bad Advice:** From an article on suits, "Big hips are best in long jackets with a high closure."

① **My Advice:** Yikes! High closures have nothing to do with making hips look smaller, firmer, or nicer in any way. AND all of the women who read this article whose hips are larger than they wish (the majority) may feel that they can't look great in other jacket styles. **All** women can wear all jacket styles—looking great in them simply depends on how they fit and what style skirt/pant you pair them with.

Classic blazers, both single- and double-breasted, tend to be a bit on the long side for many women and when they are paired with classic trousers (especially those that are a touch wide) they can shorten your leg line and make you appear frumpy. This look can also make you look "broad" at the place the jacket ends—depending on your height, leg line, and the widest part of your upper leg.

Always check your view from the side. Put on heels and check the proportion again. It should be better—unless the heels have just made your pants too short, in which case you've created another concern. Have trousers narrowed from the hip or simply wear longer jackets with slim-cut pants and pegged skirts. When your jacket and pants match, it's less noticeable than when they are two different colors.

Consider changing the look of a jacket you haven't been wearing:

◆ Switch matching buttons to gold, silver, or copper.

◆ Change metallic or odd-colored buttons to matching buttons.

◆ Change buttons to match a "bottom" that hasn't been getting much use, and you'll instantly have a new suit—the buttons "tie" the two colors together.

◆ Add some curves to a boxy-shaped jacket.

- ◆ Put crystal or rhinestone buttons on a plain jacket to turn it into one that you can wear for cocktails and the theater.

Coloring within the lines: Contrary to old notions, all colors and color combinations can be successfully worn in any place of business. If you are wearing a red suit and want it to look more "conservative," wear it with a neutral-colored top instead of one in yellow or purple, for example, which are more avant-garde color combinations.

On the other hand, if you have conservative suits or blazers and want them to appear more up-fashion, wear them in unusual color mixes. If you want them to appear a touch less *all buttoned up*, "pull them apart." What you are creating is a "mixed suit" look—you use the jacket of one suit with the skirt or trousers of another, "marrying" them in interesting color combinations. To make some of these marriages work, you'll have to learn the *secret formula*—see page 92.

> Wearing a jacket instantly makes casual attire more important. — JoAnna

---

What about wearing a leather jacket? Classic rocker chic is only appropriate when it is the *expected* attire in your field. Change the style, deleting the zippers and grunge, and you get closer to a yes for more creative business casual looks. Leather or suede in the styling of a suit jacket has a place in some casual businesses, but not in others.

How about a jeans jacket? If denim is worn freely at your place of business, then a nice denim jacket might be appropriate. A typical jeans jacket is very, very casual (add several more "very's" if it is faded or distressed).

THE RISE AND FALL OF HEMLINES

JUST THE BASICS

- ◆ Look at the business you are in and decide if short skirts and really short skirts fit with your career goals.

- ◆ Look at your legs, decide how much of them you want to show off.

- ◆ Take a third look and decide if you look stylish and elegant in them.

BEYOND THE BASICS

It took almost a century to win the battle of the hemlines. They went up and down, some say with the economy, but others know that it was at the whim of designers who seem to know when we have enough of one length in our closet that we stop buying more of the same. Now we can wear all lengths anytime we wish without being made to feel *less* stylish. This wonderful freedom has caused a concern regarding flattering footwear, but let's start at the beginning.

How much longer is a short skirt than a very short skirt? I can't tell you in inches because 2" on short legs gives a much shorter appearance than on longer legs. But, here's a fun guideline:

- ◆ Measure the distance between the top of your kneecap and your crotch—mine is 12".

- ◆ The place on your leg that is one-half of that distance is approximately where a **very short skirt** might end—for me that is 6" above my kneecap.

- ◆ One-fourth of your original measurement will give you the approximate place where your **short skirt** might end—for me it is 3" above my kneecap.

At this point, you may find it helpful to skip to the *smart tips* on shoes, boots, and stockings and then come back here to go over these general guidelines—they'll help you in deciding which stockings, and which weight and style of shoe, will work best with a specific skirt length.

Just a few years ago I was prompted to write my first letter to an editor of one of our major fashion magazines. Having just returned from the "shows," she wrote in the lead-in to the magazine's main fashion section that the newest skirt length, one that was a few inches below the knee, was fabulous and that *any other skirt length looked passe.*

Now, I'd thought that about two decades ago WE stopped letting fashion editors and designers dictate what our skirt lengths should be in order for us to look fashionable. This editor's comment sounded not only dictatorial to me, it made me furious. Why? Because she'd just told every American woman that unless she goes out and spends her hard-earned money on this new length (and tosses out all of her old lengths), she will look out of style—out of date. As I was hoping, either nobody took the time to read this editorial or most of you chose to ignore her—**thank you!**

My letter to her explained that instead of trying to once again dictate our skirt lengths, it would have been so much nicer if she had let us know that we now have an *additional* choice in the stores, and had explained *how* to best wear the new length (with very sheer stockings and heels).

Getting *smarter so you don't shoot yourself in the foot:* Women of every height can look great in both long and short skirts—it's all a matter of getting the skirt long enough or short enough; getting the shape right (pegged, for example); knowing what style top and/or jacket to combine the length with; and what stockings and shoe or boot style finishes the look perfectly for **you**. (Review the information on shoes and boots on page 102.)

◆ Skirts that hover around your knee, from just above the knee-cap to just below, need a medium to light-weight shoe and fairly sheer stockings.

◆ Lengths that fall from just below the kneecap to 2" or 3" below will look much more stylish with at least a mid-height slender heel and sheer stockings (either nude/skin tone or a sheer tint of neutral that matches your shoe or skirt—no opaques with this length, *please*).

◆ Generally, the shorter the skirt the heavier the shoe *could* be (a medium-weight is always appropriate)—but a light-weight skirt fabric (in any length) calls for a medium to lighter weight shoe.

◆ Generally, the longer the skirt, the lighter weight the shoe. Note that I did not say to wear a light-weight shoe necessarily, just that as the hemline drops, the weight of the shoe "usually" drops as well (again, the weight of the skirt fabric will affect the appropriate shoe weight).

◆ A pump with a slender heel and low vamp and side is always appropriate with skirts from just above the knee to the floor. Depending on the look you want to create and where you are going, this shoe will also work with a short skirt. And, also a "depending on," a low-cut flat will work—the most important "depend upon" here is the skirt length.

◆ Delicate and light-weight fabrics always need a light- to medium-weight shoe.

◆ Heavier weight fabrics do not necessarily need more weight in a shoe—it depends on the length and shape of your skirt. When in doubt, a medium-weight shoe will always be appropriate with heavier fabrics.

◆ Avoid spike heels with very short skirts unless this is a stylish look for your lifestyle.

◆ Avoid chunky or clunky-looking shoes unless you are wearing a short or very short skirt and creating a specific trendy look that calls for them.

Very long skirts are fabulous but what is "stylishly" long and what is *too* long for daytime? An inch or two above the ankle bone is usually long enough for the daytime. I love really long skirts (and short skirts, too), but when a skirt comes all the way down almost to the floor it can make you look like you're engulfed in fabric or living in another time. Use your mirror to help you decide—does your attire look out of place for your place of business? Do you look elegant or engulfed?

If your skirt appears just a little too long, try wearing it with a heel (shoe or boot) to raise the hem, creating more inches between the bottom of the skirt and the floor. Make sure to put on a jacket or top in a style you might wear with this skirt. Now take another look. If it still looks too long, it should be shortened —maybe only 1"—pin it up or turn the waistband over and look again.

There's sort of a "no man's land" for skirt lengths—aptly named because most men don't pay attention to women who wear their skirts this length. The reason this length often makes women look dowdy is because **women don't know how** to make it look more chic. The length in question? From 2" or 3" below the kneecap to 2" or 3" below the middle of the calf—it depends on your height and your leg length. Remember, 2" looks a lot *more* on a woman who is 5' 2" than it does on one who is 5' 9".

The very best way to look stylish in these "difficult" lengths is to wear very sheer stockings and high heels. In the fall and winter you can also wear boots—many different styles and heights will work depending on your choice of stockings and the heel height. Don't forget that skirts can also be shortened to a more flattering length and some can be let down an inch or two—sometimes all that is necessary to make the difference between looking chic and looking frumpy.

WEARING THE PANTS

JUST THE BASICS

- When trousers look good, they look very, very good, and, when they look bad, they're horrid.

- The wider the leg the longer the trousers should be—no high-water pants, *please.*

- For work, no low-rise pants so low that the skin around your "mid-section" would ever be in danger of showing if you reach for something or bend over—no exceptions unless your job requires this look. It's soooo inelegant that I don't want to mention it but I have to—no butt cleavage ever, no thong or panty tops showing to anyone other than your significant other, in private!

- No capris for classic business or classic business casual.

BEYOND THE BASICS

You've already read many *smart tips* about how to create a longer leg, to avoid spreading pockets and spreading pleats, etc. The *smart tips* in "shoes and boots" will help you with trouser styles and lengths and their best weight of footwear. Here are some more guidelines:

- The wider the trousers, the longer they should be—1" off the floor in the back (with your shoes/boots on) is an elegant length.

- More classic widths and narrower straight-legged trousers should end no *higher* than the place where the back of the shoe meets the sole of the shoe.

- Narrower cut trousers that taper toward the ankle are worn a little shorter (because they are smaller around the ankle, they won't be able to come down over the shoe any farther)—they should still definitely cover the ankle bone; some have a slit on the side that helps make this possible.

- A slight break in the front of your trousers is always nice.

- It's very difficult to look *smart* and stylish in cropped pants even when they are "in" because they are so unflattering to the leg and ankle—wearing a boot helps this style look more flattering.

- Bell bottoms are to be worn very long, but perhaps best not worn at all if you wore them when you were "younger."

- If you've "done" bell bottoms, bootleg cut trousers are a better bet—wear them long.

- Capris that are short and tapered, ending from just below the knee to mid-calf are much more enhancing than those that look more like a cropped pant.

- Cuffs are classic and can be worn by all.

- Trousers that are designed to fit with a bit of ease shouldn't be tight across your derriere or around your upper legs—learn the difference between fitting well and tight.

- Both pleated and flat-front trousers are classic and can be worn by **all** women.

- Trousers that are cut narrower in the leg (versus wide) are the most flattering to **all** women and work well with all jacket styles.

SMART TIPS FOR TOPS

JUST THE BASICS

- Buy more tops than bottoms.

- *Basic* styles coordinate more easily with a variety of bottoms.

- When possible, own a top that matches each of your skirts and trousers.

- Jewel, V, and scoop-neck tops in silk, rayon, thin merino wool, and microfibers are easier to work with and more versatile than blouses.

- You can wear nice sweaters to work if you avoid those that are so tight that you look like a Hollywood pinup girl.

Beyond the Basics

There is a true benefit to buying more tops than bottoms. A different top (i.e., blouse, sweater, shell, tank, camisole, and so on) can change the entire look/style, appropriateness, or "flavor" of an ensemble, allowing you to have "zillions" of outfits with a minimal investment in skirts and trousers. Be sure to include some tops you *feel* sexy in and one top (for play, not business) with a "zillion" buttons in the front—a friend reports that in certain situations prolonged anticipation is a delightful aphrodisiac.

Some details to be aware of:

- Blouses without pockets are more "basic" because they can be worn under more styles/cuts of jackets. Sometimes the edge of a pocket will show when you have your jacket on, requiring either a change of your top or jacket.

- We all need to be aware of pockets that are too low, but this is a special concern for petites. Low pockets can make you look like your bosom is low or, *yikes,* droopy.

- Styles that work best with all of your jackets (basics) are simple long-sleeved, short-sleeved, and sleeveless shells, tanks, jewel/scoop/rounded/V/U-necks in fine knits. You can include quality T-shirts in this group.

- Turtlenecks and mock turtlenecks will work with many jacket styles as well.

- Be aware that the texture of ribbed knits is much more limiting than knits that have a smooth or flat texture.

- Tops in prints can add wonderful variety but they are useless unless they contain the colors of your "bottoms."

- Take note of where short-sleeved tops hit on your arm. If they end too low, they may cause your bosom to look low/droopy. If they end exactly at the fullest part of your bosom, they can make you look more ample—fine for some.

- Silk, rayon, fine cotton, merino wool, light-weight cashmere, microfibers and other fine textured knits are great fabrics for tops.

- Avoid anything scratchy.

- There's more information on tops in your *smart* capsule "class."

Keeping effort to a minimum: If your blouses seem to always be in the ironing, need to be sent to the cleaners, or don't work well with the necklines of most of your jackets, you could just **stop buying them.** Purchase instead the most versatile tops listed above.

It's always a good idea to follow the laundering instructions on the labels of all of your clothing, and I think you should. But *I'm just going to whisper in your ear* that I, personally, wash all of my tops made out of the fabrics listed above in cold water on the gentle cycle in my machine.

Yes, I wash all my silks and cashmere, but, of all the fabrics listed above, rayon is the one that I hesitate to wash because it might shrink. I also hesitate to launder tops that are lined because the lining can shrink. If you take your tops out of the washer right away, most (except blouses) won't need any ironing or just a touch-up to make the silk and cotton feel silky and soft instead of "crunchy."

If you forget to take them out soon enough, you can put them in the dryer for a couple of minutes on delicate. Use padded hangers to avoid hanger marks at the shoulder and "block" (stretch) knits that need it—my arms are long so I pull on the sleeves to keep the length I need.

Have you ever considered if your arms match your body? Many women avoid sleeveless tops—they feel that their upper arms are too *generous* to show. One of my full-figured clients was going on her first cruise and I was pre-shopping for her (shopping without her) because she had so little time to spare before she was to leave. When I asked her how she felt about sleeveless tops she said that she didn't wear them because....

I suggested that she try on a sleeveless shell (that she always covers with a jacket) and look in the mirror and ask herself if her arms "go with" her body. Her answer? "Yes!" Of course, she now loves wearing sleeveless dresses and tops in the summer—but not to work because she works in a fairly conservative field.

Getting your necklines coordinated: Wearing a notched collar blouse with a shawl collar jacket does both an injustice. One easy rule is to have the neckline of your blouse or top repeat the same line as your jacket. Here are some *smart tips*:

- Jewel, scoop, U, and just slightly rounded necklines work well with most all jacket styles, which makes them very versatile.

◆ A V neckline works well with notched collar lapels and collar-less jackets that also have a V shape.

◆ A blouse with a notched collar goes well with most notched collar jackets and works even better if the "notches" fall into line or if the notch of one fills in the space between the notches of the other.

◆ Some notched collars come to a "point" and others are rounded off. *Please* don't mix them.

◆ It usually looks best if the notched collar on a blouse is a little narrower than the notched collar on your jacket.

◆ Blouses with a shawl collar are great with a shawl collar suit, as are jewel, scoop, and U-shaped necklines.

What's the difference between a **nice** T-shirt and a regular T-shirt? The apparent quality of the fabric and the feel. Think of it as a *layering piece* instead of a typical T-shirt. Picture a nice thinner fabric crewneck "sweater" with long or short sleeves in brushed mercerized cotton, silk, rayon, and blends of those. No T-shirts with your favorite sayings, sport teams, or souvenirs from your latest trip. "Brand" logos need to be very small and subtle.

When it comes to the question of wearing a sweater to work, I can't give you a blanket yes—I have to insert the words *nice* and *classic*. A "yes" would be easier but you always have to deal with the "it depends on...." stuff.

If you are a fan of long sweaters, make sure that those you are wearing are not *too* long for you—if they are, they'll shorten your leg line. Sweaters that end about mid-hip or above are generally the most flattering length for women of every height, weight, and leg length—please note that mid-hip is almost never the widest part of your hips. For those of you who want your tops to cover your thighs, wearing heels will give you a more sleek versus sloppy appearance.

Pair longer sweaters with slim pants and slim pegged skirts. Avoid sweaters that "cup" under your derriere, opting instead for those that hang straight down without the type of ribbing that makes them smaller around at the bottom.

⊘ **Bad Advice:** An article on how to minimize a large bust suggests wearing a high V-neck sweater.

① **My Advice:** It's true that a sweater like this doesn't call attention to your bosom, but it does **nothing** to minimize it. No mention was made of the fabric—if this, or any, sweater was ribbed, tight, or clingy, it would *emphasize,* not minimize, **any** bosom.

⊘ **Bad Advice:** The same article said, "The boxy shape of a sleeveless turtleneck will camouflage a big bust."

Ⓘ **My Advice:** Actually, most sleeveless turtlenecks accentuate any size bosom, but what was most alarming here was that the accompanying picture showed a clingy, curvy, not boxy, shape. Besides, most women with an ample bust do not want to box it in—boxy can look dowdy if it's not done well.

A cardigan is a terrific option to a jacket *if* it looks substantial and elegant—substantial meaning "weighty" and more structured versus a thinner merino wool cardigan that might be part of a twin set, for example. Judge it by your *smart tip*, if it looks **equally as smashing as your best jacket**, wear it to work.

Although they do not take the place of a jacket, twin sets are great for many places of business and most give a dressier appearance than just a sweater.

"Outdoorsy" looking sweaters and sweaters with lots of glitz are usually best kept for your free time unless you work in an environment where you know that they are expected and accepted attire. I would expect to see you wearing a ski sweater if you work in an outdoor sports shop that sells ski wear or backpacking and camping equipment. And I wouldn't be at all surprised to see you in a sweater with glitz if you work in a boutique that sells like items.

This doesn't mean that those of you who work in more conservative fields cannot wear sweaters that are "embellished." There are some great sweaters that are embroidered, have a few pearls or simple, subtle studs that you may be able to wear to your place of business. If you want to make something embellished look more conservative, keep everything else you are wearing very simple and understated.

Obviously, sweaters under jackets are great for even the most conservative workplace, but, if you still aren't certain about wearing just a sweater without a jacket, observe what the top women in your company are wearing and follow their lead until you get to be the leader. **Exception: Follow no frumpy or dowdy leaders.**

Some cowl neck sweaters, dolman sleeves and drop-shoulder sleeves, can make your shoulder line look narrower than it is, so consider adding small shoulder pads. Large cowl neck styles can also make a small head look even smaller in proportion to body size, and it can make a slender neck look scrawny.

No matter what you see or might have heard, tying a sweater around your hips isn't a stylish look. It is a look that makes your hips look larger and, therefore, your shoulders look smaller. It also makes everyone who looks at you think you are trying to hide your hips, therefore calling attention to them. The only time this look is acceptable is *during* athletics when you started out cold and you end up warm, or vice versa.

Dressing Smart in Dresses

Just the Basics

- A dress you wear to work needs to have the same visual *presence* as a suit.

- Dresses with matching or coordinated jackets make a super impression.

- A jumper is not a dress.

- A dress with a little tie in the back is not professional looking and is rarely flattering to any body shape or size.

Beyond the Basics

Why is it that we see so few stylish dresses in the workplace? One of the reasons is that there are so few good styles to choose from. Another is that many women seem to select dresses with a *different* part of their brain—the part that still wants to be a little girl, at a party, or living in another decade.

It's been said that a dress has to be very tailored looking to match the "authority" of a suit, but it really only has to make *you* look great, stylish, elegant, and appropriate (remember your *smart tip*, **equal to or better than the best look you have right now**).

A dress that makes a statement equal to that of your best suit doesn't have to have a jacket, but it does have to have all of the same wonderful qualities of that suit:

- The dress has presence and style.

- It is a style that is perfect for your workplace.

- It fits you well.

- Its fabric and construction are of good quality, and it doesn't bag or sag after a few wearings.

- It's a great color on you.

- You've accessorized it perfectly.

- You love it and are willing to wear it very often.

Dresses that come with matching or coordinating jackets are terrific, as are dresses that are styled so that you can wear one of your existing jackets over them. If you like a great deal of variety, look for a simple (do not read "boring") dress with beautiful lines that you can accessorize with different belts, scarves and necklaces. What does a dress like this look like?

◆ It's a solid color.

◆ It has a waistline (or shows a curve) at your natural waistline.

◆ Darts or curved seams make the top fairly fitted, like a well-tailored blouse.

◆ The neckline is one that will work with most of your jacket neck-lines and a variety of necklaces—a scoop, jewel, or V neck would be good.

◆ It could have tailored long sleeves ("puffy" or fuller-cut sleeves are difficult under jackets), short sleeves, or be sleeveless, de-pending on the time of the year and your place of business.

◆ The skirt of the dress should be darted so that it fits well through the hips (like a well-tailored skirt)—it is pegged and in one of your favorite lengths.

◆ This "dress" could come in two pieces—it could actually be a *base* (a matching top and bottom) that you create out of a skirt and top. It could be that you already have the perfect "dress" hanging in your closet.

In hot summer months when you may be tempted to wear a sleeveless dress to work, take a look around you. If you work in a conservative field where there is still a written or understood code against bare arms, play the "game" until you are in charge.

When you wear sleeveless dresses for work or play, make sure the armhole is cut high enough so that you cannot get even a glimpse of your bra. Cleavage at work is looked down upon—excuse me—*frowned* upon.

A "dress," forgotten by many women, that is *phenomenally easy* to wear and stylish, too, is the two-piece dress with a straight skirt. Think of it as a skirt with a matching top that is worn on the outside versus tucked in. Actually, think of it as a *base*. It covers tummies, hips, and unwanted bulges. If you make sure that your skirt is pegged, your top isn't too long and the shoulder line is a touch wider than your hipline (to give you that flattering V shape), you'll have a great look. The top can end anywhere from a few inches below your waist to a tunic length no longer than just barely covering your derriere, and it should skim your hips, not stand away from your body.

There are exceptions, of course, but generally, it's not a good idea to belt this look, but if the top isn't too long or made out of a thick fabric, you can tuck it in and then add a belt. You can find these "dresses" in a huge variety of fabrics from silk to knits—catalogues are often a good source. Get the same *easy elegance* and style with a top and matching narrow-leg, plain-front trousers.

Ace the Interview

Just the Basics

♠ Look credible.

♠ Wear a solid-color suit—if you wear a neutral color (probably still the safest bet for a very conservative company), you will likely look the same as everyone else, so the styling of your suit will need to set you apart. For the majority of companies, if you are confident enough to wear a color, you will stand out from the rest of the applicants as a confident woman (as long as the clarity and shade of the color, and the color combination, are great for you).

♠ Wear a femininely styled suit or a "menswear" fabric suit with a feminine cut, ladylike (but not sexy) top, and accessories.

♠ I recommend wearing pumps with a slender heel and a low-cut vamp—no heavy, chunky shoes, please.

♠ Wear makeup.

♠ Cover any "body art" if possible.

♠ No gum, obviously no smoking.

♠ Employers do not expect recent grads to be expensively dressed but they do expect them to be neat and clean.

♠ Review "Being Groomed for VIP" on page 178.

♠ Remember to smile.

Beyond the Basics

You are going to be sized up in a hurry—in just seven seconds the interviewer will make a judgment about you—do you look right for the job? When qualifications, skills, and credentials are close, the way you look will give you the edge. What you don't need is someone looking at you *wondering* if you can do the job. A huge majority of firms, regardless of the their dress codes, expect you to wear a suit for an interview.

What is "fail-safe" interview attire? Fail-safe I can't promise but if you are dressed in what is expected interview attire, you will have your second best visual shot at making a good impression. Second best? If you are also wearing colors and a color combination that are flattering to your coloring, you will have a visual edge over everyone else who hasn't learned this skill.

It used to be that different industries had completely different expected dress codes and it wasn't necessary to put it in writing because everyone understood—wearing casual clothing wasn't an option. Now, a firm in a conservative industry, like accounting, law, or banking, might have a casual Friday, or even a 24/7 business casual, *agreement* with their employees with the understanding that, regardless of what day it is, they need to wear a suit or dress if they are going to be meeting with a client. Many companies in creative industries, such as advertising, public relations, the arts, and the high tech fields, have been less buttoned up for years. With sales and marketing firms it has often depended on the product you are selling and your target audience.

Whether specifically stated or not, the appropriate attire will depend on the industry, the firm, your position in that company and what you do there, the position you want in that company, where you live (the region and/or city) and, perhaps, the person you will be meeting with on any given day. **Always be prepared for one of the most important days of your life.**

Before an interview, if you have the opportunity to check it out, stop by the company you will be interviewing with ahead of time (in the morning or over lunch) and "people watch" to get an idea of the way the employees dress. You can also call the human resources office and ask about the dress code or the *expected* attire. Regardless of what you find out, you will still want to wear a suit to your interview.

Try not to have a lot of "stuff" to gather up from the reception room (umbrella, briefcase, coat) because when someone calls your name it can feel awkward getting it all together, as it will be when your interview is finished. Keep organized.

What do you wear when you go back for your second interview? Since you will more than likely have a second and even perhaps a third interview, what you wear when you make your "next" impression is as important as the first. Why? Because you won't want to *disappoint*—you don't want to cast any doubt that their first impression of you might have been wrong. You have set a standard that you will want to maintain.

If you have a second suit, wear it. If you don't, wear the first suit again with a different top and change of accessories. The same for a third interview. Each interview is equally as important, with a reminder that you may not meet the top boss until your second or third interview.

If wearing a suit to an interview is not possible for you at this time, wear a jacket and skirt with a nice top. If you have the time to look around the discount/off-price stores, you can find some very good suits for a minimal amount of money. These stores are also a great place to buy shoes and stockings.

Should you wear a pantsuit to an interview? I think it depends on those "depends-upons" listed above: industry, company, position you are applying for, and the region of the country. How do you want to be perceived? Will their perception of you match the impression you want to leave?

Walking into an interview or a meeting, you really are sized up instantly— usually not in a "let me check this person out" way, but instinctively our eyes take it all in, our brains process, and we are predisposed to judge. Let the outside match the inside—make sure you look like you have the skills that you have. Remember to smile. No, you don't have to grin all the time, just smile once in a while.

What do you wear to work on your first day of a new job besides a smile? If your job calls for a suit or dress, you can wear the same thing you did to your first interview. If your workplace is business casual, plan to dress better than the women you will be working with, and keep reading.

BUILDING A SMART WARDROBE

JUST THE BASICS

♦ Collect tops and bottoms that match each other so you can change your entire look just by changing your jacket or your accessories.

♦ Always bringing a touch of the bottom color "up" can help you combine a variety of separates in a totally stylish way.

BEYOND THE BASICS

How much of your wardrobe do you *really* use? Two of the reasons why most women only wear about 25% of their wardrobe in any given season is that their closets are full of separates that don't go together and they don't know how to combine pieces to create great looking outfits.

To solve the first, get in the habit of buying entire ensembles—that doesn't mean that you must buy all of the pieces that were made to go together, although that's (usually) a nice, easy way to look coordinated, but not as original as some of you may like. No matter what, *please, please, always* buy the matching top to any skirt or trousers you are purchasing so that when worn together, they make a *base*. Or, immediately look for a matching top made by any other manufacturer.

I'm sure that you've noticed that certain colors are prevalent in any given season and it will be much easier to find the exact shade you need if you're looking for it in the same season. For example: If you buy a yellow skirt, buy a *basic* matching yellow top; buy a purple top to match the purple trousers you bought two years ago but haven't yet worn; and while you are at it, see if your cream-colored sleeveless shell matches the skirt of your cream-colored suit.

The easiest way to start to build a *smart wardrobe* is to keep your look uncomplicated and understated (do not read boring)—you can branch out and go "wild" (or just a little wilder) once you get your wardrobe working for you. Remember, quality, not quantity. Well tailored. Wonderful colors, in your best clarity, and super color combinations for you.

Creating a *Smart "Base"*

There's that word again—by now you know that it means a matching top and bottom, and you've probably gotten the idea that I feel that you should have as many as you can. You're right!

A *base* is an "all one-color look" made by combining a *basic* skirt or trousers with a matching *basic* blouse, tank, camisole, shell, simple sweater, or any other plain (again, do not read boring) top. How closely do the colors have to match? They can be a hint lighter or darker, but they need to be close enough so that, at a glance, they look like they are the same color. Having several *smart bases* allows you to have a *smart wardrobe*—it's **by far** the easiest way in the world to look well-coordinated and *elegant*.

Transforming your *smart base*: You can change the look of your *smart base* simply by what you choose to wear on top of it:

Different colors and styles of jackets

◆ Vests

◆ Tunics

◆ Sweaters

◆ Cardigans

◆ Another shirt

◆ Belts

◆ Scarves

◆ Different accessories

An interesting **layering piece** will have a unique shape or pattern. *Please* keep your best color combinations in mind.

The top and bottom that create your *base* should be both *basic* and, generally, classic. Basic because they can be easily combined with so many other garments, and classic because you can wear them for many years. Just a change of a jacket style or accessories can instantly update classic *bases*, keeping them *stylish*.

Collect *bases* for work, play, and romantic evenings, in all the different fabrics and colors you love. I love my denim *base* equally as well as I love my linen, wool, and silk *bases*. Try a blue jeans *base* and a cream denim *base*—wear them with shoes/boots and belt in your hair color (yes, your hair color—much more about this concept in "shoes and boots") and count the compliments. You will always look more "dressed up" in a *base,* even in denim, than you do in unmatched separates.

***Mixing* it up:** Create entirely different outfits by wearing the bottom of one *base* with the top of another—to "balance" these combinations requires bringing the bottom color "up," your *Secret Formula* for having a great *pulled-*

together look. Use a variety of jacket, top, trouser, and skirt styles—each will increase the individuality of your look and you'll have an excellent start on building a great *Smart Capsule Wardrobe.*

Learning how to combine separates to create great looking outfits is fun and not really that difficult—like learning a new "trick" on your computer that will make your life easier forever (for me, it was learning how to use "search").

Bringing the bottom color "up": An astonishingly simple way to have a pulled-together look is to bring the bottom color of your outfit "up." This easy feat allows you to marry separates that you would never have believed could be combined into unique and great looking outfits.

> Whenever you buy a new skirt or pair of trousers, immediately look for a matching neck accessory because bringing the bottom color "up" is the KEY to mixing, matching, and marrying separates. — JoAnna

One of the easiest ways to accomplish this is to own neck accessories in the colors of your "bottoms"—your skirts and trousers. Plan a special shopping expedition where you only look for:

◆ Necklaces and solid-colored scarves that match all of your favorite bottoms.

◆ Scarves that have two or more of your "core" colors. A core color is a favorite color (one that looks great on you, of course) that you wear a lot.

For example, if you own pink linen trousers and you've only been wearing them with a cream top, find matching pink beads, pink pearls, or a matching pink scarf. Now you can wear your trousers with many different colored tops—just add your pink neck accessory and watch the beautiful *balance/coordination* take place.

While you are shopping, you can also keep an eye out for scarves and necklaces that have a **fairly large** amount of these colors—just a touch isn't enough to create the needed visual *balance*. Do a mirror test to make sure that your neck accessory *obviously pulls* the bottom color "up" from a DISTANCE, not just up close.

⊘ **Bad Advice:** Don't wear light-colored pants.

① **My Advice:** Of course you can wear pants in any color that's great on you—it's all in the color combinations you choose, and your skill in bringing the bottom color "up," that gives you great balance.

The minute you find any neck accessory to match one of your bottoms, start putting this principle to work right away. Try on your skirt or trousers with a *basic* top in a different color—one that has a neckline that is compatible with your new necklace or scarf (don't forget to keep in mind your best color combinations). Before you add the neck accessory, look in the mirror. At this point, depending on the colors you are combining, you may **not** have a very coordinated looking ensemble.

Now, add your accessory (you are bringing the bottom color up) and take another look—"instant balance," beautifully coordinated looking. Now, if you like, be daring and add a jacket in a third color (again, make sure your necklines work well together). Take yet another look—even in this three-color combination, you **will still** look very pulled together. Here are some other ways to bring the bottom color up:

◆ A belt and shoe in the same color.

◆ A scarf or necklace the same color as your belt.

◆ A top the same color as the skirt or trousers—a *smart base*.

What about using a jacket, vest, or cardigan to bring the bottom color up? Absolutely, but it only counts *if* you are certain that you'll leave it on. Earrings are usually not enough to create the balance you need, and if your hair covers them, they don't help at all. Avoid dotting color here and there, jumping from your shoes all the way to your neck or ears. For instance, red shoes and red necklace or earrings, with nothing red between, looks too spotty and/or too matchy-pooh.

Sometimes your hair color can act as a neck accessory would. If your hair is very dark brown or black and you are wearing black trousers with a different color top, your hair color can appear to bring the bottom color up. If your hair color is blonde and you are wearing a camel skirt, your hair color can create the balance you need to look pulled together.

If you don't want to go the "bottom color up" avenue (perhaps you're not a scarf or necklace person), or you haven't yet found your matching accessories, what else can you do to get more of your separates to work together? Wearing colors that have like "values" (two light colors together, for example) can create a well coordinated, balanced appearance without really needing to bring the bottom color up. Keeping your best color combinations in mind, here are some examples—combine:

◆ A light color with another light color, like pastel yellow with pastel blue (if you are a Contrast Color Type, you will need to add a medium or dark accent; darker haired Muted Color Types may also need this accent).

◆ A medium color with another medium color such as medium turquoise with a medium purple.

◆ Or a dark color with another dark color, like dark gray with dark raspberry (if your coloring is delicate looking you will need to "lighten up" these darker color combinations—or just avoid them).

It's also possible to get fairly good balance by wearing white, off-white, or cream with light colors and by wearing black, charcoal gray, or navy with medium-toned colors—again, *please* keep your best color combinations in mind.

Although like values of colors balance each other, it is *always* appropriate (and fantastic looking) to bring the bottom color up. For those of you who love them, just think of how much fun it's going to be to finally wear neck accessories that really work. For those of you who don't want to be bothered with any of this, the solution is easy—always wear a *base*.

Creating a Smart Capsule Wardrobe

Just the Basics

◆ Buy 2 suits, 5 tops, and 2 neck accessories that can be interchanged, and you will have 20 different looks.

◆ Colors, fabrics, and styles need to be complimentary.

◆ A few thoughtful additions to this "core" wardrobe will give you countless further outfits.

Beyond the Basics

Some women wish they still had a "uniform" (like men do) because they'd know exactly what to put on in the morning without the last minute *STRESS* of trying to figure out what goes with what. If you want to simplify your life and still look great every day, *continue*.....

How would you like to look not only professional but fabulous every working day for an entire month and never wear the same outfit twice? Sound expensive? It's not. Here's the "formula"—2 + 2 + 5 = 20—yes, I know the math *seems* unbelievable:

2 *basic* **suits**—or 2 jackets and 2 skirts/trousers.

2 neck accessories—solid-colored scarves or necklaces that match your skirts/trousers.

5 *basic* **tops.**

The Suits

Use two *basic* suits, or two jackets and two skirts/trousers ("mixed suit" looks), whose jackets and skirts/trousers can be interchanged so that the jacket of one can be worn with the skirt/trousers of the other and vice versa. Choose solid colors—your best, of course—and **keep in mind your most flattering color combinations.**

If your workplace is *highly* conservative, you may not be as adventuresome as you could be in selecting the colors for your capsule. Starting out with one suit or jacket in a neutral (off-white, cream, beige, camel, brown, rust, navy, gray, or black) and one in a color will give you some great variety —the "bottoms," as mentioned above, can match the jackets or not. The capsule will work as well if you choose to use all neutrals or all favorite colors.

The Neck Accessories

Used to bring the bottom color up, the color of the neck accessory **IS CRITICAL** and the main reason the capsule works. You will need a necklace or solid-color scarf to match each of your skirts/trousers.

For example, navy colored or lapis beads to match a navy skirt; pearls or a cream-colored scarf to match a cream-colored skirt; a camel scarf to match camel trousers; a red necklace or scarf to match a red skirt; and so on.

The Five *Basic* Tops

Use uncomplicated blouses, shells, tanks, or pullovers. All five tops must compliment your suits or mixed suit looks from a color, texture, and a compatible neckline standpoint. The more uncomplicated the top (do not read boring), the better. For example, a pullover in a smooth or flat-weave knit is much more versatile than one that is ribbed, and a blouse without pockets works with more jacket styles.

For more variety in your tops you may use a combination of solid colors and prints. However, any print must contain **both** of the jacket colors and **both** of the colors of your skirts/trousers.

For instance, if you have built your capsule around two solid-color suits, one in cream and one in red, your print top must have both the *exact* shades of cream and red. If your capsule is built around a black suit, red jacket, and camel trousers, your print tops must contain black, red, **and** camel.

The Styling

You'll want to be certain that your jackets and skirts/trousers work well with each other from a style perspective. For example, if one of your jackets is long, your skirts will most likely need to be pegged and your trousers cut with a narrow leg. If both jackets are shorter, you can more easily combine them with a variety of skirt and trouser styles.

To make your life simple, the buttons on your capsule jackets should match the color of the jackets exactly, otherwise they can interfere with your neck accessory. What if one of your jackets already has great looking gold or silver buttons on it? Can you work around them? Yes, but the metallic color of the buttons usually needs to be "tied in" to your necklace. For example, if one of your jackets has gold buttons on it and you are wearing it with a contrasting skirt/trousers (often necessitating bringing the bottom color up), your necklace will also need to have some gold beads in it to look beautifully coordinated. If it doesn't, try twisting a gold necklace (usually a simple chain) around your capsule necklace.

Those of you who wear more trendy, up-fashion, ethnic, arty, or eccentric looks can create a capsule with more avant-garde pieces of clothing and accessories—if your workplace is strictly casual you can combine casual items using the same *concept*.

The Fabrics

All of your capsule "pieces" must work well together from a fabric standpoint. You may want to review the information about fabrics on page 100.

How Does the Capsule Work?

Essentially what you are going to be doing is wearing all five tops with each of your skirts or pants, switching jackets and always making sure that you reach for the neck accessory in the color of your "bottom." Use your best clarity and any of your most flattering colors and neutrals, remembering that the way you combine these shades is equally as important to your looking super.

If your best clarity is clear and bright, every color in the capsule would be in this clarity. On the other hand, if your best clarity is more subdued and toned down, every color in the capsule would be in that clarity.

Remember that it's a *concept* you are learning and you can vary all the colors (which were chosen at random) and styles to fit your personality and needs. If specific color combinations need to be strengthened or lightened up, you know what to do.

Suit with a skirt:	■ Pink
Mixed suit look:	■ Camel jacket and black trousers
5 Tops:	■ Pink jewel-neck blouse
	■ Black V-neck pullover
	■ Yellow scoop-neck shell
	■ Beige blouse with matching buttons
	■ Purple knit shell

★ Don't forget that the necklines of your tops must be compatible with both jacket styles and work well with both of your neck accessories.

2 neck accessories:
- Pink scarf (solid color) to match pink skirt
- Black beads to match black pants

Shoes:
- Camel
- Black

The 20 Different Looks

1. Pink suit with pink blouse and pink scarf (optional)
2. Pink jacket with black trousers, beige blouse, and black beads
3. Camel jacket with pink skirt, yellow shell, and pink scarf
4. Pink jacket with black trousers, yellow shell, and black beads
5. Camel jacket with black trousers, purple shell, and black beads
6. Pink suit with purple shell and pink scarf
7. Camel jacket with pink skirt, beige blouse, and pink scarf
8. Camel jacket with black trousers, yellow shell, and black beads
9. Pink jacket with black trousers, purple shell, and black beads
10. Pink suit with yellow blouse and pink scarf
11. Camel jacket with black trousers, beige blouse, and black beads
12. Camel jacket with pink skirt, purple shell, and pink scarf
13. Pink jacket with black trousers, black pullover, and black beads (optional)
14. Pink jacket with black trousers, pink blouse, and black beads
15. Camel jacket with black trousers, black pullover, and black beads (optional)
16. Camel jacket with black trousers, pink blouse, and black beads
17. Pink suit with black pullover and pink scarf
18. Pink suit with beige blouse and pink scarf
19. Camel jacket with pink skirt, pink blouse, and pink scarf (optional)
20. Camel jacket with pink skirt, black pullover, and pink scarf

I'm sure that you are thinking that you are going to be very tired of wearing your black beads and pink scarf. For most of you, there are other things hanging in your closet that you will be wearing as well, but the points are two: if you choose well, you can get a lot of great looks out of a few pieces of clothing and, if you have a capsule wardrobe, you are never lacking something professional, dependable, and pleasing to wear.

Your capsule also makes 10 different looks without a jacket. How different do you look without the jacket? Try it and see—you'll be surprised at the difference and you might just have discovered some good looks for business casual days.

Adding Variety to Your Capsule

If you have a capsule that includes a mixed suit look, the first items you will want to add to your capsule are a jacket that matches the odd skirt or pants and tops to make more bases. To give variety to your capsule, add patterned scarves—they **must** contain the colors that you are combining that day. For example, if you are wearing black trousers, a yellow top and a pink jacket, your scarf will include black, yellow and pink. If you aren't a scarf person, maybe always wearing a necklace could become your *signature statement*.

More variety comes with the addition of print blouses that have at least two of your capsule colors—in this example, pink and camel, black and camel, or black and pink.

Note that in this capsule I've included tops that match each bottom—automatically giving you two *bases*, which makes it easy for you to extend your capsule by wearing them with most any other odd jacket. Note, also, that the neck accessory is optional when you are wearing a *base* because you have already "brought up" the bottom color. If you are wearing jackets with matching bottoms, the neck accessory is also optional **IF** you keep your jacket *on*.

Add different *layering* pieces like vests or beautiful cardigan sweaters; use belts and matching shoes in varying colors, including those that are dressier looking for evening functions; do the same with your jewelry. You will find that your dressiest looks are those that are all one color. Next in dressiness come the two-color looks, while those with three colors, even when using classic clothing, appear more casual. This is a good tip to remember when putting together a wardrobe for classic business and classic business casual dress.

Turn one of your capsule suits into an evening look by adding a silk or lace camisole, or wear a dressy jacket over one of your *bases*. This works best if the fabrics are dressier, like a wool or rayon crepe, wool gabardine, silk, or even one of the microfibers. A change of accessories, if necessary, and you're off. If you attend many evening functions, consider creating an evening capsule.

Add uniqueness through your accessories. Just because you have a red scarf to balance a red skirt doesn't mean that you won't want to keep your eyes open for a red necklace. Also, remember to collect patterned scarves in your capsule colors. On the days when you are wearing one of your *bases*, leave off the optional accessory and add a great belt.

Make Every Purchase Count

I've already mentioned that when many women shop they just "fatten" their closets with miscellaneous stuff that doesn't go with anything else. If you go and look in your closet most of you will find that you already have several of the pieces you need to create at least one *Smart Capsule Wardrobe*. The best place to *shop* first is in your existing closet (think of it as a boutique where everything is free).

By carefully adding just 1 jacket, 1 bottom, 1 top, and 1 neck accessory that go with your *capsule*, you can make countless different looks. Remember that necklines, styles, colors, and fabrics must be compatible and you'll need a neck accessory in the color of any new skirt or pants. Your additions don't have to go with every single thing in the capsule—it would be terrific if they even coordinated with just a few of the other pieces.

CHANGE THE FABRIC—CHANGE THE STYLE

JUST THE BASICS

- ◆ Knits are great for business for all bodies and all ages—wear those that *skim*, not cling.

- ◆ No sheer, filmy, gauzy peek-a-boo fabrics.

- ◆ A silk suit can be worn for daytime business during warm weather months but is best kept for evening attire when it's cold outside.

- ◆ Combining different fabrics is fine as long as the weights are compatible.

BEYOND THE BASICS

Fabric is amazing. Just picture your favorite "businesslike" pantsuit in a totally different fabric—a brocade, for example, or velvet. It can give a subtle classic an exotic look. Here are some things about fabrics that you might like to know.

Knits are super for business wear for **all** body types as long as they are not too tight. Those that are too clingy can show bulges above and below your bra, and at your waist and hips. Some of the new "body slimming" slips, panties, and stockings can help *smooth out* this concern, as can camisoles and slips that help knit fabrics *glide* over the body instead of clinging to it.

Fabrics that bag and sag ruin the look of an otherwise great outfit. Avoid purchasing inexpensive rayons and inexpensive knits unless you are willing to give them up after one season. Wearing a slip will help them hold their shape, as will not wearing them to death.

Sheer and "peek-a-boo" fabrics are not generally considered business-like; well, maybe "monkey businesslike." How sheer is *too* sheer? You get to judge. Does it work if you wear a camisole under it? Only you know your place of business, its spoken and unspoken codes, and your career goals. When in doubt, save "it" for playtime.

Cotton-polyester knits are too casual if you work in a law firm, but they are probably perfect for you if you work in the office of a veterinarian, or if you are a doctor of veterinarian medicine. When you try something on and you *feel* casual or sporty in it, do not wear it for business attire unless sporty/casual is the look you are striving for.

For the budget conscious, or those who like a sparse wardrobe, buy garments in fabrics that you can wear year-round in your climate. Consider:

◆   Silks, including raw silks

◆   Tropical-weight woolens

◆   Good quality rayons

◆   Microfibers

◆   Knits

◆   Blends of synthetic and natural fibers

Silks can be worn day and night all year long in our warmer climates. In areas with four more distinct seasons, in cold-weather months, silk ensembles generally get relegated to evening wear. In other words, the silk pantsuit you wore to work all summer could be used for a cocktail party in the winter—with a change of accessories, of course.

Most of the new microfibers are better than ever, but a few still feel too "crisp" and won't drape well on your body. If it doesn't pass the *touch* test, leave it. Some of the most comfortable fabrics are those with a touch of spandex or lycra. Really! There are even some beautiful wools that include a small percentage and they feel terrific. On the other hand, sometimes a *small* percentage of "other" can make a fabric scratchy—no matter how cute the item, leave it because if you don't, you will just be leaving it in your closet.

Similar weights of fabrics easily balance each other, like combining two light-weight fabrics. It's also possible to combine most light-weight fabrics with medium-weight fabrics and most medium-weight fabrics with heavier weight fabrics.

If you try to combine a heavier wool flannel jacket with a wool crepe skirt/trousers, you may throw your balance off—it can depend on how "substantial" the crepe looks, the lining, and the color combination. When balance is thrown off in this way, sometimes the less substantial fabric can end up looking inexpensive—even if it isn't. This outfit has a better chance of working if the heavier fabric is on the bottom and the lighter on the top. Just a note: It's best for delicate Color Types to avoid really rough, coarse looking fabrics and very heavy-looking textures.

SMART LOOKING SHOES AND BOOTS

JUST THE BASICS

◆ Avoid shoes that look chunky, clunky, or heavy including those with a chunky heel, thick sole, or very wide square toe unless they complete a funky, faddish look you are striving for.

◆ Lighter weight looking shoes with a low-cut vamp are the most flattering styles and can be most easily paired with differing skirt lengths and trouser shapes.

◆ Shoes and boots in the color of your hair are a great option to black.

◆ Sleek-looking boots can be worn with business attire as long as the overall look fits the image you want.

◆ Very pointed toes are not flattering unless you are a witch—the kind with the pointed hat.

BEYOND THE BASICS

There are a lot of ugly shoes in the marketplace, and although there are also some really beautiful shoes available, it seems that many women are making the wrong choice. What makes a shoe ugly? Well, some are just that way, but others only *look* ugly because they are being worn with clothing styles that call for a different shoe—usually a lighter weight shoe.

There are so *many* different shoe and boot styles to choose from—what to do? If you own both your favorite heel height and flats in your hair color, other favored neutrals, and your core colors, you will probably have the appropriate shoe and boot for most any attire. The best **basic** "go with anything" shoe, in a heel or a flat, is cut low in the vamp and fairly low on the sides—giving you a longer leg line and a less heavy-looking shoe. The leather is smooth and unadorned, and the sole and heel match the shoe.

The most *basic* boots are those made in a plain smooth leather, minus buckles, chains, and sporty stitching, that fit closely to your leg. Any height below the knee is fine, but those that are at least long enough to cover your ankle bone are more versatile, as are those with a slender, versus chunky, heel that matches the boot.

Wearing shoes that are too casual, the wrong style, or too heavy for the outfit are often-seen mistakes. When your shoe or boot makes the same statement as your outfit, you are making a statement that you know what's what.

The biggest mistake, by far, is wearing a shoe that is too heavy looking for the outfit. I know that you see these looks in magazines and catalogs, but that doesn't mean it looks good. Yes, what I'm saying is that many of the designers and stylists **don't know** (hopefully it's not because they just don't care) that this look is unflattering, unbalanced, totally unsophisticated, and the opposite of *easy elegance*. And, they are definitely not sensual!

Weighty "stuff": What weight shoe looks best with which trouser shape and length? First, you'll need to know which shoe styles are light-weight looking, medium-weight looking, and heavy looking?

Light-weight shoes include:

◆ Sandals that have thin soles or medium to high slender heels and very few light-weight thin straps across the foot.

◆ Low vamp sling-backs with a narrow strap around the back of the foot and medium to high slender heels.

◆ Open-toed slides/mules with one narrow piece of leather/fabric over the foot or a few thin straps across the foot.

◆ The more slim the heel, the lighter weight the shoe/sandal (there are no chunky heels in this group.

◆ All soles will be thin, not thick, platform, or a wedge.

Light/medium-weight shoes include:

◆ Pumps with a slender, medium to high heel, low-cut vamp, low sides, and thin sole.

◆ Flats with a very flat ½" heel (like a ballet flat), low-cut vamp, low sides, and a thin sole—if the heel gets thicker, the shoe will look heavier.

◆ Slides/mules with an open toe and a low-cut vamp—medium amount of leather/fabric over the foot and a medium to high slender heel.

Please don't ever let your toes hang over the sole of your sandals (or any open-toed shoe), or let your heels hang off the sole in the back. Avoid see-through sandals and shoes unless you are Cinderella or you are going for a trendy, up-fashion, or eccentric look.

Medium-weight shoes include:

◆ Pumps with a *fairly* slim heel, fairly low vamp, and fairly low sides.

◆ Flats with a *fairly* flat heel, fairly low vamp, and fairly low sides.

◆ Pumps with a high thicker (but not chunky) heel and a low vamp.

- ◆ Slides/mules with a medium amount of coverage over the foot (the lower the vamp the better) and a slightly thicker heel, but not chunky.

- ◆ Mary-Janes and T-straps that have a low vamp, are cut low on the sides, have a slim medium to high heel, thin sole, and very narrow, small straps.

Any strap that isn't thin makes a shoe look heavier. Mary-Janes, T-straps, and other shoes and sandals with a strap across the instep really shorten your leg line and can make your ankles and calves look thick and/or "sturdy." A shoe or sandal with a strap around your ankle can do the same unless the strap is very fine and the vamp is cut very low. When it comes to any strap across your instep or ankle, it helps lengthen your leg line if your stockings are a sheer tint of the same color as your strap.

Medium/heavy-weight shoes include:

- ◆ Pumps with a medium-height thicker heel.

- ◆ Very high-cut pumps with a slender heel.

- ◆ Some loafers—those that have less coverage over the foot.

- ◆ Slides/mules that cover nearly the entire top of your foot.

- ◆ Flats that are cut very high in vamp and on the sides.

- ◆ Wedges and platforms usually fall either into this category or the heavy-weight category depending on cut of vamp and thickness of the sole.

Heavy-weight shoes include:

- ◆ Any shoe or sandal (including slides/mules) with a thick/heavy sole or very chunky heel.

- ◆ Most loafers.

- ◆ Oxfords.

- ◆ Athletic shoes.

- ◆ Most anything with a tongue or laces.

- ◆ Most wedges and platforms with thick soles.

- ◆ Any shoe or sandal that covers most of the top of your foot.

The sleeker looking a boot, the more dressy and versatile it will be. Just as with shoes, chunky heels, very square toes, and casual materials (rough leather versus smooth, for example) render any boot heavier and sportier looking.

A high vamp, higher sides, thick/heavy sole, straps across the foot or around the ankle and a chunky heel can **RAISE** the visual weight of a shoe—so can thicker, coarser materials and textures like canvas versus smooth leather. A lower vamp, lower sides, and slimmer heel can **lower** the visual weight of a shoe.

Any light-colored shoe with a dark sole or heel looks *heavier* than it would with a matching sole and heel—the exception would be a sole so thin that you didn't even notice it.

Please avoid wearing mules of any style with all covered-up looks (trousers, long sleeves, high necks). Why? Look at yourself in your mirror from the back (some women think of their full-length mirror as a best friend that can't talk back) and you'll see how silly bare heels look when all of the rest of you is covered. Check out sling-backs for the same reason.

More *weighty* subject matter: Now, which weight shoe/boot works best with a specific trouser shape and length? Although I'm going to give you a guide, it's not quite that simple because the shoe weight can depend on the weight of the trouser fabric and the occasion.

The lighter the weight and more delicate the fabric, the lighter the shoe needs to be whatever the trouser style (the same goes for skirts). For example, you know that wider leg trousers are to be worn long, nearly touching the floor in the back with your shoe on. If the trouser is wool, the perfect weight shoe is medium to heavy but never light. But if the fabric is lightweight, like rayon or silk, the shoe shouldn't be any heavier looking than medium-weight. All shoes and boots styles also need to make the same overall statement as your attire. So, all of the following **depend upon** fabric weight and overall look.

Straight wide leg approximately 10" or more across the bottom:

◆ Any weight shoe or boot.

Straight classic leg approximately 9" across bottom:

◆ Any weight shoe/boot or style.

Tapered trousers from 6" to 8" across bottom:

◆ Light, medium, to medium-heavy weight shoe/boot—the narrower the pant at the ankle, the lower the vamp and lighter weight the shoe/boot should be.

Straight narrow leg approximately 7" across:

◆ Light- to medium-weight shoe.

◆ Best with styles that have a low vamp.

◆ You can also wear a boot that's not too heavy looking, but it has to fit closely to your leg so it won't make a visible ridge under your pants.

Very narrow-cut (sometimes called cigarette) leg that is tapered to the ankle, and capris:

◆   No heavy-weight shoes of any style.

◆   Light- to medium-weight shoe with low vamp.

◆   Sleek-looking boot that fits so closely to your leg that you cannot see the top under your pants.

Bell bottoms:

◆   Any weight shoe or boot depending strongly on the fabric—wear them long.

Bootleg cut:

◆   Although any weight has the potential to work, this cut seems to work best with at least a bit of a heel in a variety of styles that are medium to heavy. Wear them long. If a so-called "bootleg cut" *looks* like bell-bottoms, remember, if it walks like a duck and quacks like a duck, it's a duck.

As you train your eye to see the best weight of shoe for an outfit, you will also notice that the top/jacket you are wearing with any of these bottoms can affect your choice. Bare or sleeveless tops can call for less weighty looking shoes, and "all covered-up" tops/jackets can call for a medium-weight shoe instead of a light-weight shoe.

EXPLODING the "myth" that a black shoe is always appropriate: One of my favorite sites in Washington is the Thomas Jefferson Memorial. Inscribed on the walls are some of Jefferson's quotes, including (I'm paraphrasing) the observation that just because something has been done a certain way for a long time doesn't mean that it's right for today—and it doesn't mean that it was **ever** right. Okay, I'm getting down off my soap box, for the moment.

⊘   **Bad Advice:** Wearing black shoes with a navy dress is good and can actually work better than a navy shoe, which is some cases looks too matchy.

①   **My Advice:** Under ALL circumstances, a navy shoe with a navy dress or suit will *always* be the far better choice—much more *elegant* and pulled-together looking. Just because it's "acceptable" for men to do it, doesn't mean that it's a great look for us (or them).

Somewhere along the way, women were taught erroneously that they could wear black shoes with anything. That's not accurate now, it never was, and it never will be unless your hair is black or very dark brown.

Example: Four women, a caramel blonde, a brunette, a redhead, and one with very, very dark brown or black hair are all wearing a medium-toned blue dress and skin tone/nude stockings. Close your eyes and "picture" each wearing black shoes. Only the very dark brown or black-haired woman will look well coordinated—pulled together, finished, polished.

Now, picture how coordinated the caramel blonde would look wearing a camel shoe that gives the illusion of being the same color as her hair. Picture the brunette wearing a brown shoe—the same shade of brown as her hair. Then, picture the redhead wearing a rust tone shoe that gives the illusion of being her hair color. Very polished, very balanced, very *elegant*, very simple—their handbags match their shoes.

Some "Demystifying" S*mart Tips*

There is an old rule you can follow which is to wear shoes the same color as your hem (skirt, dress, trousers). This can still work if you want to afford, and can find, shoes in all of the colors this would require.

A more practical easy guideline is to wear shoes and boots in your hair color and hair highlight color (if it is very apparent), lighter and darker versions of your hair color, and your skin tone, depending on how light or dark your outfit. I know, you think I've gone crazy again.

There are two colors that are already part of every outfit you put on—your hair color or hair highlight color (whichever is most visible in all lighting conditions) and your skin tone. These colors are already part of your "color scheme" no matter what, unless you're wearing a hat that totally hides your hair.

Instead of bringing in an "odd" color that doesn't relate to the colors in your outfit, or to you, bring in one that does. It only makes sense that if you repeat these body colors in accessories (and clothing, too) you will look really *pulled together*. For example, when you wear a print that has your hair color in it, you look "extra" fabulous.

Match your hair as exactly as possible—in front of a mirror, put the shoe on the floor and glance at yourself to see if it gives the "illusion" of being your hair color or your strong, highly visible highlights. Redheads and those of you with "silver" (gray) hair, do the same.

Many years ago, during a consultation, I was talking to a client about using her hair color (it was brown) as a *basic* shoe color because it would work so well with all of the colors on her chart. She made a "face" and told me that she would never wear brown shoes with navy, for instance. I told her that, of course, navy shoes would be the very best choice but asked her (I already knew the answer) why she would never wear brown shoes with navy. She said that she didn't think that navy and brown looked good together.

I asked her if she felt she looked good right that minute. She said, "Yes." I handed her a mirror and asked her to tell me what colors she was wearing. Her medium-length brown hair was touching the collar of her *navy* suit—she took one look at the beautiful harmony created by **her** best brown and navy and immediately got the point. That realization changed her life. By the way, she was wearing black patent shoes.

⊘ **Bad Advice:** Wear black boots with a red, yellow, beige, and brown print dress.

⊕ **My Advice:** The black boot looks totally unrelated to the dress, regardless of hair color. In this instance, the perfect boot or shoe matches the brown in the dress.

If your hair color is light and you need a medium or darker-colored shoe, use a camel and brown that are darker versions of your hair color (golden blondes will look for golden camels and golden browns, for example). If you need a light shoe, use your hair color or your skin tone if it is light. **If your hair color is medium** in tone and you need a darker-toned shoe, use a darker version of your hair color.

Everyone who needs a light-toned shoe can use her skin tone or, if your skin tone is darker, a lighter version of that exact color. Light-haired women can also use their hair color.

If your hair is very dark brown, you can probably use black when you need a dark shoe (it's a darker version of your hair color)—your mirror will tell you if the color balance is good. If you need a medium or light shoe, use your skin tone and/or lighter or darker versions of your skin tone.

Here are some simple, but so very pulled-together looking, examples of accessorizing a *base* with shoes in your hair color—for a super look, add a belt in the same shade. The shoe doesn't need to be exact, but it does need to be close enough to give the illusion of being the same color as your hair:

♦ **Brown hair:** A plum or raspberry base with brown shoes.

♦ **Blonde hair:** A robins egg blue or turquoise base with camel shoes.

♦ **Red hair:** A blue-purple base with coppery/rust shoes.

♦ **Black or very dark brown hair:** An emerald green base with black shoes.

♦ **Silver hair:** A red base (your best shade and clarity, of course), with gray shoes.

Besides having shoes in your hair color (and perhaps your skin tone), you will want to eventually own shoes in any neutral you wear often and in

The clarity and shade of your make-up should compliment your personal coloring (color type).

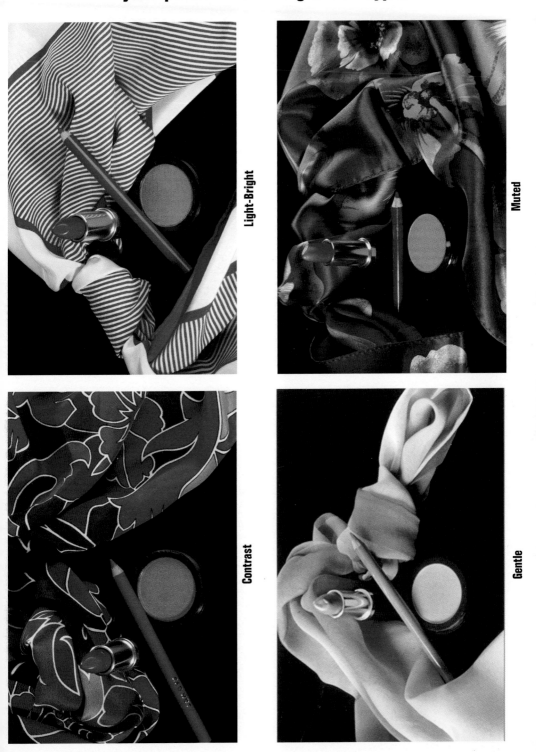

Light-Bright

Muted

Contrast

Gentle

Smart Lessons

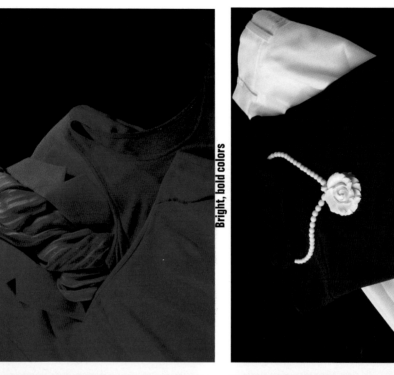

Bright, bold colors

Toned-down colors

Balance colors by bringing the bottom color "up"

High contrast

Softer contrast

Wearing a base [the top and bottom match] is a smart way to extend your wardrobe with a variety of fabulous looks.

Which flat is the most lightweight looking and flattering?

Which boot appears to be the most sleek and dressy?

Which shoe is the most versatile and flattering?

Which sandal is the most lightweight looking as well as the most flattering?

your "core colors." A core color is a favorite color (one that looks great on you, of course) that you wear all of the time. Metallics and "pearlized" finishes that give the illusion of your hair color (bronzes, golds, silvers/pewters, and coppers) are also often wonderful choices. Also check out the pearlized creamy tones to wear with pastels and other light colors.

If you plan and build your wardrobe around two favorite neutrals and one or two core colors, you can limit the number of pairs of shoes you need to look stylish, allowing you more money (for the budget conscious) to buy better quality, or to buy something else you desire. A better quality shoe can upgrade an outfit; an inexpensive shoe can downgrade an outfit.

Decisions, Decisions, and More Decisions

Work to achieve a good "color balance" between your shoe or boot and your attire by using a light- or medium-tone shoe with lighter colors; a light, medium, or dark shoe with medium-tone colors (this can depend on the season, how light or dark your hair, and the look you want to create) and medium or dark shoes with darker colors (this can also depend on those things just mentioned).

Great shoe colors to wear with cream or pastel ensembles for a woman who has light- to medium-toned hair are cream, skin tone, or camel with a light shoe. For women with medium-toned or red hair, try cream, skin tone, camel, or hair color/hair highlight color. If your hair is very dark, use cream, skin tone, camel, or black with light colors.

One of the most difficult looks to balance is a darker top with a light bottom. You can balance this look by wearing a dark shoe/boot and a dark belt—the belt could have a metallic buckle or some metallic detailing on it. This look is more easily balanced if there is "less" of the dark top, i.e., short-sleeved/sleeveless/lower neck with skin showing, than when the top has long sleeves. Wearing the top tucked in is good because less of it shows. Examples include: beige trousers with a short-sleeved black top (tucked in) worn with a black belt that has a gold buckle and black shoes; and a pale pink skirt worn with a charcoal gray long sleeve scoop-neck sweater (tucked in) with a gray belt that has a silver buckle worn with gray shoes. Add a gray and pink scarf, or pink pearls, and you have even better balance—you now know why.

You can make many combinations work by bringing the bottom color up, but if you **haven't** done that, *please* **don't** wear:

- ⊘ A light bottom and dark top with a light shoe.

- ⊘ A medium bottom with a dark top and a light shoe.

- ⊘ A medium-colored dress with a light shoe when your hair is dark.

- ⊘ A light shoe with a dark outfit.

Your shoe and boot color should always "relate" to your outfit. For example, avoid wearing a red shoe when there is no red anywhere else in your ensemble. A red belt would make the shoe work, but not just red earrings (the colors are too far apart). What if you carry a red bag? Only if it is with you at all times will it work—at a cocktail party (if you don't lay it down) or out shopping, but not at work because your bag isn't with you any longer once you get through the door.

From time to time current fashion calls for us to tuck our pants into boots and that's easy to do when the trouser is narrow—what isn't so easy to do is to wear very tapered or very slim-cut pants over a boot because the taper at the ankle usually makes it impossible to get the bottom of your pants down over the top of your boot. Hence the bootleg cut, slender in the leg but just wide enough at the bottom to fit over boots. No lightweight fabrics with boots, *please*. You know the exceptions.

It ruins your credibility to wear "sneakers" with your business attire. Don't do it, no exceptions unless your doctor insists that no other shoe made for walking will work for your "problem" (have your problem fixed ASAP). American women are still being laughed at all over the world because of this inappropriate habit. And, if that's not enough to get you to stop doing it, most men would never consider a second look (at least not an admiring look) at a woman who is dressed this way—if you don't believe me, ask them.

For centuries, women have somehow managed to walk long distances without putting on this very clunky-looking footwear. Now, some American women cannot even go out for lunch, or to and from the parking garage, without putting them on.

Several companies make great shoes that are made for walking and standing, that do not look like athletic shoes. You may not like the way they look with your outfit as well as the shoe you put on when you get to work but, believe me, they will look *1,000* times better than wearing sneakers with your business attire.

High Gloss: If you look great in clear, bright colors, shiny black patent leather will work for you. Those of you who are more enhanced by toned down colors should avoid solid shiny black patent, as the eye can be drawn to the "shine" at your feet.

Patent in toned down colors and neutrals other than black are fine, as are shoes that are a mix of small amounts of patent (even black if it's one of your best colors) and other materials such as leather, suede, faille, and canvas. Black patent in small strappy sandals may work, but it's "iffy." You are training your eye, so use your mirror to tell you if this small amount of patent still looks *unrelated* to your coloring.

You may wear trendy shoes to work if you are wearing trendy clothing to work, but using a trendy shoe with classic clothing says that you **don't** know what's what. That trendy shoe usually has a specific look it was intended for and, American women have an "unfortunate" tendency to wear/ use the latest "in" item with any previously owned item. So that I only have to say it once instead of a dozen times on the following pages, exceptions are made for trendy, eccentric, and arty dressers.

Using a casual-looking shoe with a suit or a heavy-looking shoe with a light-weight long skirt also says you don't have a clue. No boots, *please,* with serious classic suits unless the weather is bad—and then change at the office.

No loafers, oxfords, or other heavy-weight shoes with slit skirts. Also, none of these heavy-looking styles with "knee-hovering" to mid-calf length skirts. Most heavy-weight shoes are also too clunky-looking with most long skirts. No matter what the fashion, wearing heavy-looking shoes (especially those without a heel) with below-the-knee to below mid-calf lengths generally (but not always) gives a dowdy impression.

⊘ **Bad Advice:** Wear sandals with wool trousers, a turtleneck sweater, and a jacket.

① **My Advice:** It's not *smart* to look warm on top and cold on the bottom. Wear wool when it's cold outside and wear sandals when it's warm outside (except for formalwear).

In the magazines and catalogues there are many long-sleeved pantsuits shown with sandals and I have to say (again!) that it looks really absurd to be **all** covered up and then have nearly bare feet. The only way to make this look "work" is to:

◆ Wear a pantsuit that is made of a light-weight fabric, **and**

◆ Leave the jacket open **and** wear a fairly bare looking top—you need some skin showing to balance the "bare" light-weight looking sandals.

◆ Or, if the cut of the jacket allows, wear the jacket buttoned without a top under it—you need to "expose" some skin but not necessarily cleavage.

Sling-backs, or pumps with an open toe, can be worn to work if they make the same statement as your outfit and your outfit makes the right statement for your place of business. Picture a navy sling-back or navy pump with an open toe worn in the summer with a short-sleeved light beige silk or rayon suit that is trimmed with navy—beautiful, even for a conservative atmosphere.

No opaque stockings with sandals, sling-backs, open-toe or cut-out shoe styles, or with short-sleeved or sleeveless tops or dresses, *please,* no matter what you see in the fashion magazines. And when cool and cold weather comes, leave "bare" shoes in the closet until the next spring unless you are wearing them with evening clothes.

Embellished shoes and boots (embroidered, studded, etc.) are wonderful if they go with the look you are creating to further your career—usually more trendy, arty, ethnic, or up-fashion fields. Subtle metallics can be worn in many business environments, but shiny metallics are usually best kept for casual day (or evening) looks. You know the exceptions.

Those metallics that are subtle in tone, versus bright and shiny, are best for Gentle and Muted Color Types who are most flattered by toned down colors. Bright and shiny metallics look wonderful on Contrast and Light-Bright Color Types who are enhanced by clear, vibrant colors.

Silver and pewter tones will work well for all Color Types with silver/white/gray hair. They will also work for any Color Type who is wearing light gray and would like a "matching" shoe.

Very sporty looking shoes are only appropriate with casual fabrics and casual attire, but a slightly dressier shoe will go with both casual and dressier fabrics and attire. So, if you are on a budget or prefer a minimal wardrobe, which will you buy?

Speaking of budgets, if you are on one, avoid buying shoes in exaggerated styles. Many will be "out" before you get them broken in. These styles include: wide square toes, extremely long pointed toes, thick platforms, and very chunky heels.

Boots in all heights look best when they fit closely to your ankle and your leg, versus standing-out away from them. Stockings that have some weight and/or texture can be worn to create great looks with skirts of all lengths and those that match the color of your boots help give the illusion that there is less of a gap between your leg and the boot. Also, boots that come higher up on your leg (and fit closely) help prevent pants from getting caught on the top of them as you walk, sit down, or stand up.

Shoes and boots with heels covered in the same matching leather are dressier looking than those with heels that are stacked "wood."

ALLURING LEGS

JUST THE BASICS

- Never let a man, not even your husband, see you in knee-highs or trouser socks.

- No knee-highs or trouser socks, **ever**, with a skirt of any length.

- For a skin tone stocking, match the exact color of your face and arms and avoid wearing those that look like you have a tan (when you don't) or those that are paler than your skin—you are after a "nude" look.

- No sandals or open shoes of any kind with opaque stockings.

- ◆ For a classic look, no opaque stockings with skirts that hover around the knee.

- ◆ No sheer stockings with very short skirts and high heels for classic business attire.

- ◆ When you need a bone/cream stocking don't wear one so white that you look like a nurse.

BEYOND THE BASICS

Please, no knee-highs or trouser socks, **ever**, with a skirt of any length. Yes, some women do this—I've seen it with my own two eyes in the slit of a skirt and when getting in and out of cars. A super radio show in the Washington area, *Girl Talk*, had me on as a guest talking about my last two books, and a call came in from a woman who asked about wearing knee-highs. Since this particular show revolved around men, I mentioned that you don't ever want to be caught in them, even by your husband. Why? Take a look in the mirror.

Please double-check the color in natural daylight.

Have you ever walked out of the house and glanced down at your stockings to find that something's wrong with the color—they don't look the same as they did when you put them on? Natural daylight tells many truths:

- ◆ If the color of your foundation is wrong.

- ◆ If your makeup is blended well enough.

- ◆ If your hair color is flattering to your skin tone.

- ◆ If your clothing and accessory colors are working well together.

- ◆ If the color of your stockings is right.

The wrong color of stockings can ruin an otherwise great look. On the other hand, if they are right, you won't notice them except as part of your *smart* total look.

What could be the matter? Usually:

- ⊘ Wearing stockings called "suntan" which are most often too dark or reddish.

- ⊘ Wearing stockings that are too light or too white looking. Often, when stockings are too "white" (even when they may be called bone or ivory), it is because they are too opaque—not sheer enough.

- ⊘ Wearing stockings that the package said were "off-black"— way off—be aware, some actually have a muddy or green cast.

⊘ Wearing opaque stockings with skirt lengths that hover around the knee when your attire is classic.

⊘ Wearing too sheer stockings with very short skirts, definitely a "no, no" for business, *perhaps* okay at a party, and definately okay for a private party for two.

⊘ Wearing patterned or textured stockings when plain would have been more elegant.

⊘ Wearing nude/skin tone stockings when a sheer tint of color or opaque would have been much better.

⊘ Wearing dark stockings when those in a nude/skin tone or very sheer tint of color would be more flattering.

Never wear "sun tan" looking stockings unless they are the **exact** color of your skin. They are often too dark and generally too "reddish" or "orangy" looking to have a natural appearance.

Every day, during the training of Color 1 Associates, I do a wardrobe critique of each trainee in front of the class. Of course, since they are in training, I don't expect them to know everything when they start, so there are usually things that I need to mention.

One particularly stunning and stylish Black "Associate to be" came to class the first day wearing black narrow-cut trousers, a white blouse, and a black, white, and gray vest with black sling back heels—everything was perfect except for her stockings. Her feet looked "orange." After the critique, she went into the ladies room and took off her stockings.

The next day of training, she again came beautifully dressed—this time without stockings, determined not to make the same mistake. The "trouble" was, I had to tell her that she needed to wear stockings that day because she was wearing a classic business look.

Unless you are familiar with the color and the brand, check the color in natural daylight, and check it as well in the same light you work in—lighting can really make colors change drastically and you do not need to start your workday shocked to discover that the color of your stockings is not what you thought.

Sheer **decision making:** All women need a sheer nude/skin tone look with certain attire. Check every possible color to find stockings that are perfect for you. Slip one of your arms in the store's sample and hold it up next to your other arm. Your arms should match **exactly**.

When in doubt about what's best, follow these guidelines—there are exceptions, of course, but **most** of the time these *smart tips* work great IF you pay attention to your skirt length and the occasion:

◆   Wear your nude/skin tone or sheer bone/ivory with light-colored clothing.

◆   With medium-colored clothing wear your nude/skin tone if your shoe is medium in tone; your nude/skin tone or sheer bone/ivory if your shoe is light; and your nude/skin tone or a **very, very** sheer tint of the shoe color if the shoe is dark. (Almost always, the nude/skin tone will be the more appropriate choice.)

◆   With dark-colored clothing wear a sheer tint of the dark shoe color; a nude/skin tone or a sheer bone/ivory, depending on the look you'd like, the occasion, the time of year, and the length of your skirt. In the fall and the winter, with shorter skirts, opaque stockings the color of the your shoes/boots (or possibly the color of your skirt or trouser) may be perfect—it depends on the "depends upon."

◆   For a dressier effect, your stockings can be lighter or more sheer, especially at night. For example, a short skirt that requires opaque stockings in the daytime can look totally different with sheerer stockings at night.

What in the world could your age have to do with your perfect choice of stockings? How sheer, medium-opaque, or opaque you wear your stockings is dependent on the look you are creating for your place of business, the length of your skirt, the time of the day or year, the occasion, your shoe style, and your age.

"Age" is mentioned here because short skirts and very short skirts teamed with very sheer stockings can look sleazy instead of sexy on "women of a certain age"—what age is that? You get to pick the number but, if you *feel* uncertain, it's best not to wear this look because the "uncertainty" will keep you from carrying it off. What does shoe style have to do with it? A short skirt worn with sheer stockings, a low heel, or flats, although not conservative, is much more conservative than the same combination with high heels.

Opaque stockings can work well with very long skirts, short skirts, and very short skirts for both day and evening. A slightly opaque look (but not a totally opaque look) is nice with a skirt that is just above the knee. A totally opaque look is often necessary as skirts get shorter in the fall and winter, especially during the daytime.

Skirts that hover around the knee or fall just below the knee need very sheer stockings. Chose one that is just a sheer tint of your neutral shoe/boot color (navy, black, gray, etc.), sheer bone/ivory or nude/skin tone. Again, for a classic look, *please* avoid wearing opaque stockings with this length skirt.

Very thick stockings (almost as thick as wool ribbed leggings) are for trendy, arty, ethnic, eccentric, or funky looks.

Collect all *data* before making a final commitment: It's difficult to make generalizations because the color of stockings and how sheer or opaque they are often depends on:

♦ The weight of the fabric you are wearing.

♦ Whether your outfit is a light, medium, or dark color.

♦ The time of the day/year.

♦ The occasion.

♦ Your Color Type.

♦ How much skin is showing or how much is covered up.

In general, **the lighter your hair,** the more you will wear nude/skin tone (sometimes sheer bone) and sheer tints of neutrals instead of slightly opaque and opaque stockings. Examples:

♦ A camel long sleeve top and a black, just above the knee, skirt—use nude/skin tone or **very** sheer black stockings with black shoes. Because your hair is light, if you were to use more opaque black stockings, you could look bottom heavy.

♦ A navy suit with gold buttons on the jacket and a mid-knee length skirt—stockings can be nude/skin tone, or a **very** sheer tint of navy with navy shoes. With some looks such as this, a **very** sheer bone may also work.

"Generally," sleeveless and short-sleeved looks are most always more appropriate with skin tone/nude stockings. And lighter weight fabrics almost always need sheerer stockings.

It's sometimes difficult to know when to wear pale (nude/skin tone or sheer bone) stockings in the colder months. To help you figure this out, I'm giving you some examples, but I want you to continue training your eye so that when you look at yourself in the mirror you will begin to see the balance between the "uncovered" spaces and the "covered" spaces. When your body is all covered up (trousers and long sleeves) with mostly dark colors, nude/skin tone stockings can make it look as though you aren't wearing any stockings at all.

Pretend you are wearing the layered look of a cream shirt over a navy wool turtleneck, and navy wool trousers topped with a red wool jacket. The shoe is a navy loafer, and the stockings need to be an opaque navy because any stocking more sheer will appear too light weight and too dressy. This is a good time to wear opaque navy trouser socks that have a bit of a pattern.

Most of the time when I'm out and about, I am very *unobser-vant*—I don't "work" by noticing what people are wearing and if it's great or not. I think I'd "burn out" if I did. But, once in a while I'm very "naughty"! On a very cold and blustery New York evening I was having dinner in a famous steakhouse with my best friend, Phyl, and neither of us were paying any attention to anything going on around us. When we're together, we are always brainstorming and planning something to do with our businesses.

Suddenly, I felt someone's eyes on me and I glanced in that direction and met the gaze of a *gorgeous* man. At some time unknown to me, the large round table right next to us had gotten a new group of people—all guys. Exchanging glances once in a while, I couldn't help notice that he was perfectly and beautifully dressed except for his *socks*!

He was wearing a black cashmere turtleneck sweater and black flannel wool cuffed trousers (a black *base*) and over them, a subtle black and brown plaid wool jacket that had a blue line running through it. His shoes were perfect—brown suede tying in the color of his jacket. His socks were very *thin* and "looked" like a creamy white.

Something came over me and I just couldn't help myself. On the back of one of my business cards I wrote him a note that said, "Everything is perfect except for your socks—perhaps you might try blue socks, the shade that's in your jacket." I certainly could have said black or brown socks, but I knew that he already knew he could have done that. He was trying for something a touch more avant-garde. As we got up to leave, he said, "Hi." I smiled and handed him my card which he quickly tucked under his plate—as if none of his guy friends noticed.

Did he call? Because my card reflects the fact that I live in Washington, he didn't have my number in New York. But, just like *magic*, two days later, we passed each other on the street (I guess New York is really a small town sometimes) and we couldn't stop to speak because he had "company."

Did he ever call? A couple of days later I was back in Washington and he called. The first words out of his mouth were, "My socks were blue! And, I know, they were too pale and too thin." He's still gorgeous and one of my most adored men friends.

When fabrics are heavier, or you are wearing thicker looking layers, or heavy-weight shoes, you need heavier and thicker looking stockings. The opposite is also true; light-weight fabrics call for more sheer stockings. That doesn't mean that there aren't other things to consider.

For example, if you're wearing a red wool boucle suit with a just above the knee skirt length, your choices for stockings in the fall and winter include a very sheer tint of your shoe color or nude/skin tone. In the spring and summer, if you are a Light-Bright or Gentle Color Type or your hair is light, wearing a nude/skin tone is often the best option. What does your Color Type have to do with the color of your stockings or the sheerness of your stockings?

For the fall and winter, if the same suit skirt is shorter, you can go more opaque—shorter yet, totally opaque, **IF** you are a Contrast or Muted Color Type with medium to dark hair. If your hair is medium or light in tone, a semi-opaque look is dark enough and even then, if you are a Light-Bright or Gentle Color Type, you may need to find a way to lighten up this look. Glance in the mirror. If you look like a "headless person," work your magic. Yes, you do know how: metallic buttons, necklace, and earrings, and/or wear the jacket open with a light top under it—even a belt with a metallic buckle helps.

When you are wearing a longer skirt with a slit, carefully consider if your stockings would be more flattering if they were nude/skin tone (or even sheer bone), a sheer tint of your shoe color, slightly opaque or totally opaque. Remember your "it depends on," such as day or night, dressy, business or casual, and fabric weight. It also depends on whether your hair is dark, medium, or light in tone, and, of course, it depends on the color of the skirt, the height of the slit, and what you are wearing it with.

There are too many different variants for me to be able to give you specific guidelines so you will have to continue training your eye to see good balance—but I will say that if you want to showcase your legs (the reason for the slit?), do not wear totally opaque black stockings with a black skirt, for example, because your legs will get lost.

Avoid wearing opaque stockings in warm weather months. In the spring and summer months your stockings will be lighter, **very** sheer tints of neutrals, nude/skin tone and sheer bone/ivory. Sheer tints of colors (red, blue, pink, and so on) can be used when they work within the parameters of your *career goals*—you know what I mean—but they are never appropriate with classic looks.

⊘ **Bad Advice:** You can go without stockings when you are wearing a suit in the summer.

① **My Advice:** If you are going to wear a suit, especially one that has a classic cut and long sleeves, it's important to wear hose. With most suits, bare legs look *unfinished,* and with a suit at work, unprofessional. For the same reason, please remember to wear makeup.

Even when it's very hot outside, go bare-legged to work only if your workplace is very casual. Even then, if you are wearing attire that calls for stockings, put them on (working and driving in air conditioning takes away any excuse not to wear them).

How do you know if your outfit calls for stockings? If you are wearing pumps (even open-toed pumps), sling-backs, a suit, a pantsuit, or a dress that isn't casual, put on stockings. Even many casual dresses look better with stockings. Also, if you are pretty much "all covered up" (long sleeves, not much skin showing at the neck), bare legs look as totally out of place as sandals. Most of you know, but apparently some women don't, that when you wear sandals (or any open shoe) you need to wear sandalfoot stockings—no reinforced toes or heels showing, *please.*

If you don't want to wear stockings when it is hot outside, make absolutely certain that your work environment will allow you to wear the type of clothing that goes with a no-stocking look. And keep your feet, toenails, and legs beautifully groomed—**no** exceptions.

Wear opaque stockings when you are wearing boots with trousers or skirts (exceptions are made for "you know who," and some of the looks that combine sheer stockings with skirts and boots can be quite charming). Make certain that the stockings do not look *thin*. They need enough visual weight to look good with the weight of the boots. How would anyone know what stockings you are wearing with your boots and trousers? When you sit down and cross your legs, your stockings often show—this is good time to add a touch of *style* with patterned knee-highs.

The *allure*, or possible *horror*, of patterns and textures: Stockings that have visible texture and patterns come and go in fashion and are definitely more appropriate with up-fashion, trendy, funky, eccentric, arty, romantic, or ethnic looks than they are with classic looks. You can try the more *subtle* patterns with long skirts or trousers—if you have any doubts about your workplace, restraint is advised.

For those of you who can dress more creatively at work, try them with shorter skirts. Remember, within certain guidelines, the shorter the skirt the more opaque the stockings. Why am I pointing this out again? Because not all textures and patterns are "opaque"—many have a lot of open work. So, with shorter skirts, open textures become more appropriate for evening than daytime.

⊘ **Bad Advice:** Wear fishnet stockings with a classic tweed suit.

⊕ **My Advice:** Now, most of you aren't going to be wearing this look anyway, so why am I bothering to write about it? Because, it's being shown as a chic way to dress and I can't let it pass without a comment.

One of the mistakes that some American women (and obviously some fashion editors and stylists) make is *mixing statements* to the point where a woman looks like a fashion victim instead of appearing stylish. What are *mixed statements*? Well, in this instance, tweed generally summons up the images of work and warmth, while fishnet stockings bring to mind parties—two completely different statements.

Some other mixed statements: wearing sandals with a raincoat; a warm wooly sweater with a chiffon skirt; boots with a sundress; a glitzy button on a tweed jacket; boots with chiffon evening dresses; wool knee-high stockings with spike-heeled, calf-high boots; and chunky/clunky heavy-weight shoes with an evening dress.

Yes, fashion should be fun, and amazing style comes from unusual mixes like borrowing the jacket from one of our best suits to wear with jeans or cords. But when the statements are too far apart, they are best kept for trendy, funky, or eccentric dressers.

There are two *wonderful* ways to wear fishnet stockings that will bring admiring glances instead of raised eyebrows. First, choose the smallest patterned net—it's more flattering. Wear them with a solid-color dress that is the same color as your stockings; match your shoe as well.

Although it's not impossible to get a great look using a contrasting color, it's definitely beautiful to have your trouser/skirt, patterned stockings, and shoes match or be tone-on-tone of the same color. The very best way to wear textured and patterned stockings with classic styles is to pair them with pantsuits and trousers—just a touch of texture or pattern showing at the ankle adds style and interest. Can just that small touch make a difference? Yes. It might even say, "This is an interesting woman." **Sometimes the biggest "wows" come in tiny, subtle touches.**

When wearing textured and patterned stockings it's often, but not always, best to keep everything else plain and simple—it's easy to look overdone. Small subtle patterns can be worn more successfully than those that are medium and large in scale. For example, the "Swiss-dot" (sheer tint with matching dot, like sheer black with a tiny black dot or sheer bone with a tiny bone dot) is the most conservative pattern and can be worn with femininely styled suits and dresses.

"Color" down *there*? Stockings in colors like blue, purple or red come and go in fashion and are still "suspect" for classic business dress.

For the adventuresome who can wear colors to work, some great looks are created by:

◆ Wearing a totally all one-color look from shoe to earrings (everything red, for example).

◆ Putting together a monochromatic color scheme with lighter and darker tones of the same color, like mixing beige, camel, medium brown, and dark brown; or light purple, medium purple, and dark purple.

◆ "Color blocking" (definitely not for most workplaces)—using two or more blocks of colors like black shoes, red opaque stockings, short black skirt, and a red top.

No "baggy" stockings, *please:* Stockings that are too big for you, or that are very sheer, can "bag" at the ankles and knees. For all pantyhose, try to find a size where your weight and height fall in the middle of the chart, not right on the edge where you are close to needing a smaller size or larger size.

If you do end up on the edge, consider the size and length of your legs. For example, I'm 5' 8½" tall and my legs are short (for my height) and, although not skinny, they are slim. So if I'm on an edge where I'm wondering if I should buy the larger size or the smaller size, I buy the smaller.

Having even a hint of lycra in your stockings (often called lycra sheers) helps keep them from bagging, and it helps them wear longer, making them one of the best choices for work.

Keep a spare pair handy: Keep an extra pair of your most used neutrals at work and NEVER run out at home. Change the minute you get a visible run or hole. Don't start the day with stockings that have several visible snags—you won't feel you look your best and it will affect your entire day. Save snagged stockings to wear under trousers or long skirts with boots.

What's in your sock drawer? No socks with sandals unless you are eccentric (or creating a trendy, funky look). Wearing shoes with socks that show skin above them, other than for athletics or with casual shorts, is a fad unless you are 10 years old or younger—I just picked 10 arbitrarily, because if I were 11 I think I'd want to start dressing more like I was 12, which, after all, is nearly a teenager.

What do I mean by shoes with socks that show skin above them? A classic look for many women is jeans or casual pants worn with socks and loafers. It's best that you aren't able to see your bare leg above your socks, even when you are seated and cross your legs. If you are wearing athletic shoes with jeans or casual pants, the same applies. That means no short, just above the shoe, socks for anything but athletics. Even then, classic socks that you fold down look better than short, ankle socks. Don't believe me? Do a mirror test. The sock that you fold down creates a better "transition" between your leg and big, heavy-looking athletic shoes.

Carrying a Smart Handbag

Just the Basics

- Always carry a handbag that looks coordinated with your attire from both a color and "statement" standpoint.

- If you don't want to be bothered changing your handbag daily, only wear clothing that looks great with the one you want to carry.

- Best colors include your hair color, most used neutrals, and your core colors.

BEYOND THE BASICS

If everything looks great but your handbag, do you look great? Elegant? Stylish? **No.** Carrying the wrong handbag can ruin your look. No matter how much else you've done right, the wrong handbag (including your briefcase and your luggage) sends a message to the contrary.

⊘ **Bad Advice:** It's fine to carry a muted red handbag when you are wearing a vibrant red skirt and black turtleneck top.

① **My Advice:** It's always best to match clarities or brightness levels. Of course in this instance, to look coordinated, all you have to do is carry a black handbag (because of the black top), but if you want to carry red, match the brightness and shade to the skirt as closely as possible.

In years past, our bag had to match our shoes. Now it is acceptable for them to be different—both just have to go with our outfit. Actually, following the old rule is easy and "well pulled-together looking." I highly recommend it because it keeps women from reaching for an *odd* handbag that they may think works fine when it really doesn't.

The most *versatile* handbags: A bag in your hair color and/or highly visible hair highlight color is a great choice because it's always part of your color scheme—remember, unless your hair is totally hidden by a hat, it is part of every look you create. *Please* explore the first few paragraphs of your *smart tips* for shoes and boots if you do not yet understand this concept.

Other excellent possible colors: lighter and darker versions of your hair colors, your skin tone (again, always part of every color scheme you create), all neutrals you wear often, and your core colors. Just as with shoes, Gentle and Muted Color Types should avoid solid black patent.

Metallics are most often used for evening or for daytime casual, but can be used for daytime business if your "business" look calls for a metallic handbag. Bags with two tones or those with patterns only look great with an outfit in those exact colors. Likewise, bags with logos all over them only coordinate well with something in the same color(s).

Your handbag needs to make the same "statement" as your ensemble:

Here are some examples that don't:

⊘ A trendy or fashiony looking bag with classic clothing such as a fringed suede pouch or a backpack with a classic suit.

⊘ A tailored, heavy-looking leather shoulder bag with a feminine elegant linen suit.

⊘ A delicate looking skin bag with a wool plaid suit.

⊘   A classic tailored suit handbag with a trendy/funky look.

Backpacks are "classic" for students and backpacking only. They can also be quite helpful for moms with babies and toddlers. A few years ago, backpacks made mostly in leather and nylon became "fashionable" for daily use when they were carried over one shoulder, not both. No matter how beautiful and stylish, they are more appropriate for business casual and with casual and trendy attire than they are with classic business looks.

Buy the *Basics* First

Let's just suppose that you don't own even one handbag, what would you buy first? A bag without embellishment, or any metallic hardware showing, is a great *smart basic* because it works beautifully with so many different outfits. Whether your other accessories and buttons are gold, silver, pearls, etc., this bag will look good. If you lost all of your handbags, this should be the first bag you buy.

Can't find a "plain" one you like? Keep looking and meanwhile, if you wear both gold and silver jewelry, you will need one bag that has gold detailing and one that has silver.

Always coordinate any metallic color on a handbag or tote with your jewelry, buttons, and buckle. For example, *please* do not carry a bag that has gold "hardware" when you are wearing silver earrings.

Collect small plain handbags because they go with a greater variety of ensembles. If you avoid sporty leathers, sporty detailing, and sporty clasps, you have a bag that you can carry with a business look, some evening looks (not black tie) and sporty looks as well.

How small is *small?* Certainly, it depends somewhat on the shape/style of the handbag, but I'm giving you measurements, not because I want you to grab a ruler and measure your bags, but because most of you are thinking that a bag is small when it's actually medium-size or larger.

A small handbag is can be any shape but you can check out those that are **approximately** 6½" by 10½" or 8" by 8" to get an idea of what I mean; medium is around 8" by 11" (picture a piece of copy paper); and large is most anything larger than medium. Any bag that is "thick" (front to back) gives a larger look. And if you "stuff" any bag so it bulges, it obviously looks larger than it is, and it looks inelegant. Very structured handbags can look larger than bags with softer lines.

Let's say that you have a date right after work and you walk into the restaurant carrying a large bag or a tote. I don't think that you want him (or anyone else) to think that you're planning to spend the night. Having a small bag tucked into a tote allows you to check your tote and bring your small bag to the table. If you are carrying a briefcase, no problem, but I'd still check it so you won't be reminded of work while you're having dinner.

Carry the right size of handbag for your coloring: I know, crazy lady! If you have delicate coloring, a medium-sized bag *looks* larger when you carry it than when a person with strong coloring is carrying it.

If you carry a large bag it can look like you're carrying a tote. Unless you are going for the look of a tote, stay with small and medium-sized handbags. If you have strong coloring, you can carry a handbag of any size; however, when it comes to large bags, petites need to judge whether the bag looks like a purse or a tote.

Does your height really have an effect? Yes it can, but if your coloring is delicate, being taller doesn't mean you can go much larger without having your handbag look overwhelming. Delicate coloring is most enhanced by creating a delicate look in clothing and accessories. A large bag just doesn't look delicate. Don't believe me? Ask your mirror.

Now's not the time to get *lazy:* Get in the good habit of emptying your handbag into a lovely tray or basket at the end of each day (like a man empties his pockets—he could have his own tray). The next day, that will "force" you to reach for a bag that compliments your attire and fill it with only those things you need—remember, an overstuffed bag does not look *smart*.

Too much work? Won't do it? Then only wear outfits that look great with the one handbag you are willing to carry every day. No, no exceptions.

No handbags in need of repair, *please:* No "plastic" bags—you can buy quality leather goods on sale or at discount stores. Just as with shoes, a quality bag can upgrade your ensemble; an inexpensive handbag can downgrade your look.

Toting in style: Carry a briefcase or tote in your most used neutral or your hair color. If your hair is light, use a darker version of the same color— if you are a golden blonde, for instance, use a golden camel or a golden brown. If you can afford more than one briefcase or tote, add another in your second most used neutral.

I recommend less "mannish" looking briefcases—those that look less structured. Also, buy the best quality you can afford and then carry it *forever*. This will be one of your best investments because it's part of your first and last impression.

Please don't carry a large handbag or tote at the same time you are carrying a briefcase unless you're headed for a plane or train. A smaller bag (I recommend a shoulder bag) can be carried with a briefcase without making you look like a pack mule. Ideally, if you carry a small bag, it would fit inside your briefcase—in a "perfect" world. *Please* never carry bags over both shoulders.

With suits and business dresses, no casual canvas totes unless you are on your way to the gym—even then, I'd really like for you to invest in a "gym" bag that has a bit of elegance because you will be seen with it several times a week. Since my wish for you is that you always look stylish, I don't want a bag to detract from your look, especially one that you carry so often. Trust me, it's worth the investment.

YIKES! Belly bags and fanny packs: Suddenly I'm at a loss for words. I just keep shaking my head and I don't want to write about this subject. I know that these bags are "useful" at times, but when worn for other than athletics, they make the wearer look unsophisticated. What about for travel? I wouldn't if I were you—travelers fared just fine for the many years before these bags came into "fashion." If you want your hands free, wear a shoulder bag across your body.

SMART BELTS

JUST THE BASICS

- Everyone can look good in belts—I know you think I'm crazy.

- Match a metal buckle with any buttons, jewelry, and watch.

- Best colors include your hair color, most used neutrals, and your core colors.

BEYOND THE BASICS

Opening with a controversial statement is supposed to get your attention. Do I have it? Good. You can ask any *sane* woman or man if she/he thinks that all women can wear belts and look great, and they will tell you, "NO WAY."

It all has to do with the *way* a belt is worn. Let's start right off with an example so I'll have your trust once more. The woman in this example is a Contrast Color Type, probably a size 22, but she could be a 14, 16, 18, 20, or 24. She is wearing a bright blue *base* and a fairly wide great looking black and gold belt which she has been careful not to belt too tightly because she doesn't want the belt to "ride up" on her tummy. She has purposefully placed this belt where her "natural" waistline would be if it weren't for her tummy.

On top of this base with its belt, she is wearing a simple, but stylish black cardigan style jacket that hangs open (in a straight vertical line) so that several inches of the belt shows. When you look at her in this outfit, her waist only looks as wide as the part of the belt that's visible. In fact, without the belt her waist looks *bigger*. **Seeing is believing.**

Hopefully having won back your trust, here's more "stuff" about belts. Own *basic* and "statement" belts (if you love them) in your most used neutrals, your hair color, your core colors, and your best metallics. It's super to have belts in all of the colors that you use for shoes and boots because it makes coordination so very easy.

Purchase first very plain belts with just simple, but elegant, buckles. They are so *basic* that they can be worn with many different looks without greatly interfering with buttons on jackets and earrings and necklaces.

One and one-half inches is a good *classic* belt width because it fits through most belt loops. By the way, if you don't want to always have to wear a belt, carefully remove belt loops.

What's small can look medium and vice versa, and what's medium can look wide and vice versa: Every one of you can wear a wide belt—another crazy statement, you say. It all depends on *how wide* is wide for you without being overly wide, and it depends on "how" you wear it. What looks wide on me may look overly wide on you and what looks narrow on me may look more medium-size on you.

Your coloring comes into play as well, as those of you with delicate coloring should avoid heavy-looking belts whatever their size. Also be aware that medium-sized belts could look wide on you (but perhaps not too wide).

Whatever your height or weight, if you have a lot of space between your waist and bosom, you usually have the choice of wearing a belt at your natural waistline, or more loosely, letting it "sling," or angle, down lower on your hips.

If you have little space between your waist and bosom, you can use the same belt, but you will want to wear it lower (try anchoring it on one side at the waist and angling it down toward the opposite hipbone). A narrower belt at the waist will also work well. Just avoid wearing your belts too close to your bosom because it can make you look saggy, droopy, or dumpy—*yikes!* Who wants that?

A "tummy" can cause a belt to ride up in the front, creating the illusion that your bosom is lower and making your tummy look more prominent. Angling your belt, as above, always gives a better result, but sometimes all you need to do is to loosen your belt and "blouse" your top a little. How? Once your top is tucked in, raise/shrug your shoulders and this can elongate your top just enough to give you good balance. Need more? Angle your belt and blouse your top.

Matching Metallics, Again

Consider the metal color of your buckles. Lets say that navy is a basic neutral for you, and you love both gold and silver jewelry. Unless you can find a navy belt with a covered navy buckle (no metallic showing anywhere) or a buckle that mixes both gold and silver, you will need two navy belts—one with a gold buckle and one with a silver buckle.

Also consider any metallic buttons when you put on a belt—gold buttons with gold belt buckles, silver with silver, bronze with bronze, and copper with copper.

Embellish Away

Embellished belts and arty and ethnic belts are fabulous with certain attire. For some women they are a *signature statement* and they can be worn to work in creative environments.

Crystals on a belt make it more for evening or day and evening for more fashiony/funky dressers than a belt with gold or silver studs. A belt with a few metallic studs can be worn to almost any place of business, depending on what you are wearing it with. Although both are "decorative," a Chanel style chain belt is more classic—therefore more expected and accepted—than a belt that mixes leather, reptile skin, suede, crystals, and studs.

Sometimes a stunning belt need be the only focal point of your outfit for the workplace—a single major statement is enough and adding "major" statement earrings would be *too much*. Your earrings must still make the same statement as your belt, just one that is more subtle.

Getting *Smarter*, Still

If you're wearing a belt on top of a patterned garment, make certain that the color of the belt is highly visible in the print. Look in your full-length mirror from a few paces away. If you can't see the belt color in the pattern, you'll want to change to a belt that looks related from a distance, not just from close-up.

Make sure that your belt style and/or buckle style aren't "fighting with" the style of your outfit or any other accessory you are wearing, including your necklace, earrings, and any buttons. Examples of incompatibility are a contemporary rectangular shaped buckle worn with dainty filigreed round earrings; a trendy belt with a classic business suit; or a structured belt with a femininely styled dress made of a lightweight fabric.

Understanding that you are currently training your eye to see what's what, you will understand that in developing this concept I had to do the same. Many years ago, an Associate asked me what was *wrong* with what she was wearing—she knew that something wasn't working but couldn't figure out what it was. I had to study her for a minute. She was a Light-Bright Color Type who was wearing a color-perfect clear turquoise polished cotton base with a camel belt and shoes that matched her hair color. The shoes were a perfect style with her pants and the belt was very simple. The culprit? The belt. It was made out of a stiff leather and was *too structured looking* for the soft cotton fabric.

Please do not place a belt on a sweater or top that has ribbing around the bottom. Most jackets and blazers should never be belted; and *please* do not belt anything with pocket flaps or patch pockets that fall below the belt unless you are creating a safari look. Often, what you choose to "leave off" is as important as what you add. There are very rare exceptions here, so let your mirror guide you if you are tempted to try this look.

SMART BIJOU STYLE

JUST THE BASICS

◆   Your jewelry needs to make the same statement as your attire.

◆   No competing pieces—like a sporty watch with a dainty ring.

◆   Match all metals or purposely mix metals by wearing one piece that is a combination.

◆   Glitz or dangle at work is not glamourous.

◆   Get the "scale" right for your *coloring*—I know, crazy.

◆   All that *glitters* isn't gold. Everyone can wear both gold and silver. If you look best in clear, vibrant colors, avoid wearing dull, tarnished metals. If you are more enhanced by toned down, muted looking colors, avoid large amounts of bright, shiny metals.

BEYOND THE BASICS

The finishing touches are so important to your looking *smart* or *silly* that it would be better for you to go without any jewelry than it would be to make a mistake.

⊘   **Bad Advice:** Wear large hoop earrings with classic business attire.

⏻   **My Advice:** Please don't—they make different statements. You're probably wondering what's considered *large.* When it comes to hoops for business wear, it's best to stay under 1¼".

Your metallic colors need to look great together. For example, gold buttons on a jacket require the same *shade* of gold in earrings and/or necklace—not one that appears more yellowish, pinkish, or brassy.

Earrings

Earrings do call attention to your face, not a bad thing at all as long as the glances are admiring. How important are earrings? Well, let's just say that since they can make us look silly or stylish, make us look like we need a face lift (when, perhaps, we've already had one) or like we've had one (when we haven't), they are very significant.

That doesn't mean that you always have to wear them; as a matter of fact, sometimes the best move you could make would be to reach up and take them off. When? When you don't have the appropriate earrings or when wearing them gives you a more "dressed-up" or an "over-the-top" look than you want.

It is important to wear earrings that work (from a statement, style, and color standpoint), with your outfit *and* your face shape:

◆ Pair classic understated earrings, instead of dangle, ethnic, or glitzy earrings, with classic suits and dresses.

◆ Wear funky earrings with "far-out" looks instead of classic small gold knots.

◆ Marry wearable art earrings with arty or more casual looks instead of wearing them with a business suit.

Make certain that the style and shape of your earrings are compatible with any buttons on your jacket or top. For example, delicate pink and ivory cameo earrings will not enhance a pink suit that has gold geometric buttons. Obviously, necklaces and earrings must also work very well together, and with your ensemble. **If your earrings go well with your outfit, and your outfit is appropriate for your work, your earrings will be as well.**

Earrings that look large on one woman will look medium-size on the next and vice versa—it depends on the size of your head, your hairstyle, and your coloring. Yes, I know you think I'm batty, but the size of your earrings and your coloring are related.

If you have more delicate coloring, avoid large earrings (unless they are very lightweight looking) because they can easily look "overdone" on you. On the other hand, if your coloring is stronger, small earrings can look insignificant.

Also, pay attention to your hairstyle. If you wear your hair pulled back, or if it's cut quite short so that your ears totally show, earrings may be more important in achieving a finished, balanced look. But, beware (be aware) that larger earrings tend to "stand out" if you are wearing your hair in these styles because the *entire* earring shows. If your hair is styled in such a way that it covers part of your earring, a larger earring can look more subtle.

Position clip earrings so that they rest right next to your face—this way they won't "flop" around when you move your head. Instead of clipping them on your ear lobe, clip them in the space where your lobe meets your face.

If you wear glasses, finding the perfect earrings is a bit more difficult. Keeping your glasses free of embellishment and very simple (do not read boring, read *elegant*) helps. If your glasses have metallic frames, your earrings need to be the same metallic. So, if you love gold and silver jewelry, you will need two pairs of glasses or one pair that combines gold and silver.

If your glasses do make a statement of any kind, your earrings must make the same. For example, glasses that have "dainty" detailing are not compatible with earrings that have a modern design or a funky/trendy look. For more about glasses, see page 140.

If your jacket buttons, or belt buckle, are gold, use gold at your ears; if silver, use silver, and so on. Metallic colors can be mixed *if* the mix is carried out as a "color scheme"—mix your metallics on purpose. If a necklace combines silver and gold (or you twist a silver necklace and a gold necklace together), the earrings can be either one of those metallics as can your jacket buttons, bracelet, and belt buckle. **Owning earrings that combine your favorite metallics is helpful.** If your earrings are a color, make certain that the same color is apparent in your attire from a few paces away, not just up close.

What about your face shape with certain styles of earrings? It used to be that women wanted to avoid wearing earrings that repeated their face shape, unless their face was "oval" (like avoiding a round earring if you have a round face). Now that women are *finally* beginning to understand that there are vast variations on what's considered attractive, they are more likely to "play up" their face shape rather than try to change it with *illusion*.

You can do as you like, but I will make one comment. If you have a very long face, especially one that is attached to a long, slender neck, dangle or drop earrings can make your face and neck appear even longer, depending on what you are wearing and your hairstyle. If you are wearing a turtleneck or are standing up your collar, you may love the effect of long earrings, especially if they have "weight" (substance) up on your ear, before the "drop" starts (picture at least medium-sized earrings covering part of your ear with a drop/dangle attached).

Again, your hairstyle can come into play here because if you are wearing it in a style that makes your face look **broader**, you may have created enough balance (the illusion of width) to counteract the increased illusion of length created by long earrings.

Necklaces

Whether it's an old fashioned choker, a turquoise and silver squash blossom, or a tiny cord with a little pendant, there is something very romantic about necklaces. Unfortunately, like hats, necklaces are items women buy but seldom wear, although they may wear their one or two favorites all the time even if they don't really enhance an outfit. Here are some *smart tips*:

◆ A good simple rule is to have your necklace follow the same shape (or line) as the neckline of your outfit. Wearing a necklace that hangs in a V shape with a rounded or jewel neckline is an example of incompatible lines.

◆ If you would like a necklace that normally hangs in a "round" shape to work well with a V shape neckline, try hanging a pendant, or pin, on it. Hanging pins on your necklaces can create some fantastic looks.

◆ When in doubt under-accessorize.

◆ Glitzy and ornate necklaces are not part of classic business attire, but if you love them and can't wear them to work, you can enjoy them in your free time.

◆ If your place of business requires clothing that may call for an ornate or glitzy necklace, then wearing one is not a mistake for you as long as you still look *elegant*.

◆ If you need to dress more conservatively at work but still would really love to "do more," try wearing a collection of simple, small necklaces, like a few strands of pearls and small gold chains together—add pearl and gold earrings. Or,

◆ Wear a larger pendant (or pin) on one strand of pearls or one simple chain and keep your earrings simple.

When a necklace falls partially on bare skin and partially on your top, there is probably a better choice. Experiment by holding your necklace shorter or longer, so that all of it is on skin, or on your top. You can lengthen or shorten your necklaces—if your hair hangs down over the clasp in the back, simply tie a knot before you fasten it around your neck (sometimes a knot that shows in the front is nice, too). Your jewelry store may carry necklace extenders and shorteners.

It's important to get the scale right for your "coloring." *I know it sounds nutty, but,* if your coloring is delicate, wear small and medium-sized necklaces, avoiding large-scale designs unless they are very light-weight looking. If your coloring is stronger, wear medium and larger scale designs, avoiding small pieces—they can look totally insignificant on you unless you strengthen their look by combining them in a "collection."

To increase the size of a necklace, you can wear several together—try twisting a strand of pearls with a gold and/or silver chain (get daring and twist into those a strand of turquoise or coral). Need more? Knot them all together and let the knot show. If your coloring is delicate, you can do the same as long as you don't create something that is too large or bulky looking.

What about "right and wrong" when it comes to the color of your necklaces? There are two types of wrong. The first is wearing a color that doesn't enhance your attire. The second is wearing a color that doesn't enhance you.

To make certain the color of your necklace works well with your outfit, the color needs to be repeated at least once somewhere: in a print, the skirt/trouser color, the top color or the belt color (but not just the shoe color because they are too far apart to give you the good color balance you are looking for).

Make sure that you can see the relationship of the colors from a few steps away. Making the same statement is as "critical" as ever. **Avoid wearing:**

⊘ A tailored or chunky looking gold chain necklace with a floral print.

⊘ A necklace with rounded beads with a geometric print.

⊘ A trendy up-fashion necklace with a conservative dress.

⊘ Some ethnic necklaces with classic suits—it depends on the necklace, of course, and it's difficult to tell you which may work without seeing them. An example of one that wouldn't work would be a delicate necklace of beads and feathers worn with a suit that has severe or crisp tailoring. An example of an ethnic necklace that would work is a more tailored looking inlaid turquoise and silver necklace that just circles the base of the neck worn with a gray suit that has a jewel neckline.

If you are not certain that an accessory is "additive," leave it off. Remember that your necklace and earrings must look great together **and** with your attire.

Two of the most common mistakes women make is wearing a small gold chain or a strand of pearls with everything—often a gift from a loved one whom they wish to honor by wearing it all of the time. If it doesn't *add* style to your look, it may be taking some away. If you don't wish to break a *bond*, carry your loved one's gift with you in your bag (protected in a small pouch or box).

I think the idea of wearing a strand of pearls with everything is a throwback to the days when mothers told daughters that, "Pearls are always appropriate." Actually, at that time, they pretty much were because clothing choices were more limited. Remember the twin sets with the pearl or pearlized buttons? A great classic look with a strand of pearls for yesterday, and still a wonderful classic for today.

"Pearls" come in many different colors, including many shades of white, cream, and even a *champagne* color. If you are wearing beige or camel on the "bottom" and need to bring that color up, champagne or beige-toned pearls work beautifully. You can use a gold necklace to do the same—a tiny chain isn't enough to do it. Use your mirror to check for the needed balance. Use gray pearls and silver necklaces to balance gray.

Pins

Your grandmother or great-grandmother probably wouldn't have felt "dressed" without a pin. They are wonderful if you can figure out exactly where to place them, and if they work in harmony with the style and shape of your garment and your other accessories, buttons, and buckles. It's really difficult to get it right, but when you do it's marvelous and fun. Examples to **avoid**:

⊘ A square pin placed on a rounded or shawl collar (like shapes compliment each other).

⊘ A pearl pin on a jacket with gold buttons (a pin that combined pearls and gold would be great).

⊘ A delicate floral pin with a tailored chain choker (accessories need to make matching statements—you can wear the pin without the necklace or, if the pin has a touch of gold in it, try hanging it on a more *delicate* chain, or grouping of chains, to give a pendant effect).

⊘ Avoid using pins to bring the bottom color up—they are usually not large enough to give you the visual balance you'll need.

It's really fun to place a pin on a necklace—just thread it through a chain or carefully pin it between beads or links. You can get a pendant effect by hanging it on the bottom of the necklace, but you can also pinch/pull the necklace together right at the base of your neck, putting the pin through/ around both sides to create a "bolo" effect. You can do the same at any place between the base of your neck and the bottom of the necklace—whatever effect looks best with your neckline.

Big, brilliant, subtle, heirloom, ethnic, or modern, do you look like a million dollars if you wear several rings at the same time? How many rings can you wear and still look elegant? The answer depends on the person you ask. One of my elegant men friends isn't even interested in meeting a beautiful woman if she is wearing more than one ring (total). Another of my elegant men friends is perfectly charmed by women who wear more than one ring, even on the same hand.

My advice for most women is that *less is more*, but your particular *style* may say more is better—you must decide for yourself. Should you decide to wear more than one, make absolutely certain that the rings compliment each other in style and color as well as compliment your other accessories, including buttons and buckles.

A ring (one only) that is quite large, or large looking on your hand, makes an "unusual" statement, usually too much so for many places of classic business. If you can wear arty, ethnic, funky, or trendy looks to work, great. If not, wear your larger rings in your free time.

If you wear a wedding ring that has a diamond(s) set in gold, you may wear it with both gold and silver earrings, necklaces, pins, bracelets, watches, buttons, and buckles because the ring gives both a gold and "silver" look.

If you wear a ring that has a diamond(s) set in platinum or white gold, it goes best with just silver accessories, buttons, and buckles. But wait. You can wear it with gold jewelry, too. How? There are two ways. You can add small (yellow) gold guard rings on either side of your ring; or you can wear both a (yellow) gold bracelet and a silver bracelet on the same side you wear your ring.

Bracelets

From the finely crafted ethnic to the museum quality keepsake, bracelets can be wonderful. However, bracelets that clatter, tinkle, or clunk can give your co-workers a splendid headache, or just be a terrible irritant or distraction. So, unless you work alone, no bracelet noise, *please.*

Three small simple bracelets worn together can look more conservative than one large embellished cuff. Several smaller bracelets stacked up on the arm look great with an ensemble that calls for them, just as glitzy, ethnic, or other specifically styled bracelets may be worn with outfits that they enhance. Just make certain that the look you are creating makes the statement that you wish to make at *your* place of business.

Avoid wearing bracelets that compete in style and/or color with each other or with your other accessories, especially your rings, buttons, and belt buckle.

Bracelets that hang down over your hand are fine UNLESS they hang so low that they look like they are about to fall off.

Your Watch

From timeless elegance to sporty chic, some women have been inspired to start collecting watches because they have finally realized that one watch just won't work with everything, and, besides, it's fun. You don't have to collect them but you do need to consider them, just as you would your jewelry, in the overall look you are creating. Here are some of the most common mistakes that women make with their watches:

⊘ Wearing a watch that doesn't make the same statement as your outfit such as a sporty look with business attire.

⊘ Wearing one that has a band in a color that doesn't go with your attire or look good with your skin tone.

⊘ Wearing a watch that has gold on it when you are wearing silver jewelry or vice versa—"collect" one that combines both gold and silver.

⊘ Wearing a watch that has a face that is too white for your skin tone—it will look inexpensive on you if you are a Gentle or Muted Color Type. The white will be the first thing your eye goes to when you glance at it—an off-white or cream face will be *so* much richer looking.

You can always keep your watch in your handbag if it isn't "additive" to your look. I happen to love to wear men's watches so I don't have any delicate looking styles (my coloring is strong, so "dainty" styles don't really relate well to me anyway). If I happen to be wearing a femininely styled silk suit, I wouldn't wear a man's watch—if I felt I might be needing to know the time, I would slip one in my bag.

The Smart Scarf

Just the Basics

- ◆ The colors in the scarf need to match or compliment the colors in your attire.

- ◆ Tie scarves in such a way that they don't engulf the top of your body.

- ◆ Since they are a color accent right next to your face, make sure the colors and color combination are great for you.

- ◆ When it comes to selecting a scarf for your color type, judge the overall loook when the scarf is folded and tied.

Beyond the Basics

Scarves are so fun, but they seem to be a mystery for many women—they buy them but rarely wear them. Coordinating them with your outfit is half the battle; tying them in ways that flatter you and your outfit is the other half.

A scarf should always incorporate the colors of your ensemble. If you are wearing a green dress, for example, with a multicolored scarf, the scarf must have *visible* green in it—the **exact** shade of green. A tiny amount of the color in a pattern may not be able to be seen from a few paces away— check it in your trusted mirror.

And, while you're looking in the mirror, check to make sure that you are not appearing to be "engulfed" by your scarf. This can happen when you tie it in such a way that it covers most of your top.

An often-made mistake is letting a long scarf hang way down on your body. This really shortens your leg line and can create a dowdy look no matter how elegant the scarf or your ensemble. In most instances, it's best if the bottom of your scarf doesn't fall below your waistline and, generally, never below the bottom of your jacket.

The pattern size of your scarves is critical to your looking great. Those of you with delicate coloring are most enhanced by small and me- dium-sized patterns and very light-weight, airy looking larger patterns that have a light background.

I need to separate those of you who have stronger coloring. If you are one of the Contrast Color Types, you'll look great in medium and large pat- terns and very high-contrast smaller patterns. If you are one of the Muted Color Types, you'll be most flattered by medium-sized patterns, large *blended* looking patterns and gutsy smaller patterns.

Larger scarves can look pretty worn over one shoulder unless you are "fussing" with them all day long. Some fabrics are more slippery than others so you may want to secure your scarf from underneath with a safety pin. It used to be that scarves were worrisome around machinery but that was more in the day, long ago, when copying machines had handles you had to turn.

One of my favorite ways to wear my charcoal gray pin-striped suit, with its curvy jacket (the stripes are cream, as is the lace camisole I wear with it), is with a very long embroidered cream-on-cream fringed scarf over one shoulder. To shorten it and add even more *style*, I've tied a knot in the scarf about 8" above the fringe. It drops to just above the bottom of my jacket in the front and hangs a little lower in the back. Accessories are large pearl earrings (I have strong coloring), a strand of pearls, sheer bone stockings, gray suede heels trimmed with black suede, and a black suede bag.

If you have a Color 1 Associate near you, ask her to give a *Smart Scarf Tying* class for you and your friends and co-workers. To get super specific, easy-to-follow scarf tying information, go to www.DressingSmart.com.

FOCUS ON SUCCESS &⌒

JUST THE BASICS

&⌒ Glasses are a major part of looking great, and they need to look as excellent on you as your clothing.

&⌒ There are many important basics—please review the information below.

BEYOND THE BASICS

I want your glasses to be perfect for you, and this is one of the times I wish I could see you in person. What should you look for when you are trying on new glasses or evaluating those you are wearing now?

Here are some *smart tips* that will help you take control of how you look in glasses:

&⌒ Do they make your eyes appear closer together? It's not a good look.

&⌒ Do they make your nose appear bigger?

&⌒ Are your glasses so close to your face that they tend to rest on it? Smile and see if they touch your cheeks?

&⌒ Do they sit too far forward so there is too much space between the lenses and your face?

&⌒ Are they too wide for your face—coming out on the sides so far out that you can see your temples through the lenses?

&⌒ Are they too narrow for your face, making your eyes look closer together or making your face appear out of balance?

&⌒ Frames that follow the shape of your eyebrows are often more flattering than those that don't.

&⌒ Many of the smaller glasses are great looking, some are "interesting" looking, and others look far-out, but you need to make sure that **YOU** look great and interesting (or far-out if you prefer)—not just your glasses.

&⌒ **Very** small glasses that have small lenses that barely cover your eyes can possibly make your eyes look closer together and even sometimes give you a cross-eyed look. Be aware.

&⌒ **Very** large glasses are not classic, nor are **very** small glasses. Each can give you an eccentric, trendy, or funky look—just make sure it's one you want.

&⌒ If you choose to wear frames that are more "substantial" (thicker frames versus a fine metallic frame, for example) it's often best if the frame follows, and covers, your eyebrows so that you won't have a double eyebrow look.

&⌒ Avoid glasses that "droop" down on the cheek, angling toward your jaw line—they can create a "down-line" that can make you look tired and old—*yikes!*

&⌒ *Please* avoid glasses that have fancy detailing across the bridge of the nose; they definitely draw attention to the nose area and can make your eyes look closer together as well as make your nose look big or "strangely" shaped.

&⌒ Embellished or "fashiony-looking" glasses can limit your use of earrings and necklaces—if you wish to wear glasses that make a definite statement of their own, keep your earrings and necklaces very simple, or just don't wear them.

&⌒ If your glasses are like those described just above, and you can afford a second pair, you may want to invest in a simple, but elegant pair that you can wear on days when you wish to wear accessories that make their own statement.

&⌒ *Please* avoid lenses that are tinted rosy, yellowish, amber, bluish, greenish, or any other color that gives your skin a bruised look or "strange" coloration under and around the eye.

Somehow, glasses and intelligence have become so intertwined—probably having something to do with nerds becoming *cool*—that women are buying glasses when they don't need them. With or without, here are some details that will help you pick out *smart* frames:

Smart frames:

- ᕠ A simple, elegant, versatile metal frame, or half frame, that gives the illusion of being your hair color or skin tone is worth strong consideration.

- ᕠ Metallics and "frameless" looks are more versatile than colors.

- ᕠ If your skin tone is golden, or your hair has golden highlights, your best metallic will be gold.

- ᕠ Silver frames can work well with ivory and pink skin tones and platinum, ash blonde, ash brown, silver (gray), or white hair colors.

- ᕠ If you look best in toned down colors, select soft-tone metallics instead of those that are bright and shiny.

- ᕠ If you look best in bright colors, select a brighter metallic, avoiding those that look tarnished or dull.

- ᕠ For those of you who would like a "frameless" look but need more support for your lenses, consider those frames that have a minimum amount of metal.

- ᕠ Even though the new plastics are getting better looking, many typical plastic frames do not look elegant enough for all of your day and evening looks but if vintage attire is your signature style and you want it "complete," go for it because your glasses will make the same statement as your attire.

Tortoise shell frames appear more casual than metallics and frameless looks. Your most flattering tortoise tones will be a combination of your skin tone, hair colors, and maybe black (if it looks good on you). They may be fine for daytime attire **if** you are *always* wearing colors and color combinations that work well with this casual look.

However, tortoise or any tone-on-tone frames, are not dressy enough to be worn out to special dinners, cocktail parties, or black tie affairs. So if you are to only have one pair of glasses, avoid the limitations of tortoise, tone-on-tone casual looks and colors. Unless you are an eccentric dresser, frames in colors need to be worn only when your outfit is (or has in it) the same color.

GETTING THE BEST SUPPORT

JUST THE BASICS

- ⊘ What we don't want others to see:

⊘   Bulges that show above and below your bra and your panties.

⊘   A slip that shows in your kick pleat when you walk.

⊘   Your bosom appearing to be an "odd" shape.

⊘   A visible panty line.

⊘   Seams in bra cups—own seamless bras in neutrals and colors you need.

⊘   Your pulling your panties down in the back when you don't think anyone is looking.

⊘   Visible bra straps, no matter what the fashion magazines show.

⊘   A light bra under a dark top or a dark bra under a light top.

Beyond the Basics

Why is shopping for the "perfect" bra such a *PAIN?* Unfortunately, unless you are buying the identical style from the same manufacturer, you must always try them on. All 34Bs are not made equal and that's actually good—if they were all the same, few of us would ever find a good fit.

One 34B woman may be fuller at the bottom of her bosom and more shallow on the top; the next may have a wide space between her breasts but her breasts may go all the way to her underarms; and yet another woman may have literally no space between her breasts and they may not go very far toward her underarm (she's "all out-front"). *Viva la difference!*

An alluring *shape* depends on the PERFECT FIT. There are women in the underlovelies departments who have been trained to fit you in a bra—ask. A bra that fits you well:

◆   Gives you a great shape from the side and the front—always take the time to put your top back on (or drape it over your front) in the dressing room when you are trying on new bras.

◆   Does not ride up in the back.

◆   "Tacks" (touches) in the front between your breasts.

◆   Fits you well in the cup (both in the top and bottom of the cup).

◆   Gives you support from underneath your bosom so that you could actually slip the straps off your shoulders and "they" wouldn't fall.

◆   Does not dig into your skin anywhere.

They ride up, they ride down, and they can cause "VPL": Perhaps the problem in finding panties that fit just right, like a bra, has to do with the fact that our *derrieres* are all shaped differently. For the best fit, most women need to buy their panties a size or two larger than they usually do (also, some panties shrink when washed and/or dried in a dryer). Try panties on (over your own) in the store. Sit down. Stand up. If they ride up or down, don't buy them. If they make a "visible panty line" (VPL), it means that they are too tight or they have been cut too small around the leg opening for your legs. Own both beautiful briefs and bikinis.

By the way, bikinis (and bathing suit bottoms, too) are worn with the sides pulled up giving you the longest and most beautiful leg line—most important when being viewed in them by your lover.

Briefs (buy sexy styles with high-cut legs) are sometimes handy to tuck your top into when you need an extra smooth line. Tucking colored and printed tops into skin tone briefs is a great way to camouflage the top so that it doesn't show through lighter skirts and trousers.

"Slipping" one on: Slips may seem old fashioned to some of you, but they are a staple for women who wear knits, other stretchy fabrics, and for some unlined skirts and dresses. Slips help garments that would otherwise cling glide beautifully over your body, and they help knits keep their shape.

Own slips in black and beige (and white, if necessary). You'll want short slips, semi-short slips, and long slips if you wear skirts/dresses in several lengths. Buy slips that have a slit and line it up with the slit in your skirt—no slips showing in slits, *please.* Do you need a full-length slip? If you have a knit dress or a phobia, you may.

A client, the president of a multi-million dollar company, brought over a couple of suits to try on for me. I was amazed that she was wearing a full-length slip because it was 98 degrees outside and the humidity was 98%. Because her skirt was lined and she was wearing a blouse that you couldn't see through, I explained that the extra layer wasn't necessary. Missing my point, she assured me that she would never wear a "half-slip" again.

It seems that she was walking down a major avenue in one of our major cities and suddenly she felt something around her ankles. She looked down in horror to find her slip around her ankles—the elastic had given way.

I expect that all of you already know this, but just in case, if your skirt is lined, it's not necessary to wear a slip. And, except at work and church or synagogue, it isn't necessary to wear a slip under a dress or skirt that is *supposed* to be fairly transparent.

Getting even *smarter* yet: Always feel as good about your underclothes as you do your over-clothes. No safety pins in bra straps, no holes in panties. Remember what your mother taught you? You never know when you might be in an accident!

Interesting pieces and the combination of unusual textures can add style to your wardrobe.

Leather with satin.

Silk vest with denim jeans. Any earring shown on the right would work depending on your color type and the occasion.

Part of my "wild" jeans collection — one of my signature statements.

Denim and lace.

A curvy jacket, lacy camisole, and pocket square, add a feminine touch to menswear suiting.

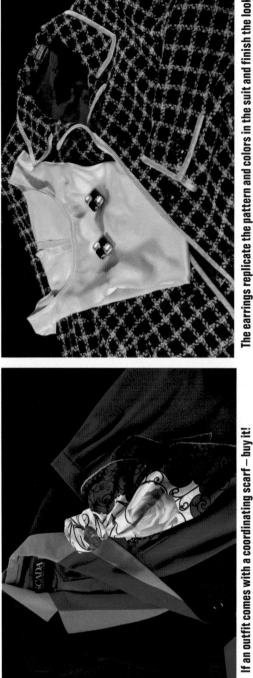

The earrings replicate the pattern and colors in the suit and finish the look.

If an outfit comes with a coordinating scarf – buy it!

The earrings and belt coordinate beautifully with the pattern in the jacket.

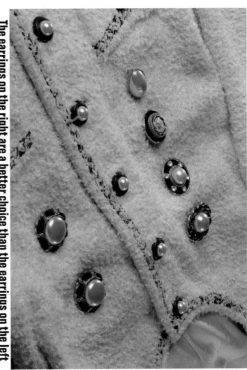

The earrings on the right are a better choice than the earrings on the left because they make the same statement as the buttons.

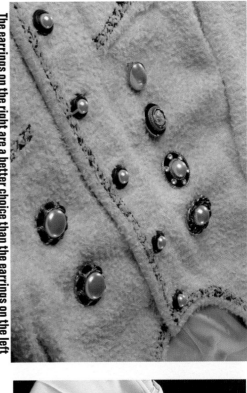

All of the earrings are appropriate depending on the occasion and your color type.

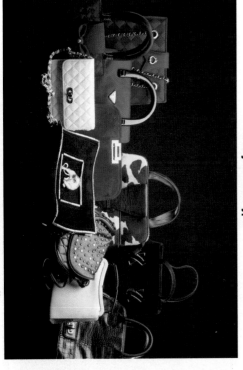

Handbags with no metal showing are most versatile.

Embellished handbags are beautiful but less versatile.

Express your own style by adding unique pieces to your wardrobe. "Wearable art" could even become your signature style.

Wear matched sets—don't be *caught* in white panties and a black bra, for example. For the times when you are wearing dark tops and light bottoms, or vice versa, own some panties that are black with a small amount of white or beige on them and some panties that are white or beige that have a little bit of black. By the way, if you don't look great in black, you won't look sexy in black underlovelies. With your darker colors, wear navy or "surprise" colors.

Matched sets also means wearing bras and panties that *look* like they are a set, like lace bras with lace panties or with panties that have a touch of lace.

Color and style coordinating your underwear (your first layer) with your inner wear (your second layer, like a *base),* your inner wear with your overwear (your third layer, like a blazer), and, your overwear with your out-erwear (your fourth layer, like a coat) can be a real puzzle at first, just like this paragraph. But, once you get the knack of it, you will be amazed at how easy it is. Other important details include:

◆ Wear "surprise" colors when you are wearing something you can't see through. A surprise color is *any* color that looks great on you that would be "unsuspected" under what you are wear-ing—like green or fuchsia under navy or black, a leopard print under black or red, or purple under pink.

◆ Nude-toned bras are often a better choice than black under sheer black fabrics (or white under sheer white fabrics) because you can't see them. Your mirror will help you decide which is best.

◆ If you have a top that's cut wide at the shoulder line and your bra strap tends to show, sew in the little snaps with the treads attached that capture your straps and keep them invisible.

◆ Small shoulder pads with velcro should be part of every woman's intimate apparel wardrobe—own them in black and beige (and white if necessary).

◆ Nearly "total body control" is available—survey the latest at your department store. The one-piece undergarments that are made to "smooth you out" from your bosom to your lower thighs are valuable under dresses or at any time when you want/need to look and feel "smooth" to the touch. These "support" garments are really great because they give you the flexibility to wear things that you wouldn't otherwise look super in.

◆ Avoid control garments that squeeze you "up and out" or "down and out," causing rolls, lumps, or bumps in places they're not welcome. Also, avoid those that will rub you raw.

◆ Keep some special lingerie designated for *play* and *passion* that is as appealing to the eye as it is to the touch—no scratchy lace, *please*.

◆ ALWAYS wear, every day, underlovelies that you would love to be *caught* in; although you may not be, *you'll* know. You'll even "walk" differently. Try it and see.

LEARNING THE ABC'S OF BUSINESS CASUAL

JUST THE BASICS

◆ You don't have to dress down.

◆ When in doubt wear a suit or mixed suit look.

◆ No jeans unless you are sure it's appropriate—if yes, dress them "up" with a jacket.

◆ No jeans *ever* that are faded, frayed, dirty looking, or ripped.

◆ No athletic shoes.

BEYOND THE BASICS

Learning the difference between classic business, classic business casual, "typical" business casual, and creative business casual can change your life. I can't stress enough that I want you to look as super (read professional and appropriate) in your casual looks as you do in your suits and dresses. Men wear the same thing, like khakis with a polo shirt or oxford button-down, all the time out of fear—they don't want to make a mistake. Fear of looking foolish or inappropriate can keep you looking humdrum and un-imaginative.

American casual wear is world renowned for its style—our U.S. designers and manufacturers do it better than anybody. Why, then, do so many American women look unstylish in their casual clothes when we have so many great styles to choose from? Part of the reason is right there—there are *soooooo* many styles to choose from. The other part is that women seem to think or feel that casual, grubby, and sloppy are synonyms.

Think casual elegance. Am I telling you that you need to dress up all of the time? No, only that I want you to look as great even in your jeans and T-shirts as you do at work or at a party. It's all a matter of d*ressing smart* and looking "pulled together."

For some companies business casual has backfired and the policy has caused firms to lose future clients and even current clients. Why? Mainly because the sloppy appearance of employees gives the impression that the company is not well run, not professional, "doesn't know their stuff"— they cannot be trusted to do the best job for the client. Guidelines have not been specific enough and are not being policed well because bosses/managers are sensitive about telling their employees how to dress. Therefore many companies have moved away from a business casual policy back to strictly formal business attire—the suit.

Whether you are entry level or the boss, and your company lets you dress any way you want, I hope the way you want to look is great versus sloppy—pulled together instead of haphazard. To care about the way you look shows respect for yourself and others wherever and whenever (even outside of work) you represent your company AND yourself.

Regardless of the differences that exist from job to job, company to company, industry to industry, and region to region, you either look good in what you are wearing or you don't—you look *professional*, or not—leadership material, or not. Here are the ABC's and D's of "strictly" business and business casual:

A **Classic Business, also known as formal business:** Suits, pantsuits, mixed suits, and dresses. Always wear stockings. Could include non-outrageous up-fashion looks, depending on industry.

B **Classic Business Casual:** The same suits as above and more casual suits and mixed suits—dressy casual attire like nice pants/skirt and sweater/blouse—when in doubt, or to stand out, wear a jacket. Always wear stockings. No denim or athletic shoes. Could include non-outrageous up-fashion looks, depending on industry.

C **Business Casual:** Typical looks include nice pants/skirt with nice blouse or sweater. To stand out, wear a jacket and also stockings. No denim unless you are sure it's *more* than appropriate. Could include non-outrageous up-fashion looks, depending on industry.

D **Creative Business Casual:** Nice pants, skirts, and nice jeans— in more unusual styles and fabrics. Again, to stand out, wear a jacket. No athletic shoes. Includes, but does not require, up-fashion (non-flashy) looks.

NICE, **nice,** and *nice* means good looking, quality fabrics including: wool in all weights, cashmere and cashmere blends, cotton in different weaves, and more silky finished cottons, mercerized cottons, linen, rayon, silk, microfibers, and blends of all of these.

One of the most important things about business casual that you should know is that you don't have to dress down. You can even wear a suit. With the guidelines above, you can always go up on the list (dressier) but be careful going down (more casual). For example, you can wear *classic* business casual attire even when everyone else is dressed more casually—but not the other way around.

If you are feeling overwhelmed or confused, just wear **A** every day because you will look appropriate no matter what and it is not a problem if you are "overdressed" in comparison to your co-workers. When you want/need a **B** look, just wear a slightly more casual suit or mixed suit look, or wear a suit from **A** with a slightly more casual top and shoe. When you have **A** and **B** down pat, and it's appropriate, you can utilize **C** and **D** looks.

Your ABCD's are more than just looks, they are a state of mind—an attitude. Also, A, B, and C can be as *creative* as D within their own framework. The uniqueness of each look will depend on the styling of each garment and the way you combine your colors, textures, and patterns. Even the most classic business look can be stylish and/or creative.

If you don't know how to coordinate separates for business casual looks, and aren't interested in learning how, just wear a *base* (see page 91) with a layering piece such as a jacket, sweater, or vest.

Even the Parisians, known worldwide for their sense of style, have become very casual, and not always in the most elegant way. Some have copied the worst of American casual—like wearing sneakers every day.

Never fear, it's not going to happen to you because you've been training your eye, and every *smart tip* you have been reading and practicing can be applied to casual attire. All of the principles are the same, only the styling, fabrics, and detailing may be more casual.

Do I think that jeans should be allowed for business casual? You get a "no" for classic, a "maybe" for typical business casual, and a "yes" for creative business casual. The "maybe" and "yes" come with strings attached—industry acceptance and only if your total look is excellent—*equal to* all of your other great looks, just *different* from them. Wearing a good jacket (borrow from a suit) becomes more important and it will set you apart. Dark blue denim and black denim are much dressier looking than medium and light blue. No fading, no fraying, no "dirty" denim, no rips, no holes, no exceptions.

If nice T-shirts are permitted, look for those of quality fabric that have a more tapered sleeve versus a square, wide boxy sleeve—the look is more refined and will fit better under your jackets. No tight tops, please.

> Synonyms for casual include: careless, haphazard, hasty, indifferent, and indiscriminate. None of these things are what any company has in mind when they tell their employees that they can "dress down." — JoAnna

---

Even if your casual dress code allows it, I don't recommend athletic shoes (sneakers), or deck shoes/topsiders for business casual attire. No, not even if they are new. Not even if they cost more than your best heels.

When it comes to your wardrobe, doubt means "no." Why? Because leaving the house unsure of how you look can affect your entire day, the way you interact with co-workers and clients, even with someone on the phone, including your significant other. Only you know your place of business, its spoken and unspoken "standards," and your career goals. When in doubt, save "it" for the weekend. What's the best business casual look? An interesting suit with an interesting blouse/top or sweater.

> Achieving easy elegance isn't difficult, and it's never a look that says "you tried too hard." — JoAnna

A quick note about personal casual clothes: Moms can be really "neat" and interesting women, too....Some women wonder why their significant other takes them for granted and why there seems to be a "respect" issue with the children. Often, your younger significant others don't have a clue as to "who" you really are, how very good you are at your job, and how admired you are by others. They probably think that you're a special "mom"— but they don't know that you are a special *person!* They just think of you as their mom, instead of a *really neat lady.* Perhaps "he" thinks the same. Could it be because most of the time you spend with them, your image is less than wonderful? Less than good? Less than okay?

Knits, microfibers, and anything with *stretch* that is washable are the answers to great looking, **comfortable,** casual clothing. They take away any excuse for not looking great ALL OF THE TIME. *Please* toss your "grubbies" so you won't be tempted to wear them ever again. Yes, even to work in the yard.

☼ SETTING THE BOUNDARIES ☾
BETWEEN DAY & EVENING

JUST THE BASICS

◆ Don't wear anything see-through, too tight, too short, too low, or too glitzy for your place of business.

BEYOND THE BASICS

Because women started wearing "embellished" clothing in the daytime, metallic shoes and belts for both casual and dressy, "statement" belts anytime, and "wearable art," the boundaries between day and evening wear have been totally blurred. But we do get to break all of the old rules, right? Yes, with two exceptions: **"Always Look Great!"** and **"Dress *Smart,* Act *Smart,* Be *Smart!*"**

With few deviations, most women appropriately attired for their workplace will avoid:

- ⊘ Sheer, see-through fabrics.

- ⊘ Showing cleavage.

- ⊘ *Very* short skirts.

- ⊘ Anything that is too bare.

- ⊘ Anything too tight.

- ⊘ Garments, or fabrics, that are too glitzy or very evening looking.

Crossovers

Velvet and silk can be used for day and evening, as can satin when it's in the form of a blouse, a camisole, or tank worn under a jacket. Warm weather allows all kinds of silk outfits in the daytime and the evening. Cold weather puts the same silk ensemble into the "evening only" category. Sueded silk can look less dressy than the smooth and shiny silks. Satin brocade trousers could be worn with a more "subtle," but stylish, jacket by those of you who can dress in a creative arty, ethnic, funky, or more trendy style at work—they are "after-hours" pants for everyone else.

Animal prints are great for everybody, day and evening, but restraint is advised when it comes to considering *how much*. Where you work depends on whether you can wear just a touch (like collar and cuff) or bit more (like an animal print skirt paired with a solid-color jacket).

A single animal print accessory, such as a handbag, shoe, or belt, can be a fun touch with otherwise solid-color attire. What about two "touches" like a belt and shoes or collar and cuffs? I'll say yes, hesitantly. The hesitancy comes from knowing that some of you will then take license to wear three "touches" at the same time and maybe even add animal print earrings. *Please, please* don't—it's easy to step over the line here and turn animal attraction into fashion victim.

STRESSING OUT ABOUT BEING OVER OR UNDERDRESSED

JUST THE BASICS

- ◆ Unless you are wearing one of the above looks to "avoid," it is almost impossible to overdress for business, but it is possible to look overdone.

BEYOND THE BASICS

One of the things that happens when you look "pulled together" and stylish is that you appear more *dressed up* even in your jeans. One of my Associates mentioned that she and her husband were out to dinner with another couple, and although the women were both dressed up, the other woman appeared to be more casually attired. Why? Because she was wearing toned down colors when her best clarity was clear, bright, and bold.

My advice is that you just get used to the fact that when you look great every day, people will notice and some will comment. It doesn't mean that you are overdressed.

Never wanting you to look less than your best, I still want you to be aware that there are times when you will want to be thoughtful about what you are going to wear. It doesn't mean that you should look less than your best, it just means that you may not want to wear your "dressed-up looking" best. Looking understated at the appropriate time can be as effective as looking WOW at the right time.

What about being "underdressed"? Since you are *now* in the habit of dressing for the occasion, when you find yourself in a situation where you appear underdressed, I'll assume that it really was an accident. When this happens, your poise, self-confidence, and *elegant* attitude will get you through. Even though you are less dressed up, you *will* still be *elegant*, won't you?

THE SUBTLETIES OF STYLE

JUST THE BASICS

♦ Mixing "statements" can cause a dislocated hodgepodge appearance.

♦ Subtle details can make or break your look, and there are too many to highlight here so please continue....

BEYOND THE BASICS

These are all small details that will need your attention—if you have questions about them, you are holding the answers in your hand:

♦ The shape of the earrings you choose to wear with your particular face shape, and with your outfit.

♦ The "placement" of your eye makeup and blush.

♦ The neckline you choose for your face shape—and, very importantly, for your neck size and length.

♦ Necklines you choose to wear together—a blouse or top with a different neckline than your jacket.

◆ The shape and length of the jacket (or top) you choose to wear with a particular skirt shape and length, or trouser shape and length.

◆ The style and weight of your shoe with a particular skirt length or trouser style and length.

◆ The color and weight—sheer to opaque—of the stockings you choose to wear with any given ensemble.

◆ Other accessories, like belts and bags, come into play as well.

⊘ **Bad Advice:** Long dangling earrings give you height.

① **My Advice:** They don't actually make you look even a hair's width taller, but they can make your neck look longer and your face look longer and narrower—something that, if you already have a long face and neck, you may not want to emphasize.

Creating *smart* style:

◆ To create a longer leg line, match shoes, stockings, and trousers or skirt.

◆ A short jacket (or tucking in your top) creates a longer leg line than a long jacket, but you can....

◆ Create a longer leg line with a long jacket by pairing it with a straight pegged skirt or narrow trousers—wearing slim high heels helps as well.

◆ **Avoid** having too many horizontal lines in one outfit—it's way too *busy*. Starting at the bottom, picture this: the top of boots or shoes next to contrasting opaque stockings, next to the hem of a skirt, topped with a contrasting top (worn out over the skirt) ringed with a contrasting belt, and all that topped with a jacket. That's *five* horizontal lines.

◆ Tunics and tops, overall, need to end *just barely* at the bottom of your derriere, otherwise they make your legs look short and you look frumpy. Most of the tops in the plus-size departments (and maternity shops) are way too long—do a mirror test and shorten tops when necessary.

◆ A sleeve that is too long will shorten your leg line and can make you look dumpy.

◆ If you have a short waist (it may seem like it starts right under your bosom) wear skirts and trousers that do not have a waistband or have a very narrow band. (From this point on, I will often be referring to skirts and trousers as "bottoms," and blouses, tanks, shells, pullovers, and so on, as "tops.") If you are short-waisted, "fool" the eye into believing otherwise by: wearing tops and bottoms that match (a _base_); "blousing" your tops (pulling them out at the waist just a little but not out so much that it looks boxy); wearing your tops out (but not long); or by matching a belt that rides down on your hips a bit to the color of your top.

◆ Having a long waist (lots of space between your bosom and waist) is generally not a concern. but if you would like it to appear higher, you can wear skirts and trousers with wider waistbands or wider looking belts that circle your waist in the same color as your bottom.

◆ If you have a very pointed chin you wish was a different shape, you may want to avoid V-necks—or you may decide to love the unique beauty of your chin and wear them as well as all other neckline shapes.

◆ For eons, women with round faces have been counseled to wear V-necks to make their faces appear less round. First of all, round faces are beautiful and exotic, just as are broad square faces and any other shaped face—and "line and design" is complex. Let's just say that you do want to try to lengthen your round face so you wear a V-neck top. If _your_ round face is attached to a long thin neck, you have just made your neck look longer and thinner—for _flattering_ line and design, **everything** has to be considered.

◆ Don't forget, if you have narrow or sloping shoulders or are wearing a style of top that gives you that look, wear small shoulder pads.

◆ If you have a long torso, which is often connected to shorter legs, you may want to avoid wearing low-rise pants with a tucked-in or short contrasting top—wearing a top that matches your bottom will give you a longer leg line.

◆ Avoid all dirndl-style skirts—they _will_ make you look dowdy.

◆ Knits and other soft fabrics that drape easily over the body are great for all body types.

◆ Hair that is tightly pulled back could be making your body look bigger than it is—look in the mirror to check for good balance.

◆ A defined waistline makes any bosom appear more ample.

◆ Pleated trousers are great for all body types as long as they fit correctly—no spreading pleats or pockets.

◆ Shoes with a high vamp make your legs look shorter; those with a low vamp lengthen them. A low vamp is when the top of the shoe is cut so that you can *almost* see the beginning of your toes—a very low-cut vamp would show a little "toe cleavage."

◆ Shoes with thick heels or soles can make full calves look larger and thin calves look like toothpicks.

◆ Be aware that single-button jackets, intended to button at the waist, may button either too high or too low on you. Too low can make your legs look short, while too high can cause your legs to look as if they start right under your bosom.

◆ If you feel your body looks better nude than clothed, you aren't wearing the right clothes.

◆ If you have broad shoulders and long legs, give thanks!

⊘ **Bad Advice:** Petites should always wear short skirts.

① **My Advice:** So untrue! You can wear any length you want, it's all a matter of the shape of the skirt and what you pair with it.

WRAPPING THE PERFECT PACKAGE

JUST THE BASICS

▪ Buy outerwear suitable for your climate.

▪ Select styles that go with the attire you wear to work.

▪ Buy solid colors in your most used neutrals first.

▪ Your coat should be large enough to fit over a jacket and, generally, long enough to cover your longest skirt.

BEYOND THE BASICS

Are you making a negative "arrival and departure" statement? Your coat needs to make a good impression because it is often your first impression, your last impression, and sometimes your only impression.

When you take your coat off, are people surprised at what you are wearing underneath? Select coats in styles and colors that go with your clothing styles and colors. Great colors are your most used neutrals, your hair color, and core colors.

The more *basic* the coat, the more versatile and the more things you can wear it over. If you want *easy elegance* with your coats, make certain that:

▪ Your coat is long enough to cover your longest skirt—I think that coats that come just about to your ankle are very elegant—in any case, it's usually best to avoid those that fall in "no man's land."

- You have an outerwear jacket that covers the length of all of your suit jackets and blazers.

- All of your coats and jackets fit with ease over your suit jackets and blazers.

- The coat or jacket has matching buttons so as not to interfere with your accessories.

- The coat or jacket is free of contrasting or sporty stitching, epaulets, and tabs.

- It is made out of a fabric that looks dressy enough to wear day and night, over a suit to work and over a beautiful little "perfect" dress out to dinner and the theater in the evening.

- You choose the style carefully. If you tend to dress more femininely, do not purchase a coat that is trendy looking or is severely tailored, for example.

- If you love long, fuller skirts, take this into account when you buy a long coat because if it is too straight, it will be difficult for you to walk without feeling "stuffed."

- If you belt your coat, *please* make sure that you don't look like a sausage—an hourglass, fine; a sausage, no! Belting styles with large or obvious pockets below the belt add to the concern.

- If your belt ends up making your bosom look "low," belt the coat more loosely and *angle* the knot down as you would a belt buckle that had the same concern.

- If you tend to wear your coat open a lot, single-breasted styles are often more flattering than double-breasted styles.

- You get the picture—make sure that everyone looking at you gets a pretty one, too.

The 3-Coat Capsule

Have you ever had to change your mind about what you wanted to wear to a party or a special event because the weather changed and you didn't have the appropriate wrap to wear over it? If you answered yes, or if you are tired of an overstuffed closet filled with coats and outerwear jackets that never seem to look great with your clothes, this capsule will set you free.

Coat 1

This "rain" coat follows the guidelines above in that it is perfectly plain with no sporty or contrasting stitching, no tabs, and no epaulets. The buttons match, and it's long enough to cover your longest skirt or dress. It will look as good over a suit as it does over a "special" little dress, jeans, or anything between— in other words, it will take you from car pooling and work to cocktails.

> **Fabric:** Your fabric is dressier rather than sporty, and choices include: silk, rayon (and the sueded versions of these), velvet, smooth dressy looking cottons, microfibers, suede, ultra suede, light-weight wool gabardine, and some leathers.

> **Color:** A solid color, because patterns aren't as versatile. Your choices include your hair color or your most used neutral. Could it ever be a core color? If one of your core colors is your *"signature color"* and if it goes well over most all of the other colors in your wardrobe, yes.

Coat 2

You may not need this coat if you live in a moderate climate where you don't need anything warmer than **Coat 1** (or **Coat 1** with a warm zip-out lining). If you do need it, follow the guidelines for **Coat 1** but find one that is as warm as you need it to be. It can be a totally different style, but the details, or lack thereof, are identical.

> **Fabric:** As warm as necessary. Will furry looks work? Maybe, but not if you ever need a really warm coat in the early fall or in the spring when (by the conventional way of thinking) it's too early or too late to wear fur.

> **Color:** The choices are the same as **Coat 1**.

Coat 3

This is really an outerwear jacket. Its purpose is to be worn with anything that you won't be wearing **Coats 1** or **2** over. What would that be? Black tie, formal event attire. Don't go to any? Then you don't really need this jacket, but you may want it anyway—if you choose *just right*, this jacket will be as great looking with jeans as it is with evening clothes.

What does it look like? The sleeves need to be big enough around to fit over the sleeves of an evening dress or beaded jacket (for those of you who don't attend dressy events, think big enough in the sleeve to wear over a bulky knit sweater or blazer). It's long enough to cover any evening top or jacket you may wear—so usually mid-hip to fingertip length. It's as plain and free of detailing as **Coats 1** and **2** and the neckline is high enough (with, or without a collar) so it covers any neckline your evening attire or suit jackets might have.

> **Fabric:** Silk, satin, velvet, dressy rayons, and some microfibers or other "dressy" fabrics that you feel would work nicely over *any* evening attire. What about fur? Of course, as long as it's not sporty looking in any way (no leather inserts, leather trim, or sporty buttons) AND you'll only be needing an evening jacket when it's *cold* outside. It depends on your lifestyle and your climate—you may want both a fur jacket and one in fabric, or perhaps you could get by with just the fur and a beautiful shawl. I love wearing my velvet "evening" jacket and my fox jacket with my jeans—it's an elegant creative look.

> **Color:** Black (only it you look great in it), cream/off-white, or other best neutrals. Consider "champagne," your best beige, or camel, especially if your hair is light to medium in tone. Women with red hair should consider coppery-looking shades an option. Furs in your hair and hair highlight colors will be exceptionally stunning on you.

Adding Variety

Of course most of you are going to own more than three coats—you probably already have three times more than that. The point is, in all of those coats and jackets that you do own, most of you don't have what you *need*—appropriate wraps to wear over any attire, for any occasion. Once you have your *basics*, you can add coats, jackets, capes, and shawls to your heart's delight.

One extra that I have found so very useful is a wool and cashmere shawl that is wide enough to cover my suit jackets and plenty long enough to wrap around me—because of its length, it almost looks like a cape. I use it mostly on those fall and spring days when the temperature in the morning starts in the mid-'50s and by afternoon, it's in the '60s. I also use it on colder days when I know that all I'm going to be doing is running from the house to the car and from the car into someplace warm.

Also useful, warm huge squares (4' to 5') that you fold corner to corner that you can wrap up in or, when it's not so cold, simply drape over one shoulder. They don't have to, but mine have a 2" fringe all the way around—I have them in black, navy, and cream.

For years, I didn't have any navy in my wardrobe until I found the most stunning jacket for 75% off the outlet price. Instead of investing in a navy coat or outerwear jacket, I decided I wanted to duplicate my huge warm square scarf/shawl, so I went to the fabric store and bought a piece of thick navy wool and cashmere fabric—I fringed it and, yes, although it is very simple to do, it takes a while. You'll want to ask someone in the fabric store how to fringe around the "corners."

A *classic* trench style is too casual to be **Coat 1 or Coat 2** (unless you are **always** dressed casually), which just happens to make it perfect for a possible addition to your capsule. Trench (and wrap styes in general) look particularly smashing when they are mid-knee or just above, or very, very long, almost all the way down to your ankles. It's important to check the length *with* the belt tied or buckled.

Avoid wearing below-the-knee length or mid-calf length coats over wider leg trousers because they can give you a dowdy appearance. Also, wearing an outerwear jacket that is shorter than your sweater, jacket/ blazer, or top is for certain funky, eccentric looks only. Avoid coats that have a "half" belt in the back that scoops down because, besides the fact that they make no sense at all, they can make your derriere look droopy and/or wide. The same goes for belts on trench coats and rain-coats that end up being tied or buckled in the back. The only exceptions are those that are tied or buckled HIGH ENOUGH so that they don't drape down over your "bum."

STORMY WEATHER

JUST THE BASICS

◆   **Scarves:** Solid color or subtle pattern and color perfect.

◆   **Hats:** Not a necessity but if you wear one, wear it as if you've worn one forever (I'm not talking about ski caps). Complimentary style and color for you and for what you are wearing.

◆   **Gloves:** Avoid ski-slope and snow-shovel styles and fabrics— for classic business and business casual, wear leather and lined leather.

◆   **Umbrellas:** Solid color, match your most used neutrals—carry one in good repair.

BEYOND THE BASICS

Scarves

Looking beautiful when it's blustery outside: When it's cold outside, many women don a warm scarf—sometimes without thought of the color combination they are creating with their coat, let alone their own coloring. All of the same color principles that apply to your most flattering clothing colors and color combinations are applicable here. "Cheery" bright red scarves don't look that way on Color Types that are best in toned down colors—any bright color can make these Color Types look overly pale, anemic, and like they had better get in out of the cold and into bed.

If you live in a climate that calls for a warm scarf at the neck nearly every day for two or three months, consider treating yourself to one or two that are really exceptional—your scarf, after all, is part of your first and last impression.

An *easy elegant* way to wear a warm scarf: fold in half so that both ends are together. Wrap around your neck and pull the ends through the fold and tuck the ends in the front of your coat or jacket. Can you still do it the way Snoopy did when he was fighting the Red Baron? Of course—just wrap the scarf around your neck and toss one end over your shoulder.

Hats

Hats can be so romantic, so dramatic, and so fun: It seems that women love to buy hats but rarely have the *nerve* to wear them. Let's bring them back in style. How? Simply by wearing them.

It used to be that a woman without her hat and gloves was not appropriately dressed and I know we don't want to go back to that strict edict anymore than we want our hemlines dictated. But, if more hats are seen "everywhere," more women will feel comfortable wearing them, and before you know it, they'll be back. Will you be the first of your friends to start the trend? Maybe they won't follow your lead, but if you love hats, they could end up being one of your *signature statements*.

Hat styles, of course, need to compliment the shape of your face (and work with your hairstyle) and, without seeing each of you in varying styles, it's hard to give advice. One thing I can say is that if your face is long, or an oval that tends to look long, avoid hats with high crowns and small brims (these styles are great for women with round or broad faces). Reach instead for a hat with a low crown and wide brim.

Since you are training your eye, go to a hat department or hat store and try them on—don't forget to check yourself from the side. Oh, another thing. If we are going to bring back hats, a veil, for certain occasions, is very romantic and exotic. Yes, I'm an incurable romantic.

Gloves: Elegant Hands

Socks and gloves have two things in common. Both keep our extremities warm and both often end up with one of the pair missing. Worn now mostly for warmth and sports, your business gloves will be leather or lined leather in your most used neutrals—consider matching your coat or the color of the shoes and boots you wear most often. The warmest are lined in wool or cashmere and will fit you like a *glove*. They need to be long enough (at least 2" or 3" above your wrist bone) so you don't get a cold or inelegant gap between your glove and your sleeve.

WHAT'S YOUR MAKEUP I.Q.?

1. Brownish looking lipsticks look good on most everyone.   T   F

2. If you can find just one lipstick that looks great on you, you can wear it with everything.   T   F

3. Wearing a blue-red lipstick, coral-red nail polish and brownish blush together is fine because in the new Millennium anything goes.   T   F

4. It's an "old-fashioned" notion that you should wear a red lipstick that matches your red suit, top, or dress.   T   F

5. If you feel you are looking washed-out, wearing a bright bold lipstick can give you a lift.   T   F

6. As a woman gets "older," she should wear less makeup.   T   F

7. Your eyebrow pencil should match your hair color.   T   F

8. Using a lip pencil that is a touch browner than your lipstick creates a fashionable look.   T   F

9. A sheer, colorless lip gloss is all a woman needs when she's dressed-down.   T   F

10. Makeup artists are trained to know what makeup colors are best for you.   T   F

ANSWERS

1. False. The brownish lip colors came in as a fad and have stayed around for several years now, but that doesn't mean they look good on most women. They actually look very bad on most women because they gray and muddy the skin and can literally make you look drab and older instead of contemporary and chic.

2. False, unless all of the clothes you wear also look great with this color.

3. False, unless your style is funky or eccentric. It is always stylish and elegant to match your lipstick, polish, and blush. Each could be a little

lighter or darker than the other, but closely matching the shade is important.

4. It may be an idea that has been around "forever" but it is still, by far, the best look you can get. If you are wearing a raspberry jacket, for example, your lip, blush, and nail color (if you are wearing one) should be the same shade of raspberry. The same goes for red, coral, fuchsia, plum, the pinky oranges, and all shades that fall in between.

5. Maybe, but depending on your coloring, this lipstick could make the problem worse.

6. Maybe, maybe not. First, we need to know how much makeup she has been wearing. Classy women of every age don't want to look *overly* made-up but neither do they want to appear washed-out. The "occasion" needs to be considered, of course, but often "older" women *need* more (but not heavier) makeup applied with a skilled hand.

7. Usually, but not always. If your eyebrows are the same color as your hair, it's perfect to have a pencil that matches. If your brows are a different color than your hair—let's say that you are coloring your hair to a medium auburn shade and your natural brow color is a medium brown—the look may be great on you. But if your brows are a dark brown, for example, you may want to bring your brow color closer to your hair color by blending in a few strokes with a hair color pencil (to extend the brow, you will need to use both a dark brown pencil and the hair color pencil). Generally speaking, your brow color can be the same, a touch lighter, or a touch darker than your hair color.

8. It may be (or may have been) "fashionable" but it is very aging, generally unbecoming, and can cause the skin around your mouth to look gray or muddy, calling attention to any lines, even the fine ones.

9. False for at least 50% of women. If your coloring is strong and gutsy looking, lip color becomes very important if you want to look radiant.

10. False. The vast majority of makeup artists are only trained in technique and they are trained to sell the latest look in color. This look is very possibly not your best.

Leather and suede gloves, unless they have sporty stitching or casual detailing, are dressier than those made of wool or microfibers. For business and business casual, please avoid those that look like you could wear them skiing or to shovel snow. No mittens, please.

If hats come back in a big way, will we carry or wear "dress" gloves with our suits and dresses, like we did in the '60s and before?

Umbrellas

Buy an umbrella large enough to keep the rain off you, and perhaps another —the smaller size is handy to carry and fine when it's just raining but not at all useful when it comes to a rainstorm. Because most umbrellas are reasonably priced, make sure you always have one that is in good repair, because, if it isn't, you won't be making a good first impression.

As far as color goes, most of you are probably thinking "basic black" but if black isn't great in a large amount on you, take a look at your coats and outerwear jackets to see what color will match, or coordinate with, the majority. Solid colors, of course, give you the most versatility.

MAKEUP MAGIC

JUST THE BASICS

- Wear it but don't wear too much or too little.

- Avoid brownish blush, lipsticks, and lip liners.

- Foundations needs to match your skin tone exactly.

- Wear colors that flatter you and what you are wearing.

BEYOND THE BASICS

If you have a plastic bag or shoe box filled with makeup you've bought (or think you got free) that you've barely touched, raise your hand. Pick which makeup trends to follow as carefully as you would a fashion or a fad. If the "experts" in the fashion and beauty magazines told you that the only way you can look stylish this year is to wear all of your skirts 5" below or above your knee, 95% of you wouldn't listen. You would go on wearing all of your most becoming skirt lengths. The same *NEEDS* to be true about makeup, but it isn't.

For the past several years, while brownish lip colors have been the trend, I've spent lots of time shaking my head. Muted and Gentle Color Types (and Cross Color Types that look best in toned down colors) have looked okay in some of the *least* brownish of them. Meanwhile, Light-Bright and Contrast Color Types (and Cross Color Types who are more flattered by clear colors) have looked *really* bad in them—drab, dull, and *older*. **WE**

WEAR MAKEUP SO WE *WON'T* LOOK DRAB AND DULL and none of us have wanted to look *older* since we were 18.

One of the oddest things about this particular lip color craze is that many women never wear brown clothing and if you ask them why they'll tell you it's because they don't look good in brown. Yet, they've been wearing it on their mouth and cheeks, thinking they look great.

ALWAYS create a makeup look for yourself that compliments your coloring, using your best shades in your best clarity. No matter what is "in" fashion, stay true to your coloring if you want to look young, fresh, and vibrant.

Wearing the "in" looks: Each of you can do *your* best version of a makeup trend, it's just that if you don't know your best makeup looks and colors, it is going to be difficult to figure out your best version of a trend. One of my beautiful Black Associates who looks great in clear, vibrant colors wanted to find her best version of a brownish lipstick. Because she is aware of how fabulous she looks in clear colors, she could judge each brownish lipstick against that radiance. Having to reject them all, but being a very creative woman, she found that she could get her best version of this look by combining just a hint of a slightly brownish lipstick with one of her clear, bright lipsticks.

Experiment, but know what looks phenomenal on you so you'll have something to judge if the new look is **"equal to, or better than, the best look you have right now."**

We are beginning to see more and more bright colors in lipsticks on the shelves and in magazine ads. The makeup companies want to sell you something "new" and everybody already has enough "browns." Now, I have the opposite *worry*. Women who are most flattered by toned down clarities are beginning to wear the "new" brights and some are looking pretty bad—overpowered, garish, overdone. But those women who look great in clear colors and are wearing the "new" brights are looking fabulous. You get to decide whether to follow a trend or pass it by.

In need of an "update"? Wearing your makeup just like you did in high school or college almost always makes you look *older* and *dated*. If you just got out of school you will want to develop a "polished" look that compliments your new work image. And, if you've been out of school *forever,* you may need to give yourself a reality check to make sure you look *modern*. I'm not talking about a fashion magazine's idea of the "latest" look (which could cause nightmares), just a finished, classically elegant face. To appear contemporary is to appear to be up to date, in the know, about *everything*.

Every few years, spend some time "playing" with an expert who can show you how to keep your look contemporary. Take what you learn and translate that new knowledge into a makeup style that will work for you—keep in mind your most flattering clarity, colors, and color combinations, as makeup artists are most often not trained on these specifics.

Looking *"Finished"*

Some workplaces don't "require" a face full of makeup, but no matter where you work, you will always want to look great, and for most of us, that means wearing at least some makeup.

How do you know how much you need? Aim for a finished, head-to-toe look. If you are wearing a suit or its equivalent, your face needs to be equally as "dressed." If you are wearing the latest trends to work, you'll be making the same statement with your makeup. A sporty-casual look certainly doesn't *require* eye shadow but you can still wear it—although there are no hard and fast rules here, a little lighter application is usually a good match. A visual alarm goes off when your face doesn't make the same statement as your outfit—it's like, "What's wrong with this picture?"

What's your "bare" minimum look? Mine is the finest line of eyeliner, mascara (but not always taking the time to use an eyelash curler), a hint of blush (just what's left over on my brush from the day before is fine), and lipstick. This takes just two minutes, and I feel so great about the way I look that I could open the door and be delighted to find a favorite movie star or my "first" husband with his wife (I've only had one husband, by choice of course, but I love referring to him as my first).

Speaking of first husbands, after a Color 1 Associates training in Tokyo I flew on to Hong Kong with my co-trainer to do a little shopping (the trip and some shopping money were a bonus for her). We got in late and I told her that the next morning I was going to dress very casually and just do my "minimum makeup look"—we had been "dressed to the nines" for 11 days of training and there was no way that I was going to do more. Besides, we were heading to the famous Stanley Market and it was really hot and humid outside.

Well, wouldn't you know! The next morning we're in the coffee shop about to order breakfast when I look up to see my first husband with three other men—all of them dressed in suits and ties. I *immediately* got up and went over to give him a kiss (yes, he's a really exceptional man). I smiled at the other men and said, "It's good for William's reputation to be kissed by strange women in coffee shops."

How did I feel about the way I looked? Fabulous! That's why I didn't hesitate for a second in going over to him. When you don't feel good about the way you look, the tendency is to hide from, or avoid, not just first husbands but life and lust. What was I wearing? The *easy elegant* casual look of black cotton shorts, black leather sandals with rubber soles, a black T-shirt with a silver metallic eagle on it, a black and silver belt and a black baseball cap. My "minimum makeup look" of lipstick, a touch of blush, a fine line of eyeliner, and mascara made the perfect matching statement to my outfit.

How little makeup can you get away with and still feel great about the way you look? Make a decision and do it for *yourself* every day. Yes, even (especially) on the weekends. Think a.m. makeup and p.m. makeup—strengthen your makeup for night lighting conditions by adding more product (stronger application of eyeliner and blush, for example) and using a slightly more vibrant lip color. No brownish lips or cheeks, please.

Developing Necessary Skills

Women are not born with the skills to apply their makeup artistically so they can end up looking overdone or underdone. Find a person who can help you learn to apply flattering colors of makeup in differing ways to fit all the parts of your lifestyle. If you know your best look for work, how do you vary that look for casual evenings and dressier evenings?

Don't trust everyone wielding a makeup brush to show you your best looks—some times makeup artists just teach the "latest" look (read fad/trend) and most are trying to sell makeup—it's their job. Hoping to sell you more, they use lots of products on you (they are trained to do so) when only a few are necessary to achieve a great look. Ask for a "classic" makeup lesson. Once you know the *smart* basics for your face, you can learn some trendy "tricks" to use from time to time, depending on your lifestyle.

Women's magazines and makeup books have some good information and some misinformation. It can be difficult to correctly relate their advice to your particular eye shape and face shape, but you will probably always learn something worthwhile. The advice in magazines is most often trendy so be aware that these makeup looks may not be your best and/or appropriate at your place of business. Also, they may be "out" just about the time you master the technique.

"Practice makes perfect" but perfecting the wrong placement or technique for your eyes and face is no help at all:

- ⊘ Is your eye shadow placement or your eyeliner making your eyes look smaller instead of larger? (I didn't wear eyeshadow until I was in my thirties because every time I tried, even working with a "professional," my eyes looked *smaller*.)

- ⊘ Is your eye makeup moving your eyes closer together instead of wider apart?

- ⊘ Is your blush placement making you look older?

- ⊘ Are the lip and blush colors you are using making you look vibrant, "hard," or drab?

Here are the *universally* most common makeup mistakes made by all women of every age—and particularly by the large population of "women of a certain age":

⊘ Foundation too dark, too pink, or peachy—it's aging and unchic.

⊘ Using concealer incorrectly—it's very aging and unchic.

⊘ Too much/too thick/too many layers of makeup—it's also very aging and unchic.

⊘ Too little makeup—it can contribute to older women looking dreary.

⊘ Too brownish or orangy blush—again, very aging and drab looking.

⊘ Wearing a lipstick and blush together that do not compliment each other.

⊘ Wearing too brownish a lipstick for your coloring—drab and aging.

⊘ Wearing lipstick that is too bright for your coloring—possibly garish and aging, depending on your Color Type.

⊘ Not matching your lipstick and blush to the red, plum, fuchsia, raspberry, or coral clothing you are wearing.

⊘ Too reddish eyebrow pencil—definitely aging and unchic.

⊘ Over-plucked/too thin eyebrows—unsophisticated and aging.

⊘ Not "sketching" in missing eyebrows at outer edge—aging and unfinished/ unpolished looking.

⊘ Too much, too dark eyebrow pencil—aging and not classy.

⊘ Not brushing your eyebrows "up"—makes you look tired.

⊘ Putting blush on forehead, nose, and chin—makes your face look blemished or burned.

⊘ Wearing too much blush—very aging and unchic.

⊘ Wearing blush in the wrong place—too high (in your smile lines); too close to your nose and below your nose (droopy); and in light hair by your ears—aging and unchic.

⊘ Too brownish lip liner—definitely aging and drab looking.

⊘ Using unflattering eye shadow colors and not getting the placement right for your eye shape—if it makes your eyes droop, it's aging.

⊘ Too much eyeliner.

⊘ Using eyeliner in such a way that makes your eyes look closer together or smaller.

⊘ Not blending eye shadow enough—aging and unchic.

⊘ Not removing dark visible hair from upper lip and chin—aging and unsexy.

Getting *Smarter* About Foundation

Your foundation must match the skin on your neck **exactly** in natural daylight —you don't *wear* it there, you only match it there. Don't let anyone talk you into "warming up" your skin tone or "canceling" out undertones. With your makeup on, you should be able to stand naked in natural daylight (*yikes!*) in front of a mirror and have the color of your face match that of your body.

It's difficult to find the perfect foundation, but getting it right is worth **immense** effort. One of the reasons it is so hard is that most makeup lines do **not** have enough (if any) golden beiges, slightly golden ivories, golden camels, golden browns, ivory beiges, or light ivories (that aren't too pink) to choose from. For color perfect foundation go to www.DressingSmart.com.

Concealer, *Itself,* Shouldn't Show

It's supposed to help hide our red spots and our brown spots, but **"it,"** also, should not show. Choose a concealer that matches your skin tone as closely as possible—mix it with some of your foundation if necessary. This mix also gives you a consistency that is easier to work with.

Placement of concealer is VERY important and almost always done **incorrectly**—*please* do not cover the entire area under your eye. If you put concealer on a puffy or swollen area, the "puff" will look bigger, not smaller—and definitely not concealed, a major concern for "women of a certain age."

Usually, what you're trying to conceal are dark circles under your eyes and other "rotten" spots. The dark circles are usually found just *under* a puffy area. Using a tiny brush, the tip of a small sponge applicator, or the tip of a cotton swab that is well-formed (not a fluffy big-headed one), apply a small amount on the darkened area **only.** *Pat* it carefully to blend—avoid rubbing it, as it can end up being spread onto areas where you don't want it.

There's a lot of discussion about whether concealer should be used under or on top of foundation. Whichever works best for you is fine with me, however, many women don't need concealer once they've skillfully applied the **right** shade of base. Also, if you apply concealer first there is a tendency to rub it off, or move it out of place, as you are applying your foundation.

Wearing *Too Much*

One of the most aging looks in the world is too much makeup, especially too much foundation and powder. How much is too much? Too much *looks* thick and if you ran your fingernails gently down your face and got foundation under them you are definitely too heavy handed. Keep your goal in mind—you are after the look of a beautiful, *even* complexion, not layers of product.

Sometimes an overly made-up look comes from wearing too bright, or dark, lip and blush colors, not too much product. Double-check your best clarity and also know if your coloring is delicate or strong looking. **On delicate coloring, less looks like more.**

I think I'd ask a perfect stranger who I felt looked very "together" if she thought I was wearing too much makeup—you can take a poll. Sometimes when you ask women you know, they have built-in perceptions of you (or their own agenda) and you don't get good or accurate advice. If you ask a makeup artist in a store, she generally has **not** been trained to know what's best for YOUR coloring (and he/she definitely has an agenda).

Wearing *Too Little*

You may also ask a stylish stranger (again, probably not a makeup artist) if he/she thinks you are wearing too little makeup. If you most often feel like you look washed-out you probably need more—makeup of different colors (perhaps brighter, clearer colors), and/or to change your clothing colors. Check your best clarity and note that **on strong coloring, less makeup looks even less.**

The Radiant Glow of a "True" Blush Color

Wearing a blush that is brownish or orangy is the fastest way to take away your radiance. You just don't blush orange! All women are very flattered by their body's natural red color—you'll see this color in your fingertips, your palms and your unmade up lips—it is the color you blush naturally. Other becoming blush colors are your best plum or fuchsia, raspberry, and red-coral (that's your body's natural red with just a touch of pinky-coral mixed in). **Avoid brownish blushes no matter what the shade, unless you want to look older and dowdy.**

Getting Coordinated

One of the things that I thought every woman already knew about makeup, but obviously doesn't, is that her lipstick and blush should be the same color, or very, very close in shade. Exceptions are made for trendy, funky, eccentric, and arty dressers.

Lipstick and blush also need to be the same *clarity*—your best. So, if you are wearing a clear, bright fuchsia lipstick, your blush will also be a "clear" fuchsia. The exception to this *smart tip* is the blush you wear with coral and pinky-orange lipsticks. Since many coral, and all orangy, blushes can sallow, gray, or muddy your skin, it is important not to wear a blush that is any more coral or orange looking than one that is just a hint more coral than your best shade of red. Think of this color as falling right between your best red and your best coral.

The *Fastest* Way to Looking "Drab" or "Fab"

Just like brownish blush, wearing too brownish a lipstick can instantly take away your healthy glow and could make you look "hard" or *older*. As in all other fads and fashions, they aren't for everyone, and you get to decide if a new trend works for you. Would you wear stockings with seams or hippie tops every day, just because they were all the rage? Twelve-inch skirts? Bejeweled glasses with "wings?" Blonde hair with 1" or 2" of dark roots showing? Grunge? The drugged-up look of "heroin chic?"

Those of you who are most enhanced by clear, vibrant colors need to avoid all brownish lipsticks. For those of you who look radiant in more subdued, toned down colors, choose your brownish lip colors carefully. If they look like mud, or gray or dull the skin around your mouth, you'll know you need a lipstick that has, at least, a little more *color* in it. Your best clothing clarity is absolutely the clue to your best lipstick and blush clarity.

Another thing I thought every woman knew is that if she is wearing a raspberry or red dress or jacket, for example, that her lipstick and blush should match that exact color. Obviously, since I've been shaking my head about this for several years now, this fundamental explanation has not been passed down from mother to daughter. Again, exceptions are made for the trendy, funky, eccentric, and arty dresser with a caution—no matter what you see, hear, or read, matching is always going to look more elegant.

When a woman wears a brownish coral lipstick and blush, for instance, with a red or raspberry suit she looks as if her head and her body belong to two different women. This is one of the reasons that so many women today do **not** look well pulled together although they may be trying their best to look great.

For *easy elegance*, it's very simple—all you have to do is have a "makeup wardrobe" and a clothing wardrobe that both go with YOU. If you do, you will automatically own a lipstick and blush that will coordinate beautifully with all of your clothing. Besides matching reds to reds, plums to plums, and so on, here are some examples of lip and blush colors that are wonderful with some of your other best colors—there are no "hard and fast" rules here, just some of my favorites—you can develop your own:

- ◆ Wear any of your best lip and blush colors with white, off-white, cream, beige, camel, brown, gray, navy, and black.

- ◆ Try your best plum, fuchsia, raspberry, or coral with greens, blue-greens, robins egg blue, and teal.

- ◆ Wear any of your best shades with blue and purple.

◆　Try your best plum, fuchsia, and raspberry with red-purples.

◆　Wear any of your best shades with yellow.

◆　Try your best plum, fuchsia, raspberry, and coral with rust.

Two-tone lips—do you look stunning or "gruesome"? Two-tone lips can be very beautiful, but they can also look really bad if you line with a lip liner that is too brownish for your coloring. For a classic makeup look, the lip pencil should match your lipstick as closely as possible. For a beautiful "fashiony" two-tone look, keep the colors and clarity fairly close to each other and at least very close to **your** best.

Keeping it on: One day after having lunch with two of my beautiful and stylish friends, they announced that they had been purposely watching me eat to see how I managed to keep my lipstick on throughout an entire meal—they'd been wondering (whispering, I'm sure) about this for years. It's easy, and I thought everybody already knew this tip, but it's in this book just in case you don't:

> Simply cover your entire lips with your lip pencil and then put lipstick on top. A lip pencil "stains" your lips so that when you eat off your lipstick you still have color on your mouth. Also, I "blot" my lips gently with my napkin instead of wiping. So, now, all of you know. — JoAnna

One day I even made it from 7:30 a.m. to 5:30 p.m. without needing a touch-up. My day? I flew from Washington to Cleveland, where I made a presentation to the president of a company, then had lunch with the chairman, and made it all the way home—I'd actually forgotten my lipstick, but thankfully, I didn't need it.

Framing Your Eyes

Your eyebrow pencil needs to match your eyebrows exactly or be just a hint lighter or darker. Many "supposedly" brown eyebrow pencils are too reddish and only work well for women with reddish hair. And some of the pencils for "blondes" *write* so "ashy" that they can instantly drab a woman's glow.

Some women need to use two different colors of pencil to get *their* eyebrow color just perfect—it's worth the effort. For example, if a "taupe" pencil is too light and a brown pencil is too dark, simply combine them. When it comes to which to put first, try both ways on the back of your hand— use your eyebrow brush to blend the colors together. If a black pencil seems too dark and the brown is definitely too light, you now know what to do. For **fabulous** shades of brown and "blonde" eyebrow pencils and brow definers (a great option that easily covers gray/silver eyebrows), check the colors on www.DressingSmart.com.

Yikes—please don't take too many! Eyebrows as thin as a line were a fad that some women continue to follow. Watch over-plucking your brows because eventually they may stop growing back and you'll wish you had more. Also avoid "drawing on" eyebrows more than just a hairline above or below your natural brow line. And, *please* don't shave them off and draw them back on—yes, some women do.

One place where most women, after a certain age, need to add two or three hairs is at the outer edge of the eyebrow. These missing hairs can make your eyes look closer together—sketch them in and watch your eyes appear to be farther apart. Your eyebrows are like frames for your eyes and if the frame stops short, they look unfinished.

How far out should they be? Hold a pencil at an angle from the bottom corner of your nose to the far outside corner of your eye. The extension of the pencil will show you a good stopping place for your brows.

Too much or too dark eyebrow pencil can make you look older or "hard": Lighten up your touch, or the color you are using if necessary, and keep your pencil sharp. Blend with an eyebrow brush. If you are using a brow-defining powder, apply it lightly just where you need it. I find this "powder" perfect for covering/coating my "silver" eyebrow hairs—I had three or four before I started writing this book and more now!

Taming the "wild ones": Many women run around with their eyebrows in "disarray," giving them a scowl or a tired or unfriendly look—especially if they are brushed down. Always brush them up (and slightly over toward your ears, if necessary)—it's like getting a free eye-lift. Try it both ways and you'll see what I mean.

Placing Blush in the Right Place—the Look of Whisker *Burn* is Not Cool

Red or rosy chins can make you look like you have whisker burn. A red nose can make you look like you have a bad cold, you've been out in the cold, or you've had a bit too much to drink. Why would anyone want to create any of these looks on purpose? That's what you are doing if you put blush in these places. Foreheads don't blush either! Brush these old myths right out of your mind.

Blush is used to create a natural glow and is best kept to your cheek area. These guidelines will work for every one of you, whatever your face shape—this "universal" *Smart Lesson* is actually very **unique** to you:

◆ Do not place blush any closer to your nose than the inside of the iris of your eye.

◆ Do not place blush close to any part of your eye—keep the "eye socket" area and smile lines (or other lines) free of blush.

◆ Do not place blush any lower than the bottom of your nose.

◆ Do not place blush as high as your temples.

◆ If you want to make your face look wider, place your blush nearly horizontal.

◆ If you want to make your face look less broad or less round, place your blush at a slight angle toward your ears.

If you follow these guidelines, you will find the exact placement for *your* face. Remember to always apply powder to your cheeks (in a downward motion) before you apply your blush; it helps the blush go on much more smoothly, keeping it out of your pores.

There are two other things that need to be mentioned here. First, *please* don't put the **tip** of your blush brush in your blush. A blush brush was meant to apply blush by stroking first the blush and then the face with the *long* hairs. If you have a small space to work with, turn the brush on its side.

Try this method and see how much easier it is to apply and blend. *Please* don't approach either your blush, or your face, with the bristles of your blush brush pointing toward them. If you do, the bristles of the brush go right into your pores, filling them with blush, making it nearly impossible to blend well.

As you approach your face with your brush, avoid starting to apply your blush at any edge of the parameters listed above. Start instead in the center of the area you want your blush to cover, and then blend out, over, and down. If, for example, you start by placing your brush at the bottom of your nose (your lowest parameter), once you've "blended" your blush, it will end up lower than your nose. The same thing happens if you start at the inside of the iris of your eye—by the time you've blended the blush, it will be too close to your nose. Practicing the *perfect placement* does make perfect.

Beautiful Eyes

I wish I could give you some good solid information on how to apply eye shadow but without seeing each of you individually, it's impossible to do a good job of it. Nevertheless, these "universal" tips will help:

◆ Avoid using colors that make your eyes look bruised.

◆ Place light colors in small spaces that you want to look larger— for many women, that means keeping your eyelid area light.

◆ Place darker colors in spaces that you want to recede.

◆ Place shadow in such a way that your eyes look more wide-spaced— lighter colors or lighter application on the inside (toward your nose), and medium or darker colors or darker/heavier application on the outside. Of course, if your eyes are "wide-set" you don't have to create this *illusion* unless you want them to look even wider apart.

◆ Those of you with strong coloring can wear more eye makeup without looking overdone than those of you with delicate coloring—each of you can have a dramatic look when you like, it's just that if your coloring is delicate, it takes less to create the drama.

Blend, blend, and then blend some more: Blend your eye shadow unless you are going for a fashion look that calls for something different. For *classic* eye makeup, you shouldn't be able to discern where the shadow stops and starts. After you've blended *really* well, blend it again.

How much is too much when it comes to eyeliner: It depends on the time of day (think a.m. makeup and p.m. makeup), where you are going, and what you want people to think about you once you get there.

What's your goal? For your eyes to be more noticeable, *not* your eyeliner. If eyeliner is all you see when you glance at your face, it's too much (which can mean too heavy or too dark). Smudge it. Look again. Narrow the line. Look again. Soften it by using a cotton swab to take some it off. Look again. When you get it right, the focus is on your eyes, not the liner.

If you want your eyes to look farther apart, don't line all the way into the inner corners. If your eyelids are hooded or show very little space above your upper lashes when you look straight on (versus looking down or up) at yourself in the mirror, skip dark liner on your upper lids or make the line very, very fine. If you don't, your eyes will look smaller, not larger, and more closed, instead of more open. Fine lines need a pencil with a very sharp point.

"Contouring" Your Face is Best Kept for Photography

You aren't fooling anyone into believing that your nose is shorter or narrower, or that you have hollows below your cheeks. You just look like you have smudges on your face, highlighter out of place, or that you were too heavy-handed with your makeup.

"Creating" Beautiful Skin

If you have beautiful skin, I hope you know how blessed you are. It's so difficult to do a good job of applying your makeup if your skin isn't in good condition. I don't care whose products you are using, if they aren't working for you, you need to change them. If you are feeling loyal, perhaps the brand you like has different formulas that you can try.

One of the most important things is finding someone who will work with you to get your skin in good shape—someone who will give you samples to try *before* selling you a bottle or jar of something that may not work.

Did you know that the greatest cause of breakouts is *over-moisturizing*? In this day and age of fear of *aging*, the first thing a woman does is reach for a moisturizer. She thinks the richer, the better. If you are breaking out, this may very well be the cause. Check it out.

BEING GROOMED FOR VIP

JUST THE BASICS

- Light fragrance when allowed.

- Clean, non-scary length, short nails—no chipped polish.

- Shower every morning.

- Use deodorant.

- Clean hair.

- Get a cut that looks good that **you** can maintain.

- Remove all facial hair as often as necessary.

- Fresh breath.

- No noticeable nose hair.

BEYOND THE BASICS

Yes, some women and men need to be told to brush their teeth and/or use deodorant—even ambassadors. Mouthwash in the morning after brushing is a good idea, as is a sugarless mint or sugarless gum, after meals.

Crowning Glory or *Serial* Bad Hair Days?

Too many women get "all dressed up" to go to work and their hair ruins their image. If you are having a bad hair day it can ruin your day, as well. Take any measures necessary to get, and keep, a hairstyle that works **for** you, not against you. Some *smart tips*:

- Dirty or uncombed hair is not appropriate in any business situation—wind-blown, messy on-purpose looks are different than uncombed hair. How? One looks uncared for, the other should look stylish.

- If you are wearing your hair like you did when you were in high school or college, the style is more than likely no longer as enhancing and contemporary looking as it could be.

- Hair that has no movement (sprayed until frozen) is not *smart*.

◆ Find a stylist who will keep your look *smart*.

◆ Always check the back of your head for "hair holes"—I believe that's a southern term. The back of you is as important as the front because if someone sees you from the back first, he may never be interested in seeing the front.

◆ A great haircut is only as good as you can make it look on a daily basis—get one that you can manage.

◆ Find someone who can cut well—*consistently*. A good haircut may cost as little as $15—a good *hairstyle* may (but not necessarily) cost more, but once it's styled you can have it *maintained* by anyone who cuts well. It's best to show it to the person who will be maintaining it (you're showing him/her a new "pattern") within the first week or two of when it was styled.

◆ "Spiked" and highly gelled hair is fine if it looks *normal*, or is expected in your business environment.

Stay away from the "brassy" and the "ashy"! There's just an awful lot of hair out there that is too ashy or too brassy looking. If your hair is brassy looking, it can sallow your skin and/or give you an "inexpensive" appearance. If it is too ashy, it can gray and dull your skin, taking away your vibrance and causing you to look washed-out.

Your hair color is critical to your image, and if the color is wrong it can really diminish your beauty, even if everything else is perfect. Find a good colorist—not necessarily the same person who cuts or styles your hair.

Damaged hair, damaged image: If your hair looks damaged, it damages your appearance. Get the damaged part cut off and then vow to keep your hair in good condition.

No obvious roots of a different color—no exceptions: If you are not going to keep your color or highlighting up, *please* don't color or highlight in the first place.

Matching "statements," again: Hairstyles are particularly effective when they look great on you *and* with what you wear on a daily basis—your hair and your attire need to make the same statement.

Trendy hair is great if you get to dress that way at work—otherwise, it may be "undoing" your career goals. And this goes for "big" hair, extreme asymmetric cuts, matronly looks, and highly dramatic and old fashioned styles (unless you are into "drama" or "retro"). Hair ornaments (bows, clips, headbands, and combs) should be understated when used with *classic* clothing and more "serious" looking business attire. Think sophisticated, not little girl!

Change your hair stylist if you don't constantly get a look you love—"loyalty" can keep you looking out of date or just plain frumpy!

Nails

No chipped polish, dirty or chewed-on nails, or ripped cuticles at any place of business, ever. Using hand lotion in the morning, every time you wash your hands (in a perfect world you would have time), and using a lot before bed will help keep your cuticles and hands from getting dry. If keeping your polish in good repair is a problem, use a clear finish only.

Wear colors AND clarities of polish that look great on you: *Please* make sure that your polish colors are neither too bright nor too toned down because, if they are, the skin on your hands can look gray or muddy—that translates to *OLD*. If you like the white tip "French" or "American" manicure, make sure that the tip isn't too white for your coloring. Also, if you wear a lot of cream instead of white, a creamy-white tip will look great.

For *classic* attire and most places of business, make sure that the color you have selected matches (fairly closely) your lipstick and/or goes with your attire. Unless you are a trendy, funky, eccentric, or arty dresser, no red polish with a coral, orange, raspberry, plum, or fuchsia outfit, for example, unless you are combining two of these colors on purpose.

With my fuchsia suit, orangy-red shell, and beautiful silk orangy-red, and fuchsia scarf I often wear fuchsia lipstick and orangy-red polish.

As I write this, the continuing fad/trend for polish is in very non-classic colors such as purple, blue, green, black, yellow, or green. Selling mostly to teens, but enough to adults that I need to mention it here, these colors should only go to work in trendy, funky, fashiony, arty, and eccentric atmospheres.

***Long* nails—alluring or "cheap"?** Sorry, I used that *cheap* word again. I guess that I must really want you to get the "point." No pun intended, but there is a point at which long nails are too long and can instantly cheapen your look. Can I give you a measurement? Yes, but some of you aren't going to like the numbers. One-quarter of an inch from the end of your finger is long enough (and perhaps too long if you want a classic elegant look or have small hands). One-half inch is definitely too long.

I know that fashion is supposed to be fun, but having jewels and art decorating your nails is a fad that only goes with some far-out trendy, funky, eccentric, or arty looks. If you are wearing embellished nails in the "wrong setting," you could very well be thought of as less elegant.

One of my Associates was judging a model search. There was a very attractive young woman who had everything going for her except that her nails were very long and decorated. They gave her a less than "classy" look and she wasn't chosen. (Judges, speaking among themselves, talked about her nails.) One would think that she could be selected anyway and someone would just tell her what "not to do" to her nails. Unfortunately the judges couldn't get past the *overall* impression.

A model is a *sales* woman. She is selling what she's wearing, what she's holding, and what she's pointing to. Top models portray a certain elegance. People automatically admire and project positive qualities and values onto an individual whose image is elegant and stylish even though these traits may not actually exist.

We all make an instant impression on others, and, based on the way we *look*, judgments are made about our character, values, wealth, importance, intellect, and personality. Once imprinted in one's mind, these impressions are hard to change. Just remember, a **positive** impression is *equally* as powerful as one that is negative—and it's equally as easy to have!

Squared-off nails look like little shovels—definitely not a *smart* look: The first time I heard that description, I think it was in the late '70s or early '80s. The square shape seemed to come into prominence with the popularity of acrylic nails. A nail that is rounded, more oval in shape, is much more beautiful for **everybody's** hands. The square shape makes your fingernails look fake, your fingers look masculine instead of feminine, and your hands look "sturdy/stocky."

One of my friends told her husband that she wanted to go back to having acrylic nails, and he fought her on the idea. When pinned down, he said that they didn't look real and that he would like it if her nails looked like mine. Well, after a short "fit," she told him that I (at the time) had an acrylic coat on my nails.

So, she went back to acrylic nails. We were having tea when she showed them to me—they were square. A discussion followed that one of the reasons my nails look "natural" is their oval shape, and I mentioned that "little shovels" are neither flattering nor *real* looking—that caused her to have another short fit.

Once she got used to the idea and the new shape—she loved it—she told one of her friends about the "little shovels" and her friend had a fit. Pass it on.

A friend of a friend (who won't tell her that her nails are sending a negative image) is a public relations executive in a large firm—she wonders why her Japanese male boss doesn't respect her. If you know her, pass it on!

Be Smart About Your Fragrance

Please avoid wearing more than a hint of fragrance to work—strong perfume is neither business-like nor sexy. A person should be able to discern another's fragrance only when in very close proximity. Use your fragrance sparingly and ask an honest friend or co-worker if he can tell when you've entered the room.

Be ultra-sensitive about co-workers who may be allergic to any amount of fragrance. If you work with someone like this, *please* refrain from wearing any at all. You should be aware that some companies and government agencies have instigated a no-fragrance policy.

A small closed-in space (like a car) can magnify the intensity, so when you are going to be in a car with others you may want to be particularly light-handed.

OTHER SMART DETAILS
WITH A BIG IMPACT

TRAVELING IN STYLE

JUST THE BASICS

- Always look *elegant* and comfortable.

- No sweat or jogging suits.

- No sneakers.

- Dress for the person who is meeting you and/or what you're doing when you arrive.

- Pack around a color theme.

BEYOND THE BASICS

How proud do you feel about telling your seat mate on a plane or train what you do when asked the inevitable question? Could he guess what you do by the way you are dressed? Would she guess executive, mid-level, entry-level, or unemployed? Art gallery or boutique owner? Fashion journalist or lawyer?

What impression are you giving others about yourself and your company when you travel? Would they want to do business with you or your firm based on the way you look? Yes, you do reflect on your company's reputation as well as your own, every time you get dressed, whether you are going around the world or just to the post office.

Travel stylishly and comfortably (remember, comfort and sloppy are not synonyms). Select your travel attire according to your arrival activities and pretend that your seat mate may be the prince you've been waiting for (forever), the president of your company, or the chairman of the major corporation you've been eager to work with.

If you are headed straight for a meeting, or are being met by an associate, dress for business. If you are traveling overseas, you may want to travel more casually—read *elegant* casual—and change into your business attire before you arrive."

Leaving and arriving in style: Although it would be nice, your luggage does not have to be the same brand or same style. But it should be the same color. Buy the best luggage you can afford and stop using any luggage that looks like it won't make it through another trip—in other words, be proud to claim your luggage, not embarrassed.

The color of your luggage is important. Select from your best neutrals and your hair color. Avoid patterns that are not likely to compliment your traveling wardrobe and be aware that some patterned luggage looks inexpensive.

Stress-free packing: We love to go places but we hate to pack. For *easy elegance*:

- Pick a color theme.

- If you take just what you need, it's a miracle, so relax because you will get better and better at judging your essentials.

- Figure out whether it's worse for you to take more than you need and be sorry about it or take less than you need and keep wishing you'd brought more.

- If you pack *well*, you will only need one pair of shoes for a week but your feet will hate you.

Some of you will end up traveling for business just once in a while and some of you will travel constantly. Pick a color theme and/or take your capsule and you'll be able to pack easily.

Many women have told me that before they became "clients" they used to hate to pack—it was such a major chore because they really didn't have anything they liked well enough to take. Also, it was tough because everything that went in the suitcase called for a different handbag and different pair of shoes.

Since learning these *smart tips*, they tell me they still hate to pack. Now, their reason is that they *love* everything they own so much that they want to take it all with them. And, although one or two pairs of shoes work with everything, they still want to take more—I'm just like them! Can you imagine loving *everything* you own so much? Soon.

What to pack, of course, always depends on where you're going and what you're going to do when you get there. If I'm going to be gone more than two days I always take at least one base and usually wear another. That way, all I have to do is change jackets and accessories. If you are traveling for more than a couple of days, don't forget your *Smart Capsule Wardrobe* and remember to pack more tops than bottoms.

There are many good ways to fill a suitcase; I slip a cleaner's plastic bag over each garment that could wrinkle. I made it all the way to Jakarta with linen and silk and didn't need an iron when I got there. Packing for this trip was easy—I just needed to take 12 different great looks for 12 *consecutive* days of work.

The purpose of my trip? To train new Color 1 Associates to become International Image and Style Consultants and to present a three-hour wardrobe seminar to 300 women, including ambassadors' wives, Indonesian fashion designers, and the press. My back-to-back schedule? Six days of Associate Training, followed by our three-day Advanced Women's Wardrobe Training and two-day Men's Wardrobe Training, followed by the seminar.

How could it possibly be easy to find, let alone pack, 12 great ensembles? I didn't buy anything new; everything I have is a million-dollar look and it was such a joy to pack it, knowing how perfectly everything would work once I got there. When you know you look great, you can forget about the way you look and get on with *life*.

Keep Your "Million-Dollar Looks" in Great Shape

Just the Basics

♦ Keep your "million-dollar looks" in good repair.

♦ Fix heels and shine shoes before they obviously need it.

♦ No loose threads.

♦ No stains.

♦ Don't over dry-clean your clothes.

Beyond the Basics

Wearing a garment or accessory that needs to be repaired ruins your look—*please* don't do it. Train yourself to immediately repair, or have repaired, anything that needs it. Keep an eye out for loose threads—trim them right away because they can make even an expensive garment look less.

Fix the heels on your shoes *before* they need it, and shine them *before* they look like they need a shine.

> Please do not dry-clean your clothes to death—it really does kill them.
> — JoAnna

First, try to remove "stuff" with a soft bristle brush. If that doesn't work, try a small amount of club soda on a clean dry white cloth. Dry-cleaning two or three times a season is enough unless you spill something. In between cleanings, use your brush, particularly on the shoulders, lapels, sleeve and trouser cuffs, and under the arms.

Pressing adds more damage (and usually shine), so steaming is what to request. Jacket lapels, especially, should never be *pressed*. Ask your best clothing stores who they recommend for dry-cleaning suits. Take drycleaner plastic off your suits, jackets, and pants the minute you get them home and hang them on good (not wire) hangers.

Keep a sewing kit at home, at work, and in the car. Also keep one lint roller (it has sticky tape on it) at home and another in your desk—it's much more effective than most lint brushes. If you own a dog who rides in your car, keep another roller in the car.

If you have even the tiniest possibility of being "hit" with moths, take precautions. Cedar chests, cedar-lined closets, cedar balls, or cedar blocks **do not kill moths**. Only use moth "blocks" or balls that say right on the package that they **kill** moths and their larva. It's fine to use a cedar chest, cedar closet, or garment bag *if* you add this protection. When it's time to wear these clothing items again, you can air them out by hanging them on the shower rod for a day or two—air needs to circulate around them. Sweaters can be put in the dryer on "fluff" (no heat) with some fabric softener sheets.

Light-weight wool items that you wear during the summer months need to be brushed every few weeks. Clothes that have been dry-cleaned are **still** susceptible to moths.

LOOKING SMART BEYOND REPROACH

JUST THE BASICS

◆   Avoid drawstrings around the bottoms of your tops and jackets.

◆   Wear menswear looks in a feminine way.

◆   Don't "save" your best looks for a special day.

◆   Carry a real handkerchief.

◆   Use a nice looking pen.

◆   Don't chew in public or on the phone.

BEYOND THE BASICS

Tidy up loose ends: Keep scissors handy where you dress and in your desk at work to trim small threads—it is amazing, but lack of attention to detail of this kind sends a message that you are careless or, perhaps worse, unaware. Never *pull* a loose thread, especially on a button. A few small dangling threads on a garment is not necessarily a sign that it was poorly made—but a lot of loose threads could be. Look all new items over carefully before wearing them for the first time, and trim as needed. Always open suit pockets and remove scratchy labels carefully, because you could cut the fabric. If your vision isn't perfect, put on your "readers" before you cut even your first thread.

Anything with a drawstring around the bottom should be avoided. None of us are flattered by the "blousing" fabric effect the drawstring creates, regardless of whether it's at the waist, anywhere in the hip area, or below the hip. Perhaps you can remove the string with happy results. No, don't even wear it loosely tied because the strings are bound to end up dangling where they shouldn't.

If you love menswear looks, consider wearing them in a very *womanly* **way.**

- A lace vest or lace shirt with all else tailored.

- All tailored but a very curvy jacket.

- All tailored but with a short pegged skirt or a longer slit skirt.

- A twin set and pearls with pleated flannel trousers or pin-striped trousers.

- Wear feminine accessories like a lace pocket square and pumps with at least a slender mid-heel height.

- If you are wearing extra-feminine looking makeup, you can wear your hair in any style, including slicked back.

Avoid dazzle in the daytime: Buttons that have crystals, rhinestones, or sequins are not appropriate for most business attire. If the buttons on your jacket or dress are keeping you from wearing it to work, you could change them. Otherwise, enjoy the jacket in your off-hours.

Too "matchy-pooh": Too many matching details can turn an otherwise fantastic look into a "didn't know when to stop" look. For example, silver detailing and silver buttons on a jacket, silver bracelet, silver earrings, and a handbag with silver studs. Trade the bag for one without any metallic details or for one with a simple silver clasp.

Are you "saving up" for a special day? If you are someone who "saves" your new clothes, or your favorite clothes, to wear for a special day or night, and you find that at the end of a season you have yet to wear them, you may have just missed some special times. Stop putting off looking great—if you feel special about the way you look every day, you'll find that every day is a special day.

Creating elegance where none existed before: Carrying with you, always, and using a *real* handkerchief makes an extraordinary impression. Ask your grandmothers, great aunts, and your mom for any extras they may have—they'll most likely be delighted to share. Yes, those with lace and tatting on the edge are what you are after, but more tailored handkerchiefs are also beautiful. You can find some super ones at estate sales or in your grandmother's dresser, but you can also buy some that are new.

Writing an *excellent* statement: *Please*, no cheap looking pens with advertising from other companies, banks, or free giveaways. A beautiful, stylish pen makes a nice impression and you don't have to pay a king's ransom for one. "Beautiful" simply means good-looking, not opulent, and a stylish pen is one that shows some personality. You can actually buy one at one of the big office supply stores for under $15—you'll want to keep track of it because, just like socks and gloves, pens tend to disappear.

It's not *smart* to "chew"! Unless you are alone and not on the phone, no gum, please. It looks unprofessional and inelegant. Also, it can be distracting and a major irritant to others—especially if you are "popping" it.

IS YOUR PERCEPTION OF YOURSELF REAL?

JUST THE BASICS

- ◆ In the mind of another person, you *are* what he or she thinks you are.

- ◆ Make sure your image is sending the message you want to be received.

- ◆ Understand that change can be unnerving (to yourself and others) because the "old" you has a certain familiarity and comfortableness.

BEYOND THE BASICS

It's very difficult to look at yourself objectively—it's almost as if you have become immune to yourself. If you feel, for example, that:

- ◆ Your five-year-old favorite lipstick and hairstyle still looks great.

- ◆ The same style clothing you've gravitated to for eons is still contemporary looking on you.

- ◆ You don't receive compliments on a regular basis.

- ◆ You've been passed over for a promotion when you have the best skills for the job.

- ◆ You lament that you continue to attract the same type of men— those that you'd rather not—

it's definitely time to change your image!

In the mind of another person, you really are what he or she thinks you are. The idea is to have the image you want "match" the image you create and have that, in turn, "match" the image, or message, that's received.

Sorry for the convoluted sentence. I'll give it another try.

You want a "Wow!" image. You go shopping and you buy what you think is a "Wow!" look. You wear it to work because you want your boss to recognize your worth or the handsome new guy to think you look fantastic. Your boss looks right through you as usual, and the new guy doesn't give you a second glance. Why didn't they get the message? If you think you are sending one message and a different one is being received, either you aren't on the same wavelength (they wouldn't notice you no matter what) or you aren't sending the message you think you are.

Eons ago, when women still wore hats, I was riding up an escalator in a department store—a woman on the down escalator said, "Miss! Miss! How much is your hat?" It took me a moment to realize that she thought I was "modeling" and that my hat was for sale. I wasn't modeling, BUT I **wanted** to look like a model every waking moment. So, the look that I had created was perfect because the message sent matched the message received.

How did I know how to look like a model? Lessons, practice, and *desire*. Truthfully, I was a model, I just wasn't modeling that day.

A well-dressed woman is never out of style, and you don't need to look like a model on a runway in New York to be considered very well dressed. — JoAnna

---

When you want to "check out" or change the message you send—your image/your look—your friends and family may not be your best resource for objectivity because they are *used* to you. Change can be unnerving because the "old" you has a certain familiarity and comfortableness. As you begin to look "different" (read more attractive) heads turn. When you first realize that someone turned to look at you, you may wonder if your slip is showing!

DEVELOPING A SIGNATURE STYLE

JUST THE BASICS

 Find a way to subtly set yourself apart.

 Individuality is always in style.

BEYOND THE BASICS

If you desire to be unique, to truly set yourself apart from other women, you'll want to learn to transform the same (or slightly different) clothes other women are wearing into your own distinctive *signature statement*.

Why did I say the "same" clothes other women are wearing? Because we all wear tops, jackets, pants, skirts, and shoes or boots every day but you willl look different—special!

Why consider a *signature statement*? It can subtly tie you to everyone you work with/for and others you come into contact with on a regular basis (the person who seats you at your favorite restaurant for lunch, your pharmacist, grocer, hairdresser, salesperson where you shop for clothes, and so on). In an interesting and pleasant way, you will be noticed.

To be noticed is to be remembered—to be remembered opens doors. Co-workers who normally wouldn't take the time may even make sure they get to see you every day so they can see what you are wearing. When they need someone on their team, you may come to mind. When you need a prescription filled extra fast, your pharmacist knows who you are. When your favorite restaurant is crowded, you will be seated. When a new item of clothing comes in that has some purple in it, or a vintage handbag gets consigned, your salesperson will call you. Purple or vintage? Read on—you can be beautifully and appropriately attired and still look unique.

What could your *signature statement* be? Anything you want it to be. Here are some ideas:

- Always wear a skirt with heels when other women mostly wear pants with flats.

- Always wear the same color—every day you are in blue or cream, for example.

- Always wear variations of the same color—for instance, you are always in different shades of purple and you mix them in the same outfit.

- Always wear an incredible belt—every new piece of clothing is purchased with a belt in mind.

- Always wear the same style—all vintage suits, all ethnic looks, always in a pantsuit, for example.

- Always wear pin-striped suits with very feminine tops and accessories.

- Always wear vintage jewelry and/or carry a vintage handbag.

- Always wear an all one-color look—one day you might be in beige (your skin tone or lighter version of your skin tone) head to toe, including stockings, shoes, and all other accessories; the next day everything is raspberry, and so on.

- Always wear a beautiful scarf, tied in both simple and amazing ways.

- Always wear a piece of ethnic jewelry.

- If appropriate for your place of business, always wear "wearable art."

There are those among you who will find this boring, but for those of you who don't, think of how easy it will be for you to develop this *signature statement* once you have decided what it will be.

Let's say you love scarves and feel that they will be a perfect *signature statement* for you. Not only will you collect scarves, but you will master the art of only buying clothing pieces (specific necklines, solid colors, *basics,* and *bases*) that work great with them.

Curious about my *signature statements?* You've been reading about them. I collect incredible belts, amazing jackets, and "wild" jeans. Because of the belts and jackets, I love *bases.* My jackets are all styles and colors from long to short and simply cut to beautifully embellished, so my favorite shape trouser is a narrower cut and my straight skirts are pegged. Because my jeans are "wild," I pair them with wonderful solid-color tops and *basic,* but interesting, jackets.

If you like the idea of a *"signature color,"* you have just made your life unbelievably easy, and fun. You can pick a color like purple, or a neutral such as cream or black (if black looks great on you head to toe). You could even pick two colors that you love to combine (that many women don't think to combine) like varying shades of pink and yellow, blue and turquoise, blue and green, or fuchsia/plum with an orangy-red, coral, or a pinky-orange.

You can even choose two neutrals, such as cream and camel (not for those of you with strong coloring), black and white (not for those of you with delicate coloring), or one color and one neutral, like red and camel—*please* remember to keep your best color combinations in mind.

Once you've established your *signature,* shopping for anything from coats to accessories becomes so easy. At a glance, when you walk into a store or up to a rack of clothing, you can instantly tell if there is anything you even want to look at, let alone try on. Think of how few shoes and handbags you'll need (unless you chose one, or both, of them as your signature statement).

There are those among you who may find wearing a *signature statement* boring, but others of you may have just found your answer to *easy elegance.* Are some of you worried about being noticed for the wrong reasons? You can **stand out** without *standing out.*

Will people think that you are eccentric? Depending on your *signature,* maybe a few. *Smile.* Others won't even realize what you are doing—they'll just think that you look super all the time. Most people will think you are a very attractive and *interesting* woman.

If anyone gets "verbal" with you about it, you can either share this book with them (a very gracious act) or ignore them and let them continue to muddle through, keeping their "hit and miss" habit of looking good one day and not so good the next.

BUILDING FROM ZERO OR PARING DOWN

JUST THE BASICS

If you:

- Don't have much or anything at all appropriate to wear,

- Your wardrobe seems out of control,

- You are feeling overwhelmed,

- You just don't know what to buy or how to start,

- You're on a tight budget, or

- You simply prefer a minimal wardrobe,

The following ideas are for you.

BEYOND THE BASICS

Having fewer good choices is liberating and something many women might wish to consider. Here are some *smart tips*:

- If you could picture yourself wearing just one color day after day, what color would it be? Build your entire wardrobe around this color—it will become your *signature color*.

- Buy only *basics* and *classics*—uncomplicated but beautiful.

- Wear *bases*.

- Review the *Smart Capsule Wardrobe*.

- Make a choice between gold and silver jewelry.

- One belt should work with everything and it should be the same color as your shoes—the buckle will be either gold or silver, depending on your decision. Remember that you can remove belt loops, eliminating the necessity of a belt.

- Your shoe and handbag color should be the same—that color should be able to be used with all of your outfits; depending on your *signature color*, consider your hair color or another color-perfect neutral.

- You may need both flats and heels; make sure that they are both cut low in the vamp and fairly low on the sides.

- Review the *Smart Coat Capsule* and choose wisely.

✎ In your "makeup wardrobe" have just one of everything you really need.

Closet Surgery 🚑

Just the Basics

🚑 For *easy elegance*, get your wardrobe organized. *NOW*.

Beyond the Basics

When you leave the house every morning feeling dynamite about the way you look, you never have to give it a second thought no matter what you might end up doing that day. Even having an unexpected meeting with the president of your firm wouldn't rattle you.

It's often said, but not always true, that you should give away those items of clothing you haven't worn for one year. It is true that *easy elegance* is more easily achieved when your closet isn't full of stuff you can't or shouldn't wear, but there may be something that you aren't wearing because you don't know how to utilize it. For a stress-free experience every morning, get organized now.

Is this elective minor surgery or major mandatory surgery? It depends on you and your closet, but if you desire a brand-new *you*, you may need to operate on, amputate, and transplant things in your closet. Before surgery, get a good mental picture of the woman you want to be, what she looks like, and your lifestyle. Steady your hand and begin—it doesn't have to be painful.

Your Goal: Dress easily in the morning without stress, then go on about your day without having to give the way you look another thought.

Step 1
Remove everything from your closet(s)—
work in natural daylight.

Step 2
Evaluate each garment and separate your clothing
into three piles.

Pile #1: Those items that are worn out, hopelessly stained, you hate, are the wrong size now and probably forever will be, are uncomfortable or scratchy, just don't look good on you, and you haven't worn in a long time.

Take a second look at all of these things. Can you figure out why you hate something? Is there anything about it that you could change that would make you like it—make it useful? If trousers are uncomfortably tight, can they be altered?

Perhaps the things that don't look good just need shoulder pads, different accessories, or need to be combined with a different style top or bottom. Maybe a jacket you don't like just needs to be paired with very slim-cut pants or a pegged skirt. Are those items you haven't been wearing out of style? Do they just need a little tailoring or new buttons to give them a modern appearance, or are they out of sync with your current life? For the time being, put these items in **Pile #2** or **#3**.

If your weight goes up and down, store (someplace other than your main closet, if possible) things you love that will possibly be useful in the future. Give away anything you feel another person could use, and toss the rest. Can't stand to give away or toss an old treasured item. Put it someplace where you can go and "visit" it.

> **Pile #2:** Those garments that you like but require mending, tailoring, or cleaning. Handle these "chores" as soon as possible.

> **Pile #3:** Clothing you feel good in; things you like but aren't terrific colors for you; and garments you would like to wear more often if only you had more things that went with them.

For those items that are not color or clarity perfect, figure out if you can "save" them by adding a color-perfect accent near your face. If not, they go in your giveaway pile. Should you keep them to wear when nothing special is going on? My advice is to give them up unless it means you'll be going naked. You'll never feel good about the way you look in them and the days you wear them will definitely not be special!

Now it's time to look at those garments you would love to wear more often "if only" you had (fill in the blank) to go with them. Make a list of things you will need to purchase to accomplish this. If you want to take them shopping with you, as soon as you finish **step #3**, you can put them in a bag and *get going.* Do I sound determined to get you organized?

Step 3
Coordinate your outfits and take notes.

First, how many *bases* can you make? If you changed contrasting buttons to matching buttons on a blouse, would it complete a base? Do you have any dresses that "look" like a base? If you'd love to make more bases, add to your shopping list the colors of tops or bottoms you'll need to accomplish this, and take the garment with you—you know that the shade of the color needs to be the same, but the value of the color can vary a little (be a little lighter or darker).

How many jackets do you have that will work over your bases? If you changed some buttons, would you have more outfits?

How many separates can you "coordinate" into intriguing looks

by bringing the bottom color up with a necklace or a scarf; by using a belt and shoe in the same color; or by combining like values of colors, such as two pastels, for example. If you need to shop for some neck accessories that match your bottoms, add the details to your list. What about other finishing touches like earrings and necklaces, shoes, and handbags? If you need shoes and a bag in your hair color, they go on your list.

Remember that mental picture of the *new* you? Keeping it in mind, are there any "holes" in your closet? If most of your things are too casual to wear to the place you spend 40 hours a week, that's a big hole! Add needs and desires to your list—the needs will make your wardrobe work for you, and the desires will help make your life work for you.

A desire? One woman may have always wanted a cashmere blazer; another is always looking for the *perfect* pair of black pants; yet another happily sorts through vintage clothes at the flea market every weekend just to see if she can find another vintage suit for her collection.

Step 4
Put your "keepers" back in your favorite boutique.

Thinking of your closet as your favorite boutique will remind you to go "shopping" there before you go out and add more miscellaneous "stuff" that you end up not liking and not wearing.

Since there is more than one good way to organize your closet, whatever works best for you is the way to do it. The most popular way is by garment—a separate section each for suits, jackets, trousers, dresses, and tops. Use good plastic hangers (not plastic tube or wire) for suits, jackets, and tops—the investment will pay you back by keeping your clothing in good shape. Also, wire and tube hangers weren't meant for knits.

I know it's not always possible, but hang as many tops as you can (including sweaters on padded hangers)—you will definitely utilize them more, as it's very easy to forget about things that are folded and put out of sight.

Placing square containers on top of your closet shelf, with the opening facing you, is a good way to keep everything else (sweaters that aren't on hangers, jeans, handbags, totes) organized and in full view—the top of the containers give you a second shelf. My cubes house heavy sweaters, T-shirts, cotton tanks, shorts, handbags (including totes and briefcase), and my collection of "wild" jeans.

Small shelves for your shoes (versus those pointy metal things) are fabulous. You'll never regret the investment—buy them at one of the big linen or hardware stores. Count how many shoes you have before you go (include your athletic shoes) so you'll know how many shelves to get. They can be stacked so that you can get several into a small space—try placing them under your tops and jackets.

In my "boutique," part of my belt collection hangs on tie-racks and the other part (larger belts) are placed on a small ratan four-shelf unit that I got at an import store. To make it look even more like a fun boutique, I've actually draped some of the belts over the top and others around the rattan wrapped side "poles" that hold up each shelf. You could do the same with scarves or handbags—for example, if you have a collection of vintage evening bags, display them.

All of my necklaces, those I wear and those I don't at the moment (they are treasured gifts or are works of art that I love), are hanging on a wall in my bathroom. If you think that your significant other might object to this "art exhibit" perhaps there is a closet wall, or a wall behind a door that you could use. It's often a hassle, and it's time consuming, to look through little boxes and bags in a drawer—if you can see your necklaces easily, you will use them more.

Earrings can be separated in any way that seems to make sense to you. Little cabinets that have lots of drawers, like apothecary chests (they are good for necklaces, too), are wonderful, as are larger jewelry boxes with drawers. I have one drawer for my earrings that have black on them (black and gold, black and silver, black crystal), one for my cream and white earrings, one for my silver and gold earrings, and one for earrings that are "colorful."

If possible, hang your scarves in your closet (or your dressing room, if you are lucky enough to have one) where you can see them. When they are tucked away in a drawer, they usually get less use and often get "messed up" as a result of having to look through them to find the one you want. Mine hang on wooden dowels whose original purpose was to hold wine glasses upside down.

Make your closet(s) as light-filled as possible. Unfortunately, many women have to deal with peering into dark closets, trying to decipher colors, especially whether the garment is black or navy. One friend solved this problem by putting little gold safety pins in the labels of everything navy. She also put little blue dots in her navy shoes—it saves her numerous "trips" to the window or a lamp.

View your closet as you would any other room in your home, with a fondness for the way it looks and for the things that are in there. Keep everything neatly hung and find little ways to "decorate" it. I have some of my more romantic evening bags and some sachets hanging here and there— the way my belts and scarves are "displayed" adds to the ambiance.

Buy a special notebook or journal (one that you love when you look at it) and write down all of the outfits/ensembles you have created—don't forget to include all of your accessories and the color of your stockings.

As you wear each of these outfits, I want you to place a little gold metallic star by those that you feel are your "million-dollar looks." Place a silver star by those you feel, at least at this time, are your thousand-dollar looks (*good* looks), a blue star by your hundred-dollar looks (*okay* looks), and a red star by all other looks (perhaps *acceptable*, but not so special). You can buy a small package that contains all of these stars at office supply stores.

As soon as you have time, try on each of your looks that has any star other than a gold star. See if you can figure out what you could *adjust* about this look that would turn it into a million-dollar look or at least one that you could give a silver star.

Change the color of the stars in your notebook when you've accomplished this. See if you can move all of your red-star outfits (in this case, red means danger) at least up to a blue. If you can't, perhaps you can do without them—that doesn't necessarily mean the *entire* outfit gets tossed, because *pieces* of it may combine with other things to create a "gold-star" look.

So, You're Going Shopping Again!

My friend Phyllis brought a friend to Washington to shop with me— the friend had just gotten divorced and was in need of both an "uplifting" experience and an "update" of her wardrobe. She had enough business suits for her executive look but needed *date* clothes.

We went to our favorite off-price store, and, after about a half hour of collecting things for both of them to try on, I put them in a larger dressing room where all of the women undress and try on in full view of everyone else. I kept going in and out, bringing more things for them to try.

On one of my trips in, a woman came over and asked me where I was finding the clothes I was bringing in. Phyllis said, "She's shopping off the same racks you are!"

One of the reasons we were causing such a stir, and why everyone was watching us, was because I was only having them try on clothing that would look good on them from a color standpoint— their best shades, clarity, and color combinations. And, of course, from a style perspective, I only brought them super-looking "stuff." The result was that they looked great in almost everything.

Some women just want to give up and wear any old thing because they are exhausted by their lives. One of the things that leads to this exhaustion is the constant hassle of trying to deal with a wardrobe that doesn't work. Shopping with a trained eye makes all the difference. Armed with all of your *smart tips* I'm sure you're going to be successful and have fun, too. Here are some reminders:

- Visit your "favorite boutique" (your closet) before you go shopping.

- Don't forget to take your list of anything you need that will complete, accessorize, or pull together something you already have.

🐚 Wear something you like that is easy to get in and out of.

🐚 Wear comfortable but good-looking shoes that are easy to slip off and on.

🐚 If you'll be wearing stockings with most of what you're shopping for, wear them when you go shopping.

🐚 Wear full makeup and make sure your hair looks good.

🐚 Don't shop when you are tired, hungry, or in a hurry.

🐚 Keep focused but keep an open mind—even when you're shopping with a list, you may find something unexpected. If it's returnable, take it home to see if it fits the "you" you want to be.

🐚 When you are attempting to change the way you look, avoid shopping with a friend who says, "That doesn't look like you," when you ask her/his opinion—it's not the "old" you who you are shopping for.

🐚 Shop with a small shoulder bag worn across your body—it gives you such freedom that once you try it you'll hate shopping any other way.

🐚 Many of us love the look of "shabby chic" when it comes to decor—now, unless we have an endless supply of money, we need to think "inexpensive chic"—buy great looks anywhere! Forget about labels; pretend that you are in a foreign country and don't have a clue as to the prestige level of the store.

Shop for style, quality, and price. I know that some of you get your self-assurance from a "label," but when you are truly confident that you look great, the fun and pride will come from knowing that you don't need a designer or brand name to make a million-dollar look!

🐚 Don't get hung up on the size marked on a label, or on the size marked on the racks you are shopping from. Learn to "eyeball" a garment and you can most always tell if it will work for you without looking at the size. When I have time, I check every size. You'll be surprised at what neat things you will find in the small and medium sizes that will fit most anybody and what you'll find among the larger sizes that will look *smart* on someone who is petite. If the size on the label bothers you, cut it out.

> Don't buy anything that isn't equal to, or better than, the best look you have right now. — JoAnna

🐝 Whatever you buy, take it back to your "favorite boutique," co-ordinate it with existing items and try everything on. If you still don't have the look **YOU** want, return it. If you did just create a new look that will bring you "oohs and ahs," write the winning combination in your notebook of million-dollar looks, *gold-star* it, and start wearing it immediately. Don't save it. Don't put off getting all of those compliments.

Then there are other women who buy "hope"... the hope of going out to more special dressy occasions (long dresses, cocktail dresses, bejeweled pantsuits); the hope of going away for special weekends and vacations (resort wear, ski wear, cruise wear); the hope of having a special fellow to entertain (you know what goes here); and so on. There is even a magazine ad that says, "In the dress of your dreams, all things become possible."

It's always wonderful to have some "hope" and some "just-in-case" in your closet, but not too much. I once helped a friend buy hope—it was a beautiful cream-colored silk pantsuit with a romantic ruffled collar. When she saw it, she said, "This is exactly what I want to wear if Mr. Right asks me to go away with him for the weekend."

Mr. "Wrong" never did. She *saved* it. It doesn't fit anymore. We still refer to it as buying "hope" and although we've had lots of giggles over it, one can't afford to do this too many times unless one has an unlimited budget. Some ensembles never have a "coming-out party"—it can be sort of sad to see too much hope hanging out in your closet just waiting for a special "moment" to come along or for that "special someone" to call.

I want for you to go through your life collecting many, many special moments and memories. You'll always have something "just right" to wear if you collect only million-dollar looks—**equal to or better than the best look you have right now.**

Keep in mind that salespeople have their oddities and that their "advice and comments" may not be true for you (after all, they don't know who you are, or who you desire to be) and their advice may also be inaccurate. I am grateful to many salespeople for their helpfulness and caring and it would be nice if they had color and wardrobe training to help clients, but few do. If the fashion magazines are offering bad advice, what can you expect from most salespeople?

Also, all color advice from salespeople is suspect—**YOU** need to take control of your most flattering colors, clarity, and color combinations.

A client, shopping with her color chart, reported her experience with a salesperson who, upon seeing her chart, said, "Oh, you have one of *those.* You don't really believe in *that,* do you?" She also told me about her experience in a different store where the salesperson ran all over the store, only bringing her things to try that were in colors on her chart. Guess which salesperson got the continued business and referrals? Helpful salespeople have found that clients are much more willing to try, **and buy**, styles that they never would have considered, just because they are in one of their best colors.

CONSULTING AN "EXPERT"

JUST THE BASICS

- To take the guesswork out of which colors and color combinations are best for **you**, visit www.DressingSmart.com for the number of the Color 1 Associate, International Image and Style Consultant, closest to you.

- Not all image consultants are authorities when it comes to personal color.

BEYOND THE BASICS

If you are not certain what colors and color combinations flatter you most, call Color1Associates, International Image and Style Consultants at (202) 293-9175 for the number of the Associate closest to you or visit our website at Color1Associates.com or DressingSmart.com. Why am I recommending them? Because they have had the best training available anywhere in the world.

An interesting and informative consultation with one of them will result in your being in charge of your best colors and color combinations forever. They can also help you build the perfect *smart* wardrobe for your current job or for the career move you would like to make. If there is not yet an Associate near you, there are excellent color charts on our website that will help you with all of your color decisions. You have to figure out your Color Type (a free online quiz will help you) so you will know which "*Smart* Chart" or "Mini *Smart* Chart" to order. There is also a print-out version available on the website.

Not all image consultants are experts in color. Some people who advise on color have had only two or three hours of color training and little or no wardrobe training. Most of their approximate two-day training is on how to sell a woman makeup.

Color 1 Associates have studied approximately four weeks before their actual technical color training which lasts six full days and is followed by five additional days of advanced wardrobe training. An apprenticeship program continues their training. Flying in from all over the world, the Associates have invested up to $5,685 *plus* airfare, hotel, and dining expenses in their training versus the $250, or less, other companies charge for their two-day "color" (makeup sales) training.

Just the Basics: A Quick Reference 📖

An exceptional look is attained, in part, by paying attention to all of the little details that make up the total picture of you. This abbreviated *Just the Basics* list is also printed on the last page of the book so you can tear it out and take it shopping with you as a reminder that these small components are a huge consideration when it comes to looking great.

- 📖 **Mirror:** Use one that is full length and check your front, side, and back views.

- 📖 **Your look:** *Easy and elegant,* professional yet stylish, perfect for your career and personal goals. Well coordinated, pulled together, totally elegant "million-dollar look," whether strictly business, business casual, or creative.

- 📖 **Color:** Great shades for you.

- 📖 **Clarity:** Not too bright and not too toned down for your specific coloring.

- 📖 **Color combination:** Not too strong or overpowering and not too weak or washed-out looking on you—again, perfect for your coloring.

- 📖 **Pattern size:** Perfect for your Color Type.

- 📖 **Fit:** Well tailored for you; shoulder line a tiny bit wider than your hipline—creating a "V" shape that keeps you from looking dowdy.

- 📖 **Jackets/tops:** Paired with the perfect style skirt or trousers for jacket shape and fabric.

- 📖 **Necklines:** Compatible.

- 📖 **Skirt hemline:** Any of your best lengths (and not too short or too tight for the occasion) paired with perfect jacket or top, stockings, and shoes for skirt shape and fabric.

- 📖 **Trousers:** Long enough; paired with perfect jacket or top, stockings, and shoes for trouser shape and fabric.

- 📖 **Stockings:** Perfect color, weight, texture, and statement for your outfit.

- 📖 **Shoes:** Perfect style, weight, color, and condition.

- **Handbag:** Perfect style, color, size, and condition; same statement as attire; metallics match.

- **Belt:** Color perfect; same statement; metallics match.

- **Underlovelies:** Always beautiful; not too tight, giving you a flattering silhouette under your clothes.

- **Hair:** Clean, flattering, and stylish.

- **Facial/body hair:** Not noticeable.

- **Makeup:** On—neither too much nor too little—a "finished" look.

- **Earrings:** Right statement and color for your attire; right shape for your face; right size for your Color Type and hairstyle; metallics match.

- **Necklace:** Right statement, color, and size; works with your earrings and with the shape of your jacket/top neckline; metallics match.

- **Bracelet:** "Quietly" perfect; same statement; metallics match.

- **Watch:** Color-perfect band and face; same statement; metallics match.

- **Ring(s):** Compatible styles; same statement; metallics match.

- **Pin:** Perfect placement; right shape; same statement; metallics match.

- **Handkerchief:** Clean.

- **Coat:** Same statement; compatible color.

- **Briefcase/laptop bag:** Match most used shoe color or your hair color.

- **Other personal grooming:** Clean body; wear deodorant; clean teeth; fresh breath; clean nails and no chipped polish; no nose hair showing.

- **Posture:** Good.

- **Train your eye:** Don't believe everything you see, read, or hear.

- **Comfort level:** Good or great, but great is preferred.

- **The way you feel:** Like a "million dollars."

The Unexpected Gifts of 🎁
Dressing Smart With Easy Elegance

What you will have when you _feel_ like you look like a million dollars:

- 🎁 Confidence. A job or a better job.

- 🎁 More credibility, respect, and authority.

- 🎁 Compliments from men and women.

- 🎁 Praise and a raise.

- 🎁 Notice and recognition.

- 🎁 A more secure future.

- 🎁 You'll **feel** _smart_, **act** _smart_, and you **will be** _smart_.

Contrary to what some experts advise, in a more casual workplace, clothes are MORE important than ever—what you are wearing sends a message to others about how you feel about yourself.

When you feel great about the way you look, you _interact_ differently with **everyone,** and the impact of your self-assured behavior can touch many lives, especially your own.

Your truly extraordinary _gift_ to others, and to yourself, is the positive radiating effect you can have on everyone whose life you touch and on those people whose lives they touch.

Beyond doubt, the way you feel about yourself will have an amazing impact on your life now (and your future), your family, your work performance, your co-workers, and the lives of the people they touch. When things go smoothly at work, everyone has a more positive feeling about life and work in general—less stress brings more productivity and a better working environment for all. Co-workers, including your boss, go home happier, and that happily impacts their relationships with the people in their lives.

Think about how your self-esteem affects your children, the way they feel about themselves, their happiness, the way they interact with you, their father, and each other, and the way they behave and succeed at school. If a child is doing better in school, that adds to his or her self-confidence; that self-confidence inspires his/her teacher, affecting the teacher's work (with your child and all the others) and the teacher's home life, and so on, and the spiral continues.

When you feel confident about the way you look, your relationship with your significant other is more "delicious" (okay, maybe just better). But, when you feel good about yourself—attractive—it's easier to show him how special you think he is and that makes him feel great. When *things* are better at home, he's different at work and that impacts on his job performance, his relationship with his boss and co-workers, and their relationships with others. When his boss and co-workers are happier, he's happier at work and the circle comes back to you, touching your life, radiating out again, and so on, and, we hope some day, so goes the world.

What makes a woman feel confident—attractive? On the "outside" it's taking the time to dress and use makeup in a way that is flattering to you. On the "inside" it's about your attitude, kindness, sense of humor, honesty, disposition, your approach to life, and the way you carry yourself—all integral parts of your loveliness. But you need to be **very aware** of how much your inside can affect your outside and your outside can affect your intimate inside. **All** women can appear confident and attractive—attractive women can also appear *unattractive*.

> I recently went through a very difficult time, and when I looked in the mirror, I didn't like the way I looked—I didn't feel attractive anymore. My body was the same size and shape, and my clothes were the same—I love them! So, like most women, I focused first on my hairstyle—it was fine—and then on my face which seemed the same but I decided that it must just be showing my age. This went on for two or three weeks until one day I figured it out—it was my face— the *expression* on my face. It was clearly showing the **anger** I was feeling. I instantly got rid of the anger, and the terrible expression, by being so honestly grateful for my life. I felt attractive again.

If you can't *yet* think of yourself as attractive, I want you to start the process by thinking of yourself as having at least one of the following attributes: style, an enchanting, captivating personality, elegance, an enticing intellect, grace, a subtle aura of sensual mystery, allure.

How can you become a more interesting, confident, attractive, and fascinating female? **Draw upon every asset at your disposal.** — JoAnna

---

It is the *feeling* of being confident that can help you accomplish your dreams—and it's that *feeling* of not being sure that can undermine your self-confidence. Many fine resources are available, so tackle any concern that might sabotage your confidence. For example, if you feel your table manners and your introduction skills are good, BUT you're not absolutely sure you have every detail correct, read an up-to-date etiquette book.

When one of my last books, **Dressing Smart in the New Millennium: 200 Quick Tips for Great Style**, came out, I received many emails from women thanking me for writing the book and, although each note made me feel that my effort was worth it, one letter, in particular, let me understand that my guidance can make a significant difference in a person's life. She wrote that after reading the book she decided she would give my advice a two-week trial—every day, for two weeks, she did everything I recommended. This is what she said happened: She was told that she is pretty for the first time in her life; neighbors where she has lived for two years didn't recognize her; co-workers spontaneously asked her to join them for lunch (something that none had done in the past); she was asked to sit on an important committee—a step, she wrote, that would have a huge impact on her career. **She *felt* attractive— she changed the way the world looked at her, and her life changed.**

I didn't write this book to show you how to be beautiful, I wrote it to show you that you already are. I wish you easy elegance and more personal and professional success than you dare to dream.

JoAnna

THE RESOURCE CENTER

JoAnna's websites

DressingSmart.com

- Take a free quiz to find your Dressing Smart I.Q.

- Order a *Mini Color Chart* to find your best colors of the season

- Print out your own Mini Chart in just a few minutes for just a few dollars

- Read articles about JoAnna's books in national magazines

- Check out the great pictures that will help you get the look you want

Color1Associates.com

- Find the Color 1 Associate nearest you

- Take a free quiz to find your Color I.Q.

- Take a free quiz to find your Color Type

- If you don't have an Associate near you, order the *Smart Chart*

- Change your career, change your life—click on Color 1 Careers

- Find the color-perfect foundation and other great Color 1 products

Career1Makeovers.com

- Take a free quiz to find your Makeup I.Q.

- Check out the Career1 Makeup Kits just for your Color Type

- Change your career, change your life—click on Color 1 Careers

- Check out the great pictures that will help you get the look you want

- Print out a super Scarf Tying booklet in just a few minutes, for just a few dollars

- Print out JoAnna's book *110 Mistakes Working Women Make & How to Avoid Them*

Sexy1Makeovers.com and Sexy1Makeup.com

- Take a free quiz to check your Sexy I.Q.

- Check out the Sexy1 Makeup Kits just for your Color Type

- Order *Secrets Men Have Told Me* (see below)

- Read articles about JoAnna's books and Color 1 in magazines like *Cosmopolitan* and *Glamour*

- Check out the great pictures that will help you get the look you want

The *Smart* Chart
This full-sized chart, coupled with the information in this book, will help you greatly in attaining the look you want. With at least one shade of every color in the spectrum that will flatter your Color Type, this chart is the *next* best thing to having a personal consultation with a Color 1 Associate. Take the free online quiz to help you figure out your Color Type—if you can't, you can send JoAnna a picture and she will do it for you.

The *Mini* Color Chart
Order this fun and helpful chart from the website if you are curious to know which of the latest "in-fashion" colors being shown in the stores each season are best for your Color Type. It's also available in a format that you can print out yourself—in just a few minutes, for just a few dollars. Take the free online quiz to help you figure out your Color Type.

Secrets Men Have Told Me: What Turns Men On & What Turns Them Off
Although this little book has an amusing title, it is a *gem*! You can order it from any bookstore, or get a signed copy from the website—you can even get it right now as an e-book in just a few minutes, for just a few dollars. JoAnna interviewed men from all over the world, asking them what *they* find sexy and what they find *over the top,* and she wrote this book for *conservative* women who wish to look more sensual without stepping over the sometimes fine line between sexy and sleazy. It has been featured in several magazines and newspapers including *Cosmopolitan* and *The Washington Post*.

For gifts, you can order signed copies of JoAnna's books by sending a separate email to JoAnna@DressingSmart.com with the name(s) you would like the book(s) signed to. All books are 25% off the retail price.

Color 1 Associates International Image and Style Consultants
To "change the way the world looks at you" by working with one of the most talented, experienced, and most respected color and image consultants in the world, visit Color1Associates.com, or telephone Color 1 at (202) 293-9175, to find the Associate nearest you.

For the *smart* men in your life, check out JoAnna's book ***Dressing Smart for Men: 101 Mistakes You Can't Afford to Make & How to Avoid Them***. Purchase from any bookstore or order from <u>DressingSmart.com</u>, then send a separate email to <u>JoAnna@DressingSmart.com</u> with the name(s) you would like the book(s) signed to. You'll save 25% off the retail price.

THE AUTHOR

President of Color 1 Associates, International Image & Style Consultants, JoAnna Nicholson is one of the founders of the image industry. She is a recipient of the prestigious Image Industry Council International (IICI) Award of Excellence and the IMMIE Award for Commitment.

JoAnna, the author of seven books, has trained image and style consultants all over the world. Lecturing internationally and nationally on color, style, wardrobe, makeup, and interior design, she has conducted seminars at the invitation of the American Embassy in Paris. Her television and radio appearances include the Montel Williams Show and the Larry King Show. She is a former model and co-founder of an interior design studio. Her home, which she designed using the Color 1 concept, has been featured in *Architectural Digest* and *Italian Architectural Digest.*

JoAnna's latest books are **Dressing Smart for Men: 101 Mistakes You Can't Afford to Make and How to Avoid Them** and **Secrets Men Have Told Me: What Turns Men On & What Turns Them Off**. Her company and books have been featured in numerous magazines including *Harper's Bazaar, GQ, Cosmopolitan, Glamour, Forbes, Black Elegance, Money, and Redbook,* and in over 100 newspapers including *The Washington Post.* Personal clients include ambassadors, cabinet secretaries, senators, congressmen, Fortune 500 companies, rock stars, actors, and a former Miss America.

Career Resources

The following Career Resources are available directly from Impact Publications. Full descriptions of each title as well as downloadable catalogs, videos, and software can be found on our website: www.impactpublications.com. Complete the following form or list the titles, include shipping (see formula at the end), enclose payment, and send your order to:

IMPACT PUBLICATIONS
9104 Manassas Drive, Suite N
Manassas Park, VA 20111-5211 USA
1-800-361-1055 (orders only)
Tel. 703-361-7300 or Fax 703-335-9486
Email address: info@impactpublications.com
Quick & easy online ordering: www.impactpublications.com

Orders from individuals must be prepaid by check, money order, or major credit card. We accept telephone, fax, and email orders.

Qty.	Titles	Price	Total
Books By Author			
_____	Dressing Smart for Men	$16.95	_____
_____	Dressing Smart for Women	16.95	_____
_____	Dressing Smart for the New Millennium	15.95	_____
Networking			
_____	A Foot in the Door	14.95	_____
_____	How to Work a Room	14.00	_____
_____	Masters of Networking	16.95	_____
_____	Power Networking	14.95	_____
_____	Power Schmoozing	12.95	_____
_____	The Savvy Networker	13.95	_____
Interviews			
_____	Interview for Success (8th Edition)	15.95	_____
_____	Nail the Job Interview	13.95	_____
_____	The Savvy Interviewer	10.95	_____

5921

Inspiration and Empowerment

_____ 101 Secrets of Highly Effective Speakers	15.95	_____
_____ Life Strategies	13.95	_____
_____ Seven Habits of Highly Effective People	14.00	_____
_____ Who Moved My Cheese?	19.95	_____

Job Strategies

_____ 95 Mistakes Job Seekers Make	13.95	_____
_____ Change Your Job, Change Your Life (8th Edition)	17.95	_____
_____ No One Will Hire Me!	13.95	_____
_____ Quit Your Job and Grow Some Hair	15.95	_____
_____ What Color Is Your Parachute?	17.95	_____

SUBTOTAL _____

Virginia residents add 4½% sales tax _____

POSTAGE/HANDLING ($5 for first product and 8% of SUBTOTAL) _____

8% of SUBTOTAL _____

TOTAL ENCLOSED _____

SHIP TO:

NAME _____

ADDRESS _____

_____

_____

PAYMENT METHOD:

❑ I enclose check/money order for $ _____ made payable to IMPACT PUBLICATIONS.

❑ Please charge $ _____ to my credit card:

❑ Visa   ❑ MasterCard   ❑ American Express ❑ Discover

Card # _____ Expiration date: ___ /___

Signature _____

Keep in Touch . . .
On the Web!